746·2 博

PAT EARNSHAW

Bobbin & Needle Laces

Identification & Care

B.T. Batsford Ltd, London

ISBN 0 7134 4139 9

Typeset by Servis Filmsetting Ltd, Manchester
and printed in Great Britain by
The Pitman Press, Bath
for the publishers
B.T. Batsford Ltd
4 Fitzhardinge Street
London W1H 0AH

Contents

Acknowledgements

Photographic Acknowledgements

I am grateful to all those who, by their enjoyment of my two previous books, encouraged me to write more.

Specifically, I am indebted to the following:

For advice on lace making, to Winifred Millar, MBE (the history and traditional techniques of the Northants and other East Midlands bobbin laces); Margaret Susans of the Royal School of Needlework; and Suzanne Van Ruymbeke-Deraedt (discussions of the continental European methods of making prickings).

For advice on fibres used in lace making, and their measurement, to Dr D.F. Cutler and Miss R.M.O. Gale of the Jodrell Laboratory, Royal Botanic Gardens, Kew; and Dr Roger Trout and Miss Lois Lelliot of the Ministry of Agriculture, Fisheries and Food.

For advice on conservation to Judith Doré; Mary Ballard, conservator to the Detroit Institute of Arts; Joan Kendall of the Textile Conservation Rooms, Hatfield House; and Liz Flintoff of the Textile Conservation Centre, Hampton Court Palace.

For recollections of the working of lace machines, to Tom Stevenson.

And finally, yet primarily, to Ronald Brown for his indispensable photography.

Acknowledgements of other photographs and of the people who lent lace to be photographed are given in the Photographic Acknowledgements.

The illustration of Lady Drake on the front jacket is by courtesy of the Plymouth City Museum and Art Gallery, and is housed at Buckland Abbey.

Eleanor Adams, fig. 176. American Institute of Textile Arts, Boston, Mass., fig. 214(b)(c). Art Institute of Chicago, fig. 137(a). Joslyn Baker, figs. 9, 17, 18, 34, 70, 91(b), 132(f), 135, 144(b), 148(b), 188(a), 191, 195(b), 202, 211(a)(b), 218(a)(b), key photos 6, 17.1, 20, 30.1, 35.2, 58.1. Broholm and Hald, *Costume of the Bronze Age in Denmark*, 1940 (Nyt Nordisk Forlag Arnold Busek), fig. 2. Christie's South Kensington, London, fig. 195(a). Cooper-Hewitt Museum, New York, fig. 131(c). Detroit Institute of Art, figs. 109, 186(b), 189(a), 193(a). Dover Publications Inc., fig. 16. Lise Helvard, fig. 127. Hillwood Museum, Washington DC, fig. 149. Kent, Kate Peck, 'The Cultivation and Weaving of Cotton in the Prehistoric Southwestern United States', *Trans. Am. Philosophical Soc.*, new series, vol. 47, part 3, figs. 3, 19. Livrustkammaren, Stockholm, fig. 145(a). Luton Museum, Wardown Park, figs. 104(b), 113(d). Doris May, figs. 56, 122(e). Metropolitan Museum of Art, figs. 165, 166. Winifred Millar, MBE, key photo 36.1. Musées Royaux d'Art et d'Histoire, Brussels, fig. 134(a). Museum of Art, Rhode Island School of Design, fig. 204. Museum of Fine Art, Boston, Mass., figs. 148, 203(b). Northampton Record Office, fig. 141. Phillips, Fine Art Auctioneers, figs. 6, 12, 14, 15, 62(b), 138(b), 147(c)(d)(f), 148(a), 181(a), 192(b), 194, 199, 203, key photos 2, 5, 12.2, 13.1, 16.2, 17.2, 18, 27.3, 30.1, 30.2, 35.1, 42.1, 47.1, 51.1. Gabrielle Pond, fig. 150, key photo 44.1. Molly Redmore, fig. 88. Royal Albert Memorial Museum, Exeter, key photo 44.2. Royal School of Needlework, figs. 132(e), 177(b), 212(a), key photo 38.2. Smithsonian Institution, figs. 137, 186(a), 189(c), 205, key photo 22 (Flemish collar lace). Elvira Strong, figs. 107(b), 121. Textilmuseum, St Gallen, figs. 56, 197(b). Victoria and Albert Museum, London, figs. 4, 196(b). *Weldon's Practical Needlework*, c1900, figs. 97, 108(b)(c), 111(a)(b)(c).

PART 1 IDENTIFICATION

ONE

Bobbin & Needle Laces in Context

The Relationship of Various Techniques

Lace is a form of textile. Although the term 'textile' originally referred only to woven fabrics, it is now generally regarded as having a vastly wider application, and as being a useful blanket-term for any flexible or draping fabric constructed by the manipulation of threads. What is meant by 'threads' will be examined in chapter 5; at this moment we are less concerned with their precise nature than with how they are worked.

Basically, a textile can be worked by a single thread, by one set of threads, or by multiple sets of threads. The group names for these are : Single Element, One Set of Element, Two or More Sets of Element, were defined by Irene Emery, and are now fairly generally accepted.

In fig. 1 the first two are represented as 'Single Elements' and the third as 'Double Elements'.

If a *single thread* is used, it may be knotted or looped. Looping is the more basic movement, and knotting can be regarded as a loop fixed in place by a knot. Single thread knotting can produce three forms of lacey fabric (i.e. with an openwork design): **a** tatting **b** bebilla **c** netting. Single thread looping can also produce three forms of lacey fabric: **a** knitting **b** crochet **c** closed loop.

The closed loop is the embroidery stitch known as

Fig. 1 *The relationship of lace techniques.*

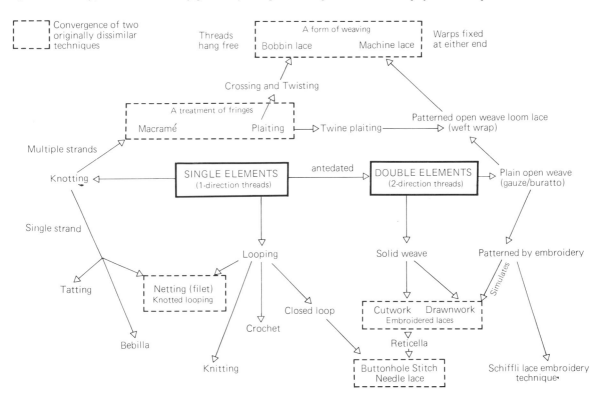

5

detached buttonhole stitch (see page 17). As a surface stitch of regular uniformity it occurs in an aery lining to the woollen caps of skeletons in Bronze Age tombs in Denmark (fig. 2) and in Pueblo settlements of northeast Arizona from the twelfth to the fifteenth century (fig. 3) and, with the addition of a slight twist, in the cylindrical 'waangk mee' bags of Australian aborigines (Nunn and West). While in a slightly more complex form it constructs the three-dimensional gowns of the tiny mannikins caught in their frozen tableaux of Biblical scenes in English stumpwork embroideries of the seventeenth century (fig. 4). When this stitch is used independently of any woven surface, and produces a pattern incorporating holes, it forms a buttonhole stitch lace, otherwise known as 'needlepoint', or 'needle', lace.

If One Set of Element, i.e. a *single set of threads*, is used, the threads are arranged to hang all in one direction, like fringes, before being manipulated.

Manipulation of these threads by knotting produces macramé (fig. 5). Manipulation by plaiting, oblique braiding, or oblique twining involves their being crossed over, or twisted around, each other, but not fixed by knots.

When crossing and twisting produce a decorative openwork fabric, involving somewhere between eight and 1000 threads, a form of lace traditionally worked with bobbins rather than with the fingers results, and this is known as 'bobbin' lace (fig. 6).

The completed appearance of a bobbin lace is often remarkably like weaving, and so it links closely to Two or More Sets of Element, or *two or more sets of threads*, in which there are initially longitudinal warps with completely distinct weft(s) arranged to cross them more or less at right angles. In the production of such fabrics, the warps must be fixed at either end to provide stability while they are separated by a heddle, or by hand, for the passage of the weft. Preferential selection of warps during this separation can produce patterning, such as damasks (fig. 7).

When there is no pattern and no holeyness the product is a plain weave (indicated in fig. 1 as 'solid' in contradistinction to 'open'). This is woven as a continuous surface, but can be rendered holey at a later stage by removal of, or interference with the course of, groups of threads (fig. 8). Actual cutting out of sections of the fabric produces cutwork (fig. 9) which, carried to its extreme, forms within the cloth an open band several inches wide crossed only at intervals by fragile strands of weft and warp. These spaces can then be filled with patterns of buttonhole stitches, producing an embroidered lace known as 'reticella' (figs. 10 & 11), which makes an easy transition into the pure needle laces constructed of buttonhole stitches only, with no woven foundation (fig. 12).

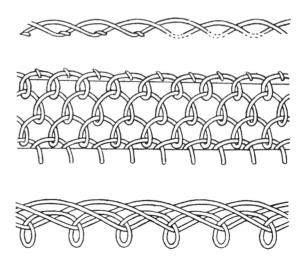

Fig. 2 *Closed loop stitches from the inside of a cap found in a prehistoric grave at Trindhøj.*

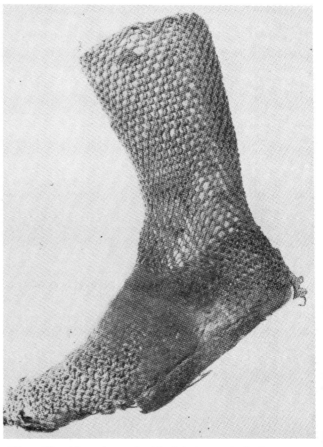

Fig. 3 *Closed loop shoe-sock with plaited yucca leaf sole, made of multiple-ply cotton and wool string upper. Length of sole $11\frac{1}{2}$ inches. Two Mummy Ruin, Nitsie Canyon, Arizona,* AD *1100–1300.*

Fig. 4 *The Judgment of Solomon, worked in buttonhole stitches. English, seventeenth century.*

Fig. 6 *A lace-maker's pillow dressed with pricking and bobbins for making a torchon border.*

Fig. 5 *An Assyrian with a macramé-fringed tunic, carrying in one hand a baby antelope and in the other a branch of the holy tree, the cedar of Lebanon. From a bas relief 8 foot high, Ninevah,* c1000 BC.

Two or More Sets of Element set-ups can also produce plain open weaves, commonly referred to as 'leno', 'gauze' or 'buratto'. Such are not in their plain state laces, but when patterned by hand embroidery, for example in a running stitch, they develop a design on an open ground which justifies their inclusion. A similarity of patterns used by open-weave buratto (fig. 13), by plain weave with small groups of threads pulled (drawn) together or pulled (drawn) out (drawnwork, fig. 14), and embroidered knotted netting (filet, fig. 15), can render the three completely distinct techniques almost indistinguishable from each other unless they are closely examined, the mesh of each being a square, and the designs often identical (fig. 16).

Apart from this embroidered decoration, the open weave can also be patterned on a loom, by interference with the straightforward right-angled intersection of weft and warp. Such weaving is sometimes called 'weft wrap' since the weft is to some extent wrapped around small groups of warps (figs. 17 & 18). The eventual appearance of the fabric made by this technique is very similar to a modified One Set of Element plaiting, known as 'twine plaiting'. In this, modification of the rigid sequence of thread movement produces either a closely textured patterned braid, or an openwork lace (fig. 19). Weft wrap can also look something like drawnwork. Techniques of this kind may be significant as bobbin lace forerunners.

Fig. 7 *A damask patterned weave showing the Seige of Lille (Flemish, Rissel) when, in 1708, Prince Eugène wrested the city from the French.*

Fig. 8 *A decorative flower centre made by deflecting some threads and removing others from the loosely woven muslin.*

Fig. 9 *Cutwork from a sixteenth-century cloth.*

Fig. 10 *Patterns for cutwork/reticella bavari (bodice tops). Vecellio.*

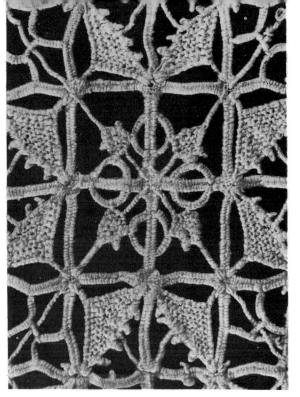

Fig. 11 *The reticella technique. The residual warps and wefts which make up the frames can be seen at the points of crossing. The decorative triangles are made with buttonhole stitches.*

Fig. 12 *Needle lace made without any fabric foundation, sometimes called punto in aria. Seventeenth century.*

Fig. 13 *Buratto, seventeenth century.*

Fig. 14 *Drawn threadwork, seventeenth century.*

Fig. 15 *Filet, seventeenth century.*

Fig. 16 *A design which, with its squared background, could be adapted for either buratto, drawnwork or filet. Vinciolo's pattern book, 1587.*

Fig. 17 *The use of openwork cotton material in an 1830s dress.*

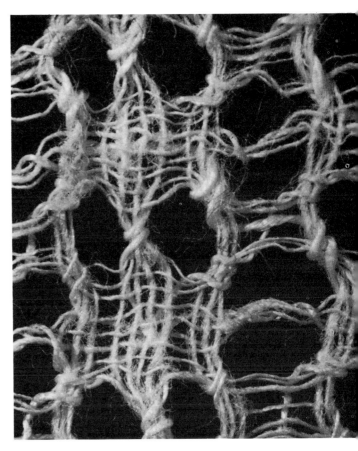

Fig. 18 *A close-up of the material showing the complex course of the woven threads.*

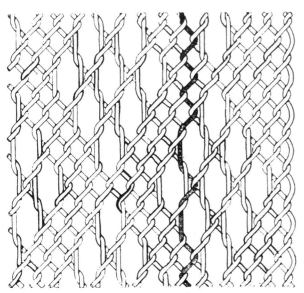

Fig. 19 *A sketch to show how a pattern of holes can be made by twine plaiting. A technique found in an ancient shirt of white cotton from Tonto, Arizona, AD 1300–1550.*

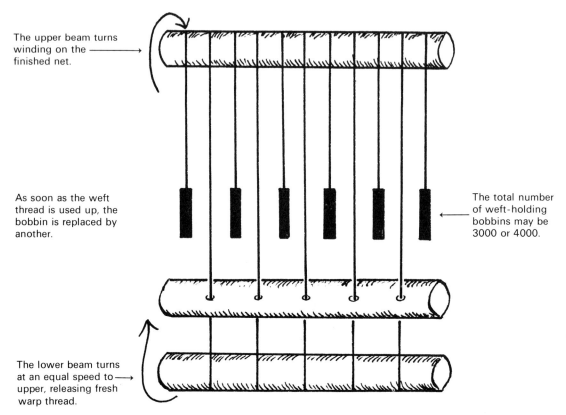

The upper beam turns winding on the finished net.

As soon as the weft thread is used up, the bobbin is replaced by another.

The total number of weft-holding bobbins may be 3000 or 4000.

The lower beam turns at an equal speed to upper, releasing fresh warp thread.

Fig. 20 *The twist-net set-up, invented by Heathcoat, 1808. The warp and weft threads are fixed alternately along the upper beam. The middle bar controls the slight lateral movements of the warp threads which is essential to produce the twist. Not to scale: the distance between the threads is much exaggerated.*

The twist net and all its subsequent patterning (i.e. machine lace) is a variation of the open weave produced on a very specialized loom. In this, the vertical warps still have to be fixed securely at either end, but the versatility of movement of the separate wefts, which are equal in number to the warps, and the slight sideways movements of the parallel warps themselves, combined with a complex selection of warps in each course, or row, can produce astonishingly intricate designs, often closely resembling bobbin laces (fig. 20).

Thus the two major lace techniques, bobbin and needle, with which this book is concerned, are neither self-contained nor isolated. They merge on all sides into relationships with other techniques which produce their own openwork patterned fabrics known as laces, and from which, if they are to be identified, they must be distinguished.

Note: The Schiffli technique refers to an embroidery machine which can copy not only the forms of bobbin laces, as ordinary lace machines can, but also with great

effectiveness the designs and appearance of needle laces. Worked on net, the Schiffli embroidery can give the appearance of Brussels point de gaze (fig. 21); worked on a backing fabric which is later destroyed it produces 'guipures' which imitate everything from Irish crochet to Venetian gros point. It is not closely related to any other lace technique, but has the ability to imitate the appearance of all of them (figs. 22 & 23).

The Preliminary Questions of Identification

Identification is concerned with putting a name to a lace, a stitch, or a technique, so that when we refer to it other people will know what we are talking about. In effect, it is a method of labelling. The word 'lace' itself has also to be treated in this way. In other words, before the question 'What sort of lace is it?' can be answered, the preliminary question 'Is it lace?' must be looked into.

Lace is a kind of cloth, or textile in its broadest sense. It is made by threads outlining holes to form a design. All lace has holes in it, but not every textile with holes in it is lace. The holes must be part of the structure of the cloth, sufficiently numerous to produce an openwork

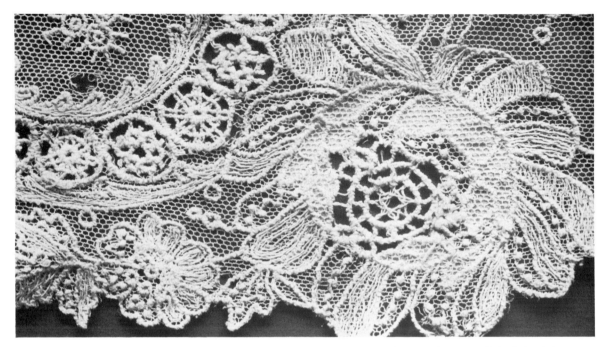

Fig. 21 *Counterfeit point de gaze made by lock-stitch embroidery on net, c1910. Reverse side.*

Figs. 22 and 23 *Two 'guipures' made on the Schiffli machine by the chemical lace technique: (22) imitation Irish crochet; (23) imitation Venetian gros point.*

fabric, and arranged not haphazardly but so as to form a pattern which is most often repetitive at longer or shorter intervals. The design is made possible by some parts of the lace being more solid than others. This can be expressed by saying that there are areas of varying density. The more solid parts make the motifs, the more open parts the background (usually abbreviated to 'ground').

Lace is made up of threads and the way in which the threads have been manipulated is called the *technique*. In identification we are concerned less with the actual process of making than with what can be discovered of the technique from the finished product. This end product provides, for everyone, first-hand observations from which conclusions can be drawn in a fairly simple and straightforward manner.

Although no one is likely to quarrel with the definition of lace set out above, there is a certain amount of disagreement as to the precise placing of the boundary between lace and not-lace. Channer, for example, defines lace in terms of 'the whole pattern is the fabric, and the fabric is the pattern', that is the working of the threads produces at the same time both the material and its patterning. This definition separates lace sharply from openwork embroidery in which patterning is added to the surface of an already-made material, and so excludes all that antique group commonly called the embroidered laces, such as cutwork, buratto, drawnwork and filet (figs. 9, 13, 14 & 15), and all the nineteenth- and twentieth-century embroidered lace derivatives such as the decorated nets (figs. 24 & 25), Carrickmacross and Ayrshire work, while validating crochet, knitting, tatting, macramé and other crafts (fig. 26), along with most, though not all, of the machine laces. As already explained, the interrelationship of the various lace techniques is so close and so complex that a discrimination of this kind is likely to create more problems than it solves, and lead to fatuous disagreements which, though purporting to be about lace, are really only about words. However, since we are concerned just with bobbin and needle laces, the point will not be argued here.

So, to return to the basics: the three essential words are 'threads', 'holes', 'design'. Lace was made by the movement of threads at a time and in a place. This, in essence, is the information which must be given when a lace is identified. What must be considered now, therefore, is how to determine the technique, the dating and the geography of laces by a consideration of the threads, the holes and the designs.

Fig. 24 *A decorated net. The design is produced by chain stitch embroidery. Tambour work, Limerick, 1830s.*

Fig. 25 *An application of shaped pieces of muslin couched to the net. Carrickmacross, c1890.*

Fig. 26 *Left, a crochet watch mat for hanging a hunter; right, a knitted lace pin cushion cover. Both c1850.*

Techniques and Appearances

A short trial run on the course of threads in a lace will demonstrate that magnification is not only helpful, but in many cases essential, in order to follow them. Whether the lace makers of ancient times used magnifying lenses as they worked, or whether the most expert were short-sighted so that their eyes magnified of their own accord, is not known. Spectacles were available in the sixteenth century, but were probably expensive.

A number of different types of magnifier are available nowadays. Six are shown in fig. 27:

a Watchmaker's eyeglass. Available in $\times 2\frac{1}{2}$, $\times 6$, $\times 8$ magnifications.

b Plastic magnifier which can be hung around the neck and has two lenses, a higher and lower magnification, approximately $\times 1\frac{1}{2}$ and $\times 2$.

c A large magnifier on a heavyweight stand. It gives a relatively wide field of view, but only an approximately $\times 1\frac{1}{2}$ magnification.

d Lens set in a plastic arch, to rest on the lace. $\times 2$ or less.

e A $\times 10$ thread counter on a stand, with linear measurement.

f A $\times 30$ lightscope with its own illumination.

Two other forms of magnification involve projection:

g A video camera with a zoom lens, the image from which appears on a television screen. There is automated movement of the camera over different parts of the lace.

h An epidiascope projecting on to a screen.

Fig. 27 *A selection of magnifiers.*

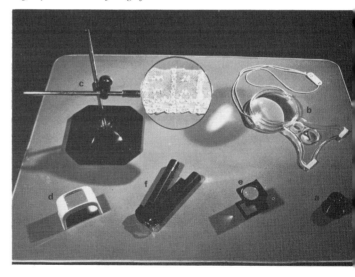

All have advantages and disadvantages. While **g** is certainly the most comfortable method, the equipment is costly, and its use exposes the lace to quite strong illumination. **h**, while making the lace visible to many people at the same time, is a conservation disaster with its combination of intense heat and intense light. **d**, **e** and **f**, have to stand on the lace, which invites undue pressure on the fibres. **a** has no disadvantage except that

Fig. 28 *A fragment of lace made of braid with buttonhole stitch fillings.*

it completely occupies one hand, inciting in the other an inclination to take hold of the lace and bring it to the eye, instead of lowering the eye to the lace, thus straining the threads, and soiling them with skin secretions.

Equipped then with magnifiers we may turn back to the lace, and attempt now to analyze the minute shapes which the threads construct. Fig. 28 shows a fragment of lace, and figs. 29(a) and 30(a) portions of it enlarged × $6\frac{2}{3}$. This lace in fact has mixed techniques, but it has been chosen here for the simple looping movements pursued in parts by the thread.

It is helpful to draw these shapes, taking careful note of where the thread passes over, and where under; where it curves around to the left, and where to the right. It would be even more instructive to take a crewel needle and a length of coloured wool and to copy those looping movements, using a backing fabric solely as a support for the first row, and for the final stitches at either end of each following row. In both (A) and (B) the stitches are worked from left to right, and then back from right to left so that the direction of the twined-

around threads is reversed (figs. 29b and 30b). The loops may be made with the needle pointing either towards or away from the worker.

These two loop-arrangements are forms of buttonhole stitch. A. has been called detached buttonhole stitch (Nordfors), Brussels stitch (Needlecraft), single Brussels stitch (Dillmont's 1st lace stitch), open buttonhole filling when spaced, or detached buttonhole stitch when worked very close together (Thomas), close buttonhole stitch (DMC), and single net stitch (Readers Digest).
B. has been called Spanish point (Readers Digest), 22nd lace stitch or a kind of Spanish stitch or point d'Espagne (Dillmont) and tulle stitch (Stringer).

There is thus some need for standardization, and while we are on this tender subject, the opposition of the terms 'needle lace' and 'needlepoint lace' might be brought into the open. 'Needle lace' as a generic term for lace constructed of buttonhole stitches is accepted usage in Europe and North America (compare the French 'dentelle à l'aiguille' and the Italian 'trine ad ago'). The only objection to it is that there are other

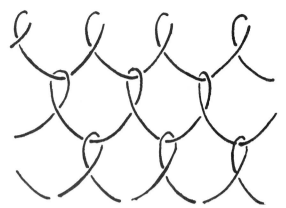

Fig. 29a and b *Photograph and sketch of stitch* A.

laces made with a needle, for example the embroidered laces buratto, drawnwork and filet; and the Armenian and puncetto laces in which a needle tightens non-buttonhole stitch loopings into a decorative knotted fabric. In short, used literally, it encompasses a large and ill-assorted conglomeration. 'Needlepoint', however, is just as ambiguous. Despite its long-established usage in Britain for buttonhole stitch laces, it has been rudely displaced by the adoption of this term for canvas work embroidery.

In figs. 31 and 32 there is no sign of the threads looping. The appearance is rather that they weave in and out of each other. This is a distinctive feature of the bobbin laces, just as looping is of the needle laces. Also, just as the needle laces have one basic stitch, the buttonhole stitch, so the bobbin laces – in all their immense complexity – have only two basic movements, known as the twist and cross. While this is a constructional point which may be far from obvious in the finished lace to the eyes of a non-lace maker, the two movements will none the less be described here since

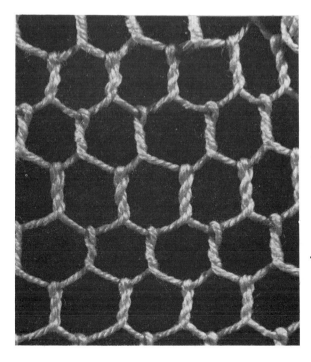

Fig. 30a and b *Photograph and sketch of stitch* B.

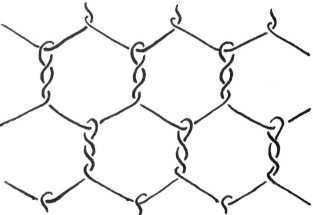

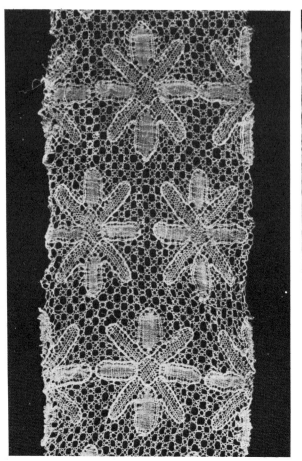

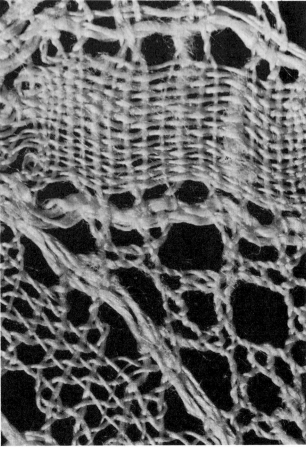

Fig. 31 *A bobbin lace showing three different appearances, or stitches, caused by different combinations of thread movements.*

Fig. 32 *A ×10 magnification of the three stitches showing the woven look (upper right) and the grilled look (lower left).*

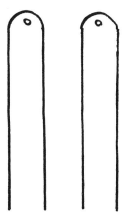

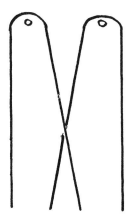

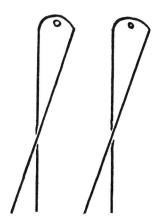

a *The threads as hung;*　　　　　**b** *the cross;*　　　　　**c** *the twist.*

Fig. 33

they constitute as it were the alphabet from which the prolific vocabulary of bobbin lace stitches is built up. The bobbin lace movements are a good deal less simple to follow than those of needle laces because a larger number of threads is used – usually between eight and 1000 – instead of only one.

The threads are arranged in pairs. In making the lace they are hung from pins near the far side of a cushion or pillow. To understand the basic movements, use a polystyrene block, and thickish thread weighted with anything convenient, such as small pencils. Hang two pairs of threads straight (fig. 33a), then place the inner left-hand thread over the inner right-hand thread. This simple movement constitutes a cross (croiser) (b). Straighten the threads again (a) and this time place the right thread of each pair over the left of each pair (c). This constitutes a twist (tordre). If more pairs of threads are added, and the movement continued across them, a cross-twist-cross sequence will produce the closely woven appearance shown on the right in fig. 32. Similarly, if the sequence across several threads is restricted to an alternation of cross and twist, the grill-like appearance to the left of fig. 32 will be formed. If on the other hand the number of threads is restricted to four or so, the result is not a large surface but a plait or braid, and such structures too are characteristic of bobbin laces.

The woven look of laces is thus very easily distinguished from the looped look when the course of the threads is followed, and there should be no problem about recognizing a needle lace. Unfortunately as far as the bobbin laces are concerned, the woven look is not their monopoly, but is shared by two quite separate groups:

1 Embroidered laces which are based on a plain fabric subsequently converted to openwork (figs. 34 & 35).
2 The patterned twist laces of the Heathcoat, Levers, Pusher and Barmen machines, and their variations (figs. 36 & 37).

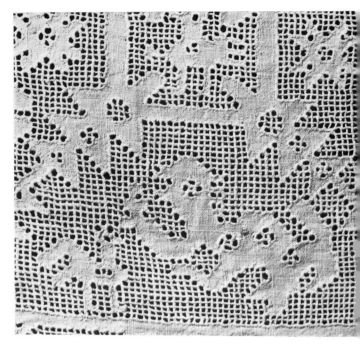

Fig. 34 *Drawnwork, seventeenth century. A cat admonishes a bird. The removal of threads has created an openwork background, and attractive detail in the design.*

Fig. 35 *A plain weave fabric showing how the cutting away of warps and wefts in parts produces a perforated (lace-like) fabric. × 10.*

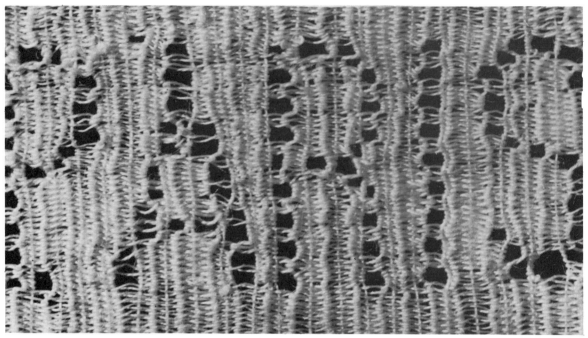

Fig. 36 (above) *A woven look made on the Levers machine for the Paris exhibition of 1900.* × 10.

Fig. 37 (below) *A woven-look imitation of a Brussels bobbin lace cleverly imitated by the Schiffli embroidery machine* c1900. × 10.

TWO

Fabrics Which May Resemble Bobbin Laces

This book is not concerned with the detailed identification of either embroidered or machine laces. They need to be identified only in order to be eliminated from the discussion. Their technique must be understood with sufficient clarity that any possibility of confusing them with either bobbin or needle laces is avoided. This is not always easy because hand and machine counterparts can resemble each other in an almost uncanny manner. The resemblance is of course the result of deliberate copying, and what is uncanny is not so much the resemblance itself as the absoluteness of its success. Perhaps even more unnerving is the fact that hand laces can be mistaken for machine. The more precise, perfect and regular a bobbin or needle lace is, the more disbelief do we feel that any mind could have been so perseveratingly unvariable, or any human hand so robotically precise, as to construct it.

In none of the three groups – bobbin, embroidered or machine laces – does the woven look extend throughout. It is rather restricted to isolated patches. This, on consideration, must be obvious: the distinctive attribute of lace is its holeyness, and in those blank holes threads, woven or otherwise, will be absent.

a *Embroidered laces* (see figs. 9, 13, 14 & 15). Four types are usually distinguished, and their comparative features are indicated in fig. 38.

Thus to eliminate embroidered laces from further consideration, it is only necessary to exclude all woven-look laces with a knotted square-meshed ground; all where the design is produced by darning; all where the ground is made of warps and wefts bound around with thread; and all where the design consists of holes cut in a woven cloth (fig. 39). Their techniques thus are quite distinct, and their designs too are quite unlike any bobbin lace.

b In *machine laces* the situation is rather less straightforward. The primary aim of the machine was to copy the bobbin laces to the extent of being indistiguishable from them, and the differences are not obvious.

Heathcoat's inspiration for the first twist-net machine came from observing an East Midlands bobbin lace maker at work. Each movement of the threads as

Fig. 38 *A table summarizing the characteristics of embroidered laces.*

Embroidered lace	Single/double element	Fabric constructed first, design added	Ground made by	Design made by	Woven effect present in
Filet	S	✓	Knotted mesh	Darning	Design
Buratto	D	✓	Woven gauze	Darning	Design
Drawnwork	D	✓	Removal of threads from plain weave cloth	Plain cloth sometimes overdarned	Design
Cutwork	D	✓	Plain weave cloth	Cutting holes	Ground

39a **39b** **39c**

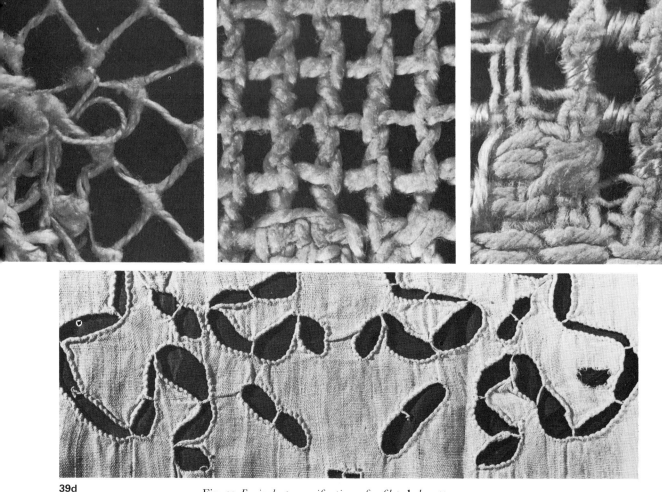

39d

Fig. 39 *Equivalent magnifications of* **a** *filet;* **b** *buratto;* **c** *drawnwork. Actual size* **d** *cutwork.*

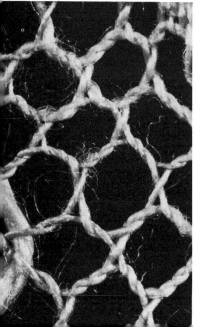

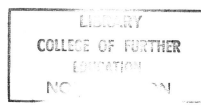

Fig. 40 *Bucks point ground, the stitch first copied by Heathcoat.* × 10.

Fig. 41 *Heathcoat's two-twist bobbinet.* × 10.

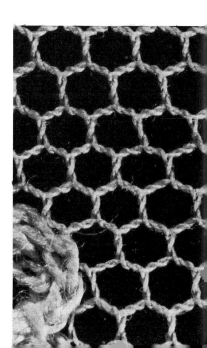

the mesh ground of the lace was constructed was analyzed, and this information adapted, with the most painstaking mechanical aptitude, for a complex system of shuttles and levers. These with miraculous precision produced the exact same movements, which are representable in bobbin lace language as a repeated sequence of CTTT (or cross-twist-twist-twist). See page 22 (figs. 40 & 41).

The actual machine set-up is, in Emery's terms, a double element construction (fig. 20). To the large roller, or beam, at the top are fixed alternately warp threads and weft threads. Both hang vertically downwards side by side, but their actions are quite distinct. While the warps are restricted to a fairly discreet sideways movement, the wefts or 'bobbin' threads swing vigorously back and forth between them, interweaving and twisting around to form firmly locked meshes of a more or less hexagonal shape.

The bobbin lace set-up is, on the other hand, regarded as a single element construction. The straight threads running down the pillow (fig. 6) are interchangeable in action. At any one time a pair of workers is distinguishable from many other pairs of nonworkers or passives, but pairs of passives can at intervals take over the work of crossing and twisting about the other threads, and the former workers are then themselves transformed into passives.

When the twist machines, slightly later in the century, came to make patterned laces the analytical procedure was adhered to. Specimens of bobbin laces, from any time and place so long as their designs looked marketable, were examined thread by thread until every twist and cross could be translated into row-by-row movements of the machine's ever-increasing multiplicity of wefts and warps. This reduction of the lace fabric to individual thread passages was made possible by their extreme clarity so that they were easily traced (fig. 32). The two-element set-up of the machine on the other hand obscures the thread-movement sequence. In this lies the key to the recognition of machine laces. Obscurity may seem a rather negative characteristic, and the obstructed pathway of threads a somewhat unsatisfactory observation, on which to base farreaching conclusions, but fortunately plenty of other indications of machine origin are available:

1 On a wide, for example 230 inch, Levers machine, edgings or insertions are frequently arranged in a vertical manner so that immense yardages are obtainable, and fifty or more can lie side by side like multiplying clones. These lengths can later be isolated from each other simply by pulling out the thickened warp which links them. Alternatively, lace can be made crosswise of the loom, that is across the whole 6-yard width. Such broad flounces would have to be sub-

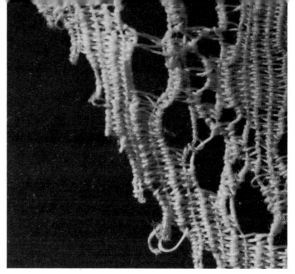

Fig. 42 *The raw cut warps at the edge of a machine lace.*

Fig. 43 *The traversed (diagonal) course of the threads in a Pusher machine lace.*

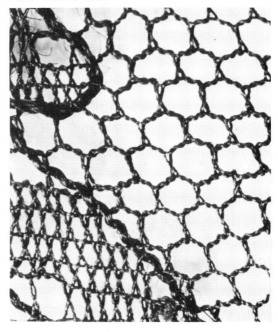

sequently separated by the cutting of the warps which, in the making, will have continued downward from the bottom of one flounce into the top of the next (fig. 43). Cut ends of this kind would never occur in bobbin laces.

2 The fixed arrangement of the warp threads gives to the finished lace a faintly ribbed effect (figs. 37 & 43). These ribs are always present, but not always equally obvious.

3 In bobbin laces the progress of the active threads across the ground of the lace is almost invariably diagonal, though the angle of the slope varies (see pages 50–60). This diagonal passage is reproduced in Heathcoat and Pusher laces, but in the Levers there is no thread-slope (fig. 43).

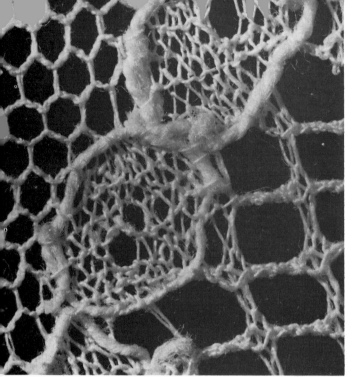

Fig. 44 *A typical machine lace appearance where the course of the threads cannot be followed through. Note that the outlining thread can be seen to be cut on both sides of the design.*

Fig. 45 *The clear course of the threads in a bobbin lace. Note the continuity in the gimp thread.*

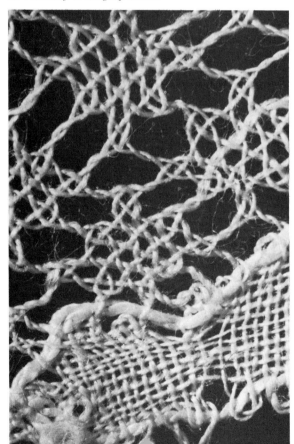

4 A very tight twisting together of threads especially in the ground of the lace is in marked contrast to the lucid course of bobbin laces (figs. 44 & 45).

5 Closely connected with point **4** is a negative feature: machine laces resist unravelling, bobbin do not. However, the unpicking of any lace to investigate this feature has not much to recommend it.

6 In some laces outlining threads may be used to strengthen the form of an indeterminate design. In bobbin laces these gimps are put in as the work progresses, and the thread will be neatly cut when the encirclement is completed. Outlines put in by the machine as the lace is made are less manipulatable. The lace as manufactured goes only upwards: an outlining thread must begin at the top and end at the bottom of each circle, petal or leaf segment, thus it will have two cuts, one above and one below the motif, instead of one cut as in bobbin laces. Sometimes, for the sake of the status value provided by additional hand finishing, or for a variation of effect, the outlining thread was not put in until after the lace had left the loom. Then it might be run in by hand with a needle and thicker thread, or it might be added by a sewing machine, operated by hand. In the former case the running stitch which was used has no counterpart in bobbin laces. In the latter, neither does the couched-down appearance of the superficial cordonnet which, being applied to one surface of the lace only, gives it a right and wrong side (figs. 44, 45, 46 & 47; and see pages 33–6).

7 Laces of all kinds are often decorated along the heading with little loops of thread, which are known as picots. In machine laces a string of these may be made separately, and then stitched on. This does not happen in bobbin laces, except in the rare instances where eighteenth-century laces have been cannibalized to pander to nineteenth-century tastes. In cases where the machine adds the picot border to the lace as it is being made, that is the border and the main fabric of the lace are continuous, the difference between hand and machine is less noticeable, but a certain clumsiness of manoeuvre may discover it (figs. 45, 48, 49 & 50).

8 Occasionally a machine stitch appears which has no bobbin counterpart, for example Levers' so-called 'fining' (figs. 46 & 49), where the threads of the solid parts interlock in a zigzag manner.

9 Because machine patterns are entirely controlled mechanically, they are not subject to whim, mood, impatience, or freedom of choice. They were programmed, by the perforated Jacquard cards, to ceaseless unvarying repetition, and there was no way that one pattern could differ from the next, except as the result of mechanical breakdown. The chance of such unvarying precision in a hand-made fabric is remote indeed but, as has been pointed out already, the more

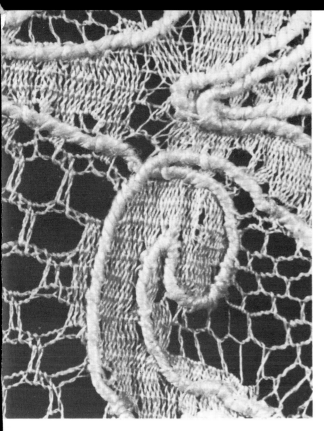

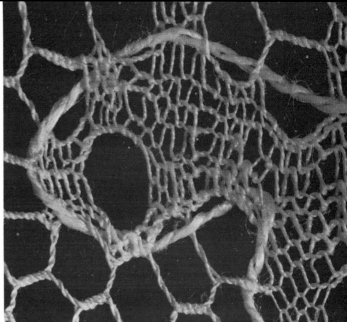

Fig. 46 *A needlerun outline.* ×10.

Fig. 47 *A couched-on outline.*

Fig. 48 *A nineteenth-century machine picot border chain-stitched to a c1700 bobbin lace.* ×10.

Fig. 49 *A picot border caught by over-sewing stitches to the machine lace edge.* ×10.

Fig. 50 *A picot border made in one with the machine lace.* ×10.

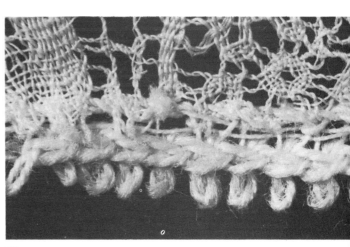

48

49

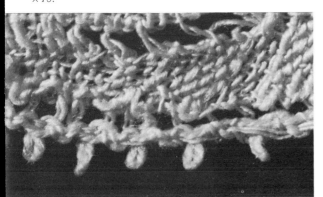

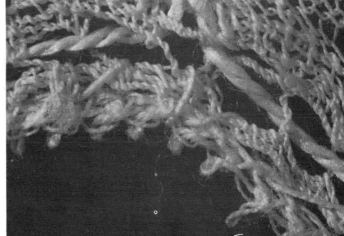

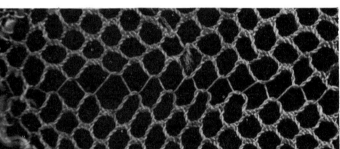

Fig. 51 *How larger pieces of bobbin lace can be built up* **a** *Two pieces of Mechlin lace are joined down the centre to make a lappet. The join is visible only where it is giving way.* **b** *A ×10 enlargement to show the course of the joining thread – a great strain on the eyes when the individual meshes were so minute.*

competent the lace maker the greater will be her control, persistence, and steadfastness, and the more nearly will her work approximate to that of a very de luxe machine.

10 Machine laces are often harsh and stiff to the touch, especially the larger pieces. They were made of cotton, and needed 'finishing' to give them body, to hold them firm and extended, so that they did not collapse in wear, or crumple when handled in a shop. Good laces, hand made in linen thread, seldom needed this treatment, but it was given to some, and therefore too great an importance should never be attached to this kind of texture.

11 Machines can make lace in 5- or 6-yard widths. Continuous bobbin laces are usually not more than five inches wide, very rarely indeed up to 10 or 12 inches, since this necessitates a huge number of bobbins, perhaps more than 1000, which is extraordinarily difficult to handle, and makes the work despairingly slow, such as two years to complete one metre (fig. 51).

12 Machines, after about 1900, were producing their own original and often charming designs – of railway engines, hot air balloons, the Battle of Britain, and the United States' Declaration of Independence (fig. 52).

Fig. 52 *A commemmorative piece made on the Raschel machine, Nottingham, 1981.*

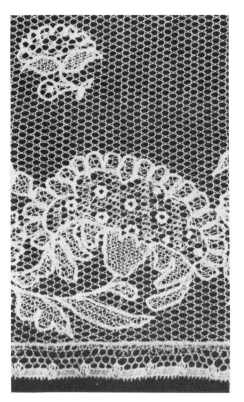

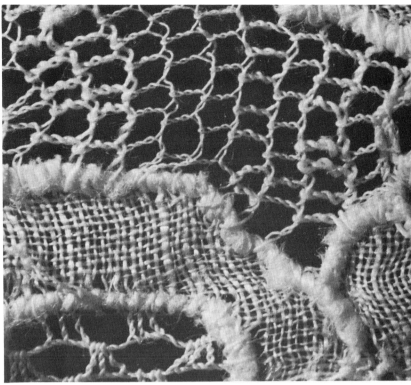

Fig. 53 *Darned net. A fine thread ducks regularly in and out of the meshes, manufacturing a delicate floral design.*

Fig. 54 *The raw edges of the muslin held by a couched outlining thread. A form of Carrickmacross with a most unusual buttonhole stitch ground.*

Fig. 55 *A sketch to show cording. An outline similar to a gros point flower has been constructed and the centre is in process of being filled with darning. As in mending a sock threads are laid down in one direction, and then the needle is woven in and out across them.*

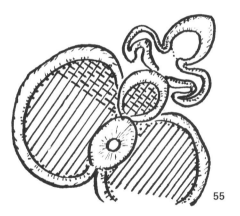

55

These, however, were late developers. For the most part the machines were conscientiously imitative, so that to judge a lace by design alone must involve more errors of identification than any other single factor.

What else approximates to a woven look, and so could conceivably be mistaken for a bobbin lace?

Firstly, there are *decorated nets*. The twist machines just described produced initially a plain net which had, because the technique for machine patterning had not yet been invented, to be patterned by hand. This was done in various ways. Tambour work used a chain stitch. Needlerun uses a darning stitch, and so is excluded from consideration in the same manner as filet and buratto (fig. 53). The net could also be patterned by the application of shapes of woven material. Since these shapes were cut out they always had raw edges which were only partially concealed by a couched thread (figs. 25 & 54), or a line of chain stitching. The nineteenth-century fabric appliqué from Ireland, known as Carrickmacross, and the seventeenth-century fabric guipure from Italy known as intagliatela, were both – to make the situation further complicated – copied by machines in Switzerland and Austria.

Secondly, another kind of needlework, sometimes

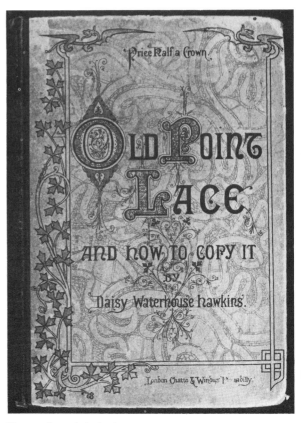

Fig. 56 *A head of William Tell, part of a picture of the man and his son, within a border of Edelweiss. Made on the hand embroidery machine by Emil Nef, St Gallen, 1917. Designed by Johannes Oertli, the picture was originally presented as a prize to the winners of the National Shooting Competition held in St Gallen in 1904.*

Fig. 57 *One of the books introducing the renaissance of 'point' laces, or at least of their designs.*

called *cording*, involved the use of a darning stitch (punto a cordella) and copied mainly the patterns of needle laces while producing incongruously an appearance of weaving. This type of work was done in Burano in the 1870s (Urbani) (figs. 55 & 215); and was copied in turn by the ponderously ingenious Swiss hand embroidery machine (fig. 56).

Thirdly, woven- or bobbin-made *braids* are sometimes linked by buttonhole stitch fillings to form hybrid laces copying antique bobbin or needle lace designs (figs. 57, 58). However, provided more than a quick glance is given to them, there is little likelihood of their proving deceptive.

Fourthly, a very complex embroidery machine known as the Schiffli was able from the 1880s to imitate the designs of many, indeed most, bobbin laces, and though the technique overall was quite different, the counterfeit appearance was marvellously rendered (fig. 59).

Lastly, on an ordinary weaving loom the wefts, while still in the main passing in a direction at right angles to the warps, may be manipulated to form an openwork pattern. At its simplest this method produces a plain gauze weave such as that used as a foundation for buratto lace. A rather more complex manipulation of wefts can produce a wide range of patternings which are known as *loom laces* (fig. 60). The near-consistent 90° angle of the threads in itself distinguishes them from all but an extremely small number of bobbin laces (see also weft wrap, figs. 17 & 18).

It may seem a reversal of the natural order, even a putting of the horse after the cart, to consider the forgeries and imitations when as yet so little has been said about the bobbin laces themselves. Rest assured that the study of bobbin laces is vastly simplified just by knowing what *not* to consider.

Fig. 58 **a** *A design from D.W. Hawkins' book indicating how braid can be applied to an outline sketch.* **b** *A close-up of a seventeenth-century braid lace which used a woven-look tape, and buttonhole stitch fillings.* × *10.*

Fig. 59 **a** *An Edwardian dress giving the impression of a hem and yoke of Honiton lace.* **b** *Part of the hem enlarged showing the slightly fuzzy appearance characteristic of a Schiffli chemical lace.*

Fig. 60 *A simple twentieth-century loom lace. No warp or weft threads have been removed, they have simply been manipulated to make the intervening meshes.*

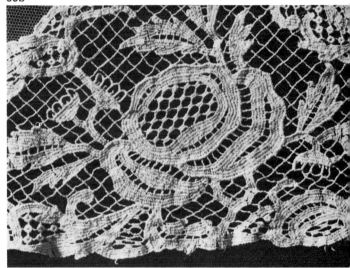

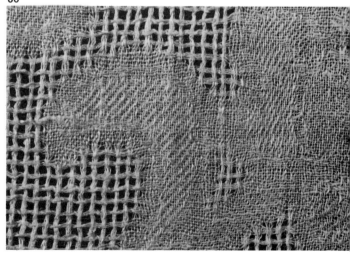

THREE
The Technique of Bobbin Laces

The Parts of a Lace: Continuity and Outlines

The terms 'design' and 'ground' have already been used freely. It is time to look at the parts of a lace (fig. 61).

It can be seen that in this bobbin lace the threads pass from the ground, over an outlining thread, into the design motif, through it and out on the other side, crossing the gimp once more, and weaving their way into the next expanse of ground. In other words, the threads of the ground and of the solid parts are *continuous* (fig. 62a).

This means that the entire width of the lace would

have to be worked in continuity, and the wider it was the more bobbins it would need, and the longer it would all take. According to Carlier (1902) a pair of Valenciennes lappets in the third quarter of the eighteenth century would require 1200 bobbins, and would occupy a worker for ten months. They would cost between £40 and £960 (1000 and 24,000 livres) while the workers would receive for each 15-hour day between 20 and 30 sous (between 4p and 6p).

The disadvantage of the continuous method can be overcome to some extent by making narrow strips, and then joining them (fig. 51). Alternatively, when the lace

Fig. 61 *The terms used for the parts of a lace.*

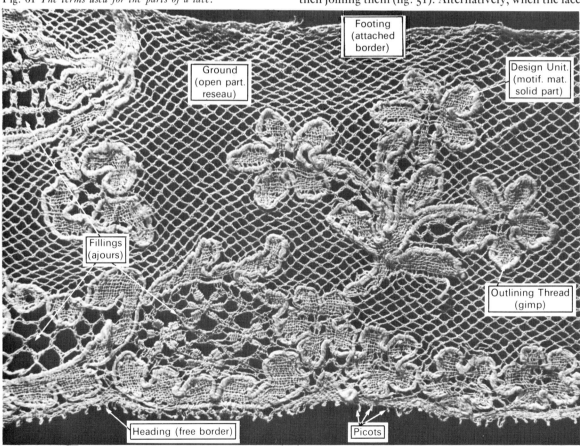

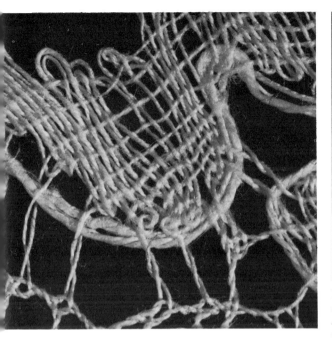

Fig. 62 **a** *The continuity of threads between the more solid and more open parts of a lace.* × 10. **b** *A parasol cover of Maltese lace. The large and complex shape is made possible by the invisible joining of odd-shaped segments.* **c** *The jigsaw technique used in Honiton lace.*

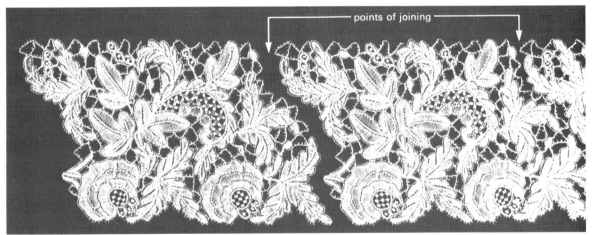

points of joining

has a large design, odd shapes comprising sprays of flowers, garlands or geometric blocks can be worked and then fitted together like a giant jigsaw, so that the joins are inconspicuous (fig. 62b & c). These laces are still continuous since, in each piece, ground and motifs are made from the same threads. The piece-work technique enables a number of workers to co-operate in making a large article so that it can be completed more quickly. For example, orders by the Empress Eugenie in 1854 for a large Chantilly shawl from Lefebure, and for a Chantilly flounce from Pigache and Mallat, were completed remarkably quickly, in time for the Exhibition of 1855 (Morris and Hague).

Another means of acceleration is to make the design

motifs self-contained so that their threads are kept inside them and do not extend beyond. Then all the separate motifs have to be joined by a ground before a lace is created. This joining can be done in various ways, but most commonly by 'sewings' (accrochetage). A minute needle or hook is used, and the threads for the ground are drawn one at a time through the hundreds, even thousands, of tiny loops made along the edges of the motifs as they were worked. Fig. 63 is a × 10 enlargement: reduce it by ten and you will have some idea of the near invisibility and appalling eye strain which the workers had to endure. Fig. 64, also × 10, but of a much thicker lace, shows the sewings and the technique of *non-continuity* more clearly.

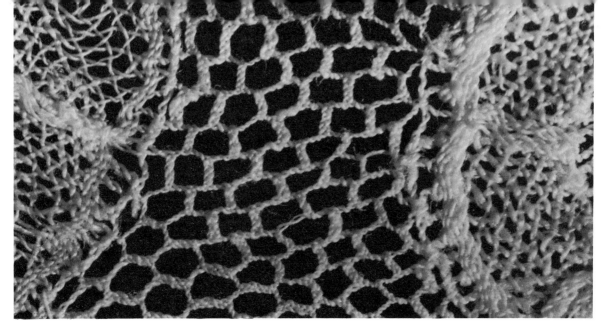

Fig. 63 *Non-continuity. Each mesh of the ground must be joined by sewings to the margin threads of the motifs.* × 10.

Fig. 64 *A much heavier lace. 1 to 6 are sewings.*

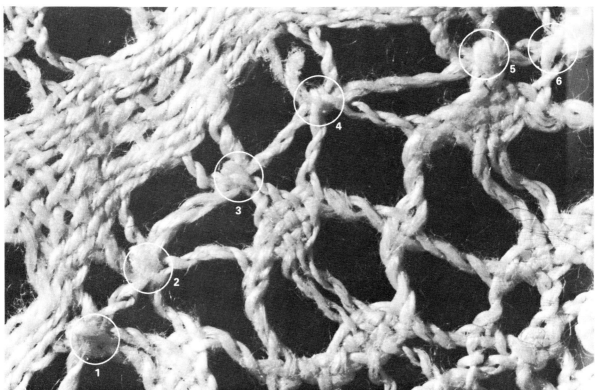

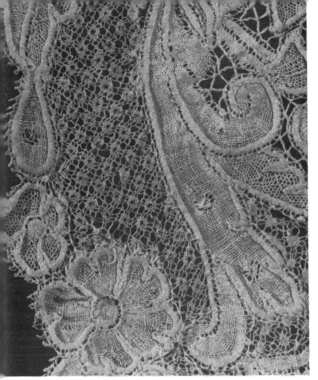

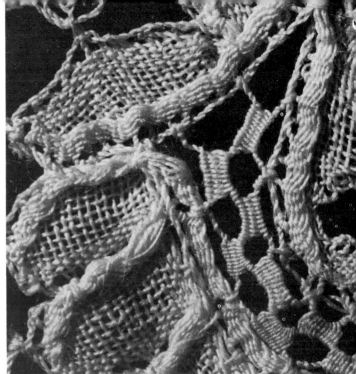

In non-continuous laces, apart from the increased speed consequent upon the large number of independent workers who could be employed on one piece (200 reputedly for Queen Victoria's wedding lace), there is in addition no restriction on shape. Wedges, arcs, or cylinders pose no problem: it is simply a question of arranging the motifs in the desired manner and then linking them together. For continuous laces on the other hand, even the construction of the corner of a handkerchief, the arc of a fan leaf, or the segment of a parasol cover, can present severe technical problems.

The continuity and non-continuity of bobbin laces are characteristic of specific geographical locations, and so are helpful in identification. This aspect will be referred to again in pages 50–60 and 67.

Occasionally the *outline* of the motifs is emphasized, for example by a heavy thread or gimp which hugs the border flatly like a heavily pencilled line (figs. 61 & 62). In non-continuous laces the outline may in addition appear like a raised prominence, giving to the forms of leaves, petals, birds or butterflies a slightly bolstered vitality: this is called 'raised work'. It is rare in bobbin laces, which are generally regarded as flat, and occurs almost exclusively in the so-called Honiton and Brussels laces. It gives a two-sided (front and reverse) aspect to the lace so that it is not fully reversible (fig. 65). Only very seldom is a gimp asymmetrically placed, for example in rare early eighteenth-century Mechlin pieces where the heavy thread is caught unevenly on the two sides (fig. 66); or in Katherine of Aragon laces where the gimp lies centrally along the trail (fig. 67).

The negative feature, the absence of an outlining

Fig. 65 a *An early eighteenth-century Brussels lace, the outline emphasized with raised work.* **b** *Detail of the raised work. Sewings can also be seen along both sides of the decorative filling.*

thread, may also have diagnostic value, as in the continuous laces of Binche and Valenciennes (fig. 68), or the non-continuous lace of Milan (fig. 64).

Sometimes the gimp is an inconsistent feature: it may appear in some Beds laces, and not others (fig. 69); in some early eighteenth-century Antwerp (fig. 70); and rarely in a non-continuous form of nineteenth-century lace known as 'Brabant Valenciennes', its designs being inspired by those of the eighteenth-century Brabant laces from Flanders (Carlier). Since both outlining thread and non-continuity are uncharacteristic of Valenciennes as normally defined, the adoption of a quite different name might be preferable.

The *heading* of the lace may be straight, dentate or scalloped, in varying degrees, but not often sufficiently exclusively or consistently to be very helpful in identification (fig. 71).

The precise structure of the *footing* is variable, and of limited help. Frequently there is a kind of secondary footing, an added narrow band, which is sometimes contemporary and sometimes a later addition. This is simply a protective attachment through which the sewing thread catching the lace to the garment would pass, and which therefore, rather than the lace itself, would suffer the drags, tears and stresses of being worn. It could be replaced inexpensively, and frequently was. It therefore may play only a misleading part in identification.

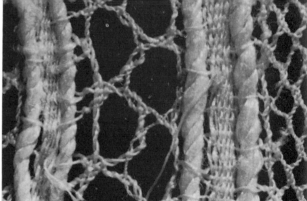

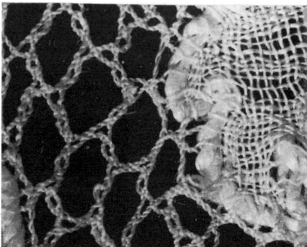

Fig. 66 **a** *A mid-eighteenth-century Mechlin lace with a prominent gimp.* **b** *The gimp bulges on the front side, and* **c** *is flat on the reverse side.*

Fig. 67 *The central superficial gimp of Katherine of Aragon lace.*

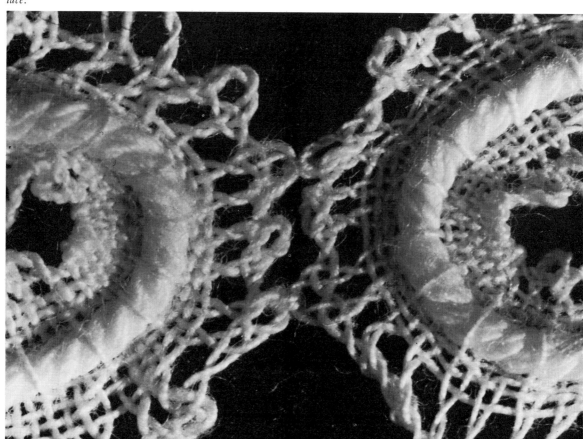

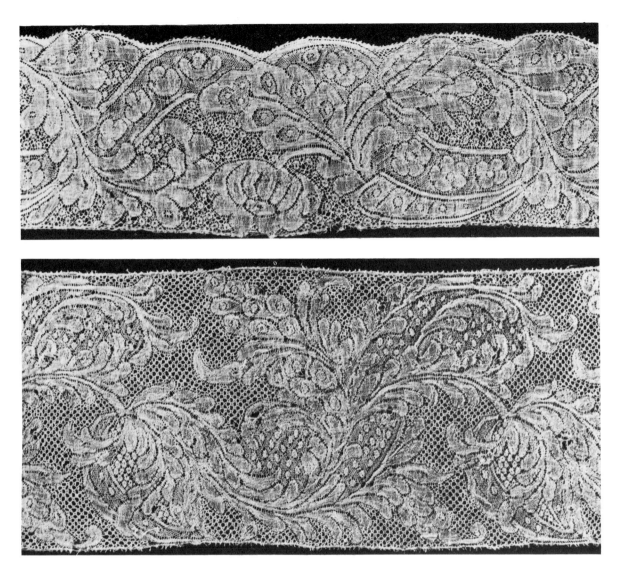

Fig. 68 **a** *Binche;* **b** *Valenciennes. Both actual size.* **c** *Detail of Valenciennes to show the lack of an outlining thread.* ×*10.*

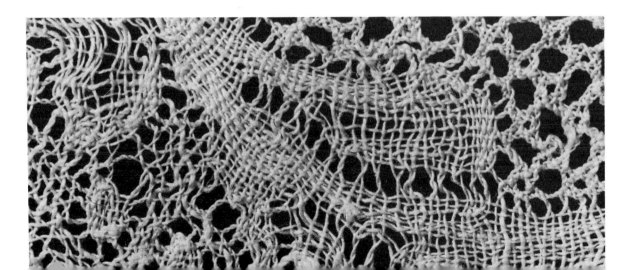

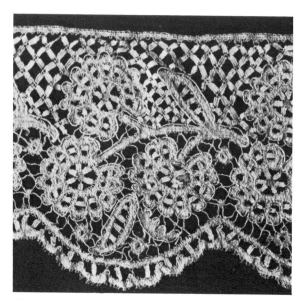

69a

Fig. 69 **a** *Beds with a plaited ground;* **b** *Detail of gimp and 'plaits'.* × 10. **c** *Beds with gimps running through as well as around the solid parts;* **d** *Detail,* × 10; **e** *Honiton with a leadwork ground.*

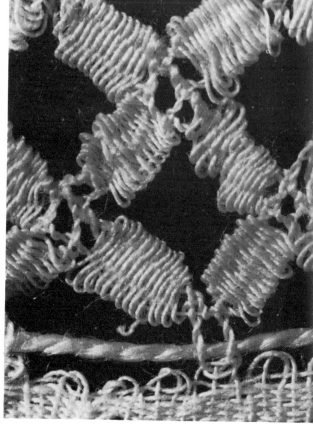

69b

69c

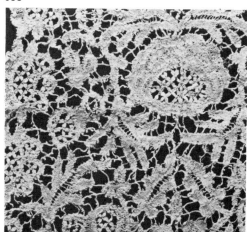

69d

69e

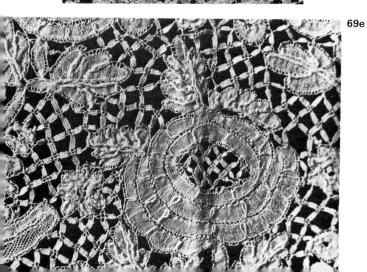

70a

70b

Fig. 70 *Early eighteenth-century Antwerp lace of the 'potten kant' variety:* **a** *with a gimp;* **b** *without gimp.*

71a

71c

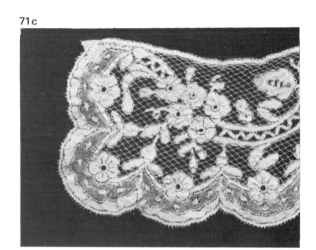

Fig. 71 *Headings* **a** *straight;* **b** *dentate;* **c** *and* **d** *scalloped.*

71b

71d

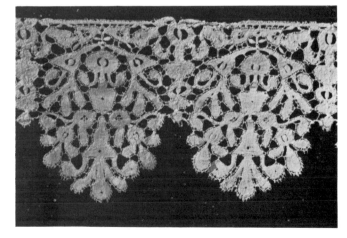

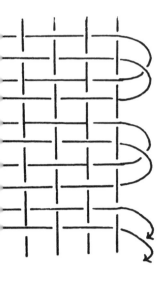 

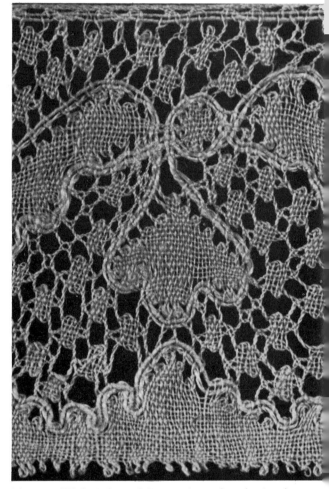

Fig. 72 **a** *The double worker threads at the edge of a wholestitch area.* **b** *The single worker threads at the edge of a halfstitch area.*

Fig. 73 **a** *Wholestitch motifs in a continuous lace showing the right-angled crossing of threads parallel to the long and short axes.* **b** *Part of a non-continuous lace showing how the wholestitch threads curve around to follow the design.*

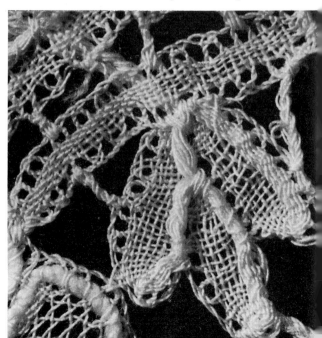

The Stitches of the Motifs (Plats)

The two basic thread movements of bobbin laces were explored in the previous chapter. Known as the cross and the twist (fig. 33), they are in themselves quite the simplest of actions: it is the permutations and combinations of sequence which make them complex.

In the structural work of the motifs only two basic stitches occur. These are wholestitch (clothwork, mat, toilé) and halfstitch (grille, half-linnen). The clothwork comprises a repetition of the single wholestitch (passée) sequence CTC (i.e. cross-twist-cross) as two worker bobbins (voyageurs) gyrate their way across a variable number of passives. Where they turn about at the end, before retracing their steps, their two threads can be clearly seen (figs. 33, 62a & 72). In continuous laces the woven threads of wholestitch run parallel to the long and short axes of the lace, crossing each other at right angles; in non-continuous laces they more frequently follow the shape of the motif (fig. 73).

The grille comprises a repetition of the halfstitch (demi-passée) CT only. A single worker passes over and around the passive threads and its path can be traced where it curves back at the border of the halfstitch area.

Wholestitch is found in a vast range of laces and so is not in itself helpful in identification. Halfstitch is less common. It is particularly associated with black laces, notably those of the Chantilly type. Black lace is a good deal more trying for the eyes, and slower to make, and so more expensive, than comparable white pieces. This is because of the difficulty of seeing the threads clearly

Fig. 74 *The sombre appearance of a black lace worked in wholestitch.*

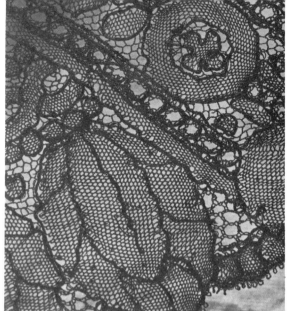

Fig. 75 *The lighter effect of halfstitch.*

Fig. 76 *Halfstitch in a Pusher lace.*

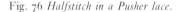

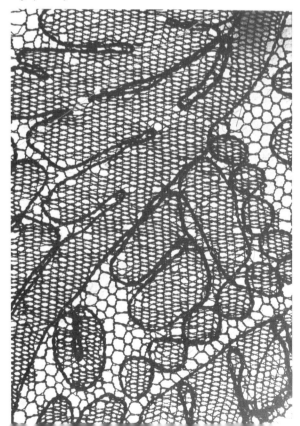

and judging their tension as the work progresses. The use of halfstitch speeds the making, while at the same time it introduces a delicacy which counteracts the heaviness of colour (figs. 74 & 75).

White laces made of halfstitch are rare, though some white Chantilly was made at Bayeux in the first half of the nineteenth century. Other halfstitch white laces, often with an open 'fond chant' ground – named after the original eighteenth-century Chantilly – may have been worked on patterns originally intended for black thread. Laces with halfstitch motifs are always continuous, and always have a gimp outline, the first being necessary to give strength and substance to the rather insubstantial design; the second to form a line of demarcation between the open design and the open ground.

Caution is needed in identifying halfstitch laces as hand made. The Pusher machine in the mid-nineteenth century made marvellously accurate copies of Chantilly both in black and off-white, using a silky thread the elasticity of which produced a slight irregularity – a feature often taken to indicate a hand-made lace (fig. 76, and compare fig. 32). Note, however, that the gimp has been run in by hand, the thread ducks in and out of the meshes, and the parallel warps can be picked out. In the hand-made lace on the contrary, the gimp is held between design and ground by the threads linking them together, there are no regularly straight threads, and the direction of the work can change a little from one part of the lace to another as the worker moves the pillow to find the most convenient position.

Fig. 77 *Wholestitch and halfstitch in a Chantilly lace, nineteenth century.*

In the 1870s and after, experimental designs combining wholestitch and halfstitch produced some delightful impressions of sunlight and shade (figs. 77 & 78). This was not entirely a new idea since it occurred in some eighteenth-century laces, but it was not until the late nineteenth century that it really caught on.

To summarize: Motifs can be made of

a wholestitch (many laces)

b halfstitch (Chantilly-type black laces, and a few white. All are continuous, and have an outlining gimp)

c a mixture of wholestitch and halfstitch, post 1870, in most countries, but especially northern France in the Bayeux area.

The Stitches of the Decorative Fillings

The fillings form the central part of the design motifs, and their function is not to establish the shapes, but to enliven them with decoration. While the 'crust' of each motif is invariably formed of plain wholestitch or halfstitch the fillings, like those of a pie, may be many, extensive and extremely varied (fig. 79).

Altogether there must be hundreds of filling stitches but, to date, their value in identification is limited. The stitches must wait to be matched reliably with specific dates or localities before we can begin to argue in the reverse direction: because such and such a stitch is present, therefore it is such and such a lace.

Fig. 80 shows the mayflower filling, characteristic of Bucks laces. Fig. 81 shows honeycomb, also characteristic of Bucks, but found in addition in Chantilly-type laces of the nineteenth century. Quatrefoil (fig. 82), and snowball (fig. 83) are characteristic of late

Fig. 77 *Wholestitch and halfstitch in a Chantilly lace, nineteenth century.*

Fig. 78 *Blended wholestitch and halfstitch in late nineteenth-century Belgian lace.*

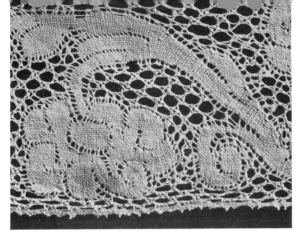

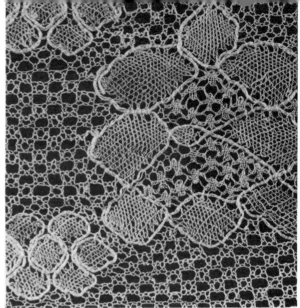

Fig. 79 **a** *Lace with no fillings;* **b** *with one filling;* **c** *with many.*

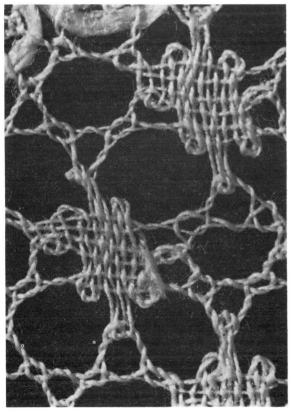

Fig. 80 *Mayflower filling stitch.* ×10.

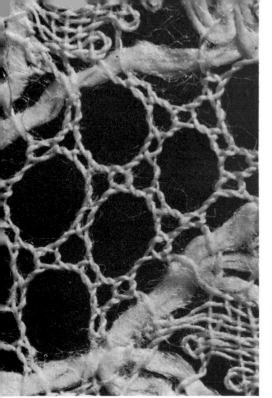

Fig. 81 a *Honeycomb;* b *Bucks to show several characteristic filling stitches.*

Fig. 82 *Quatrefoil and a kind of snowball filling called partridge eye.*

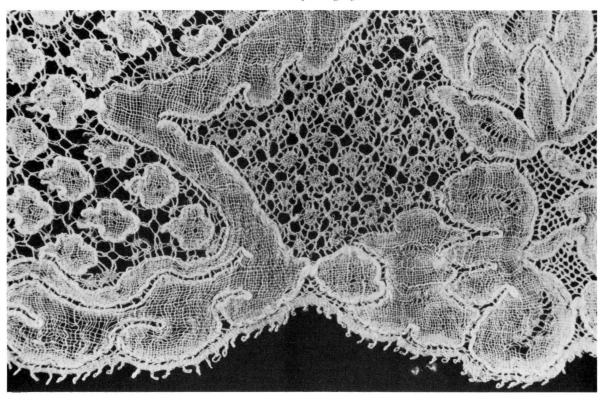

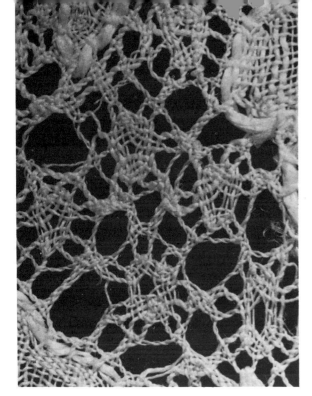
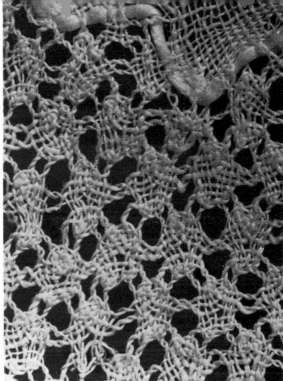

Fig. 83 *Detail of two types of snowball filling.*

Fig. 84 *Milanese c1700 with numerous fillings.*

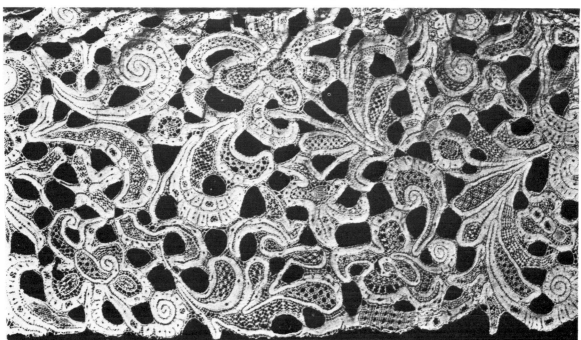

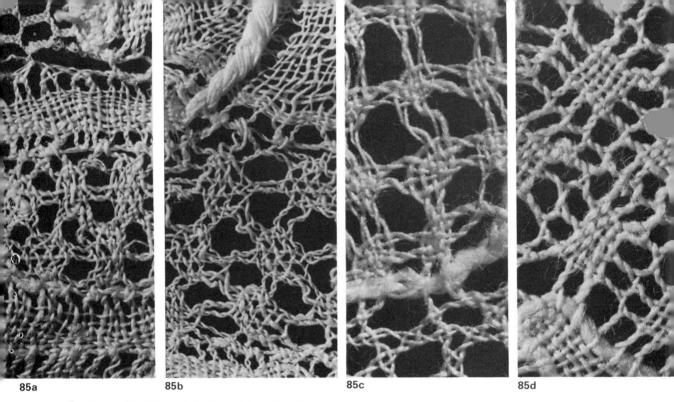

85a 85b 85c 85d

Fig. 85 a *and* b *Filling stitches from eighteenth-century*
Devon lace; c *from point de Paris;* d *and* e *from Antwerp;*
f *Bayeux;* g *old Bucks.*

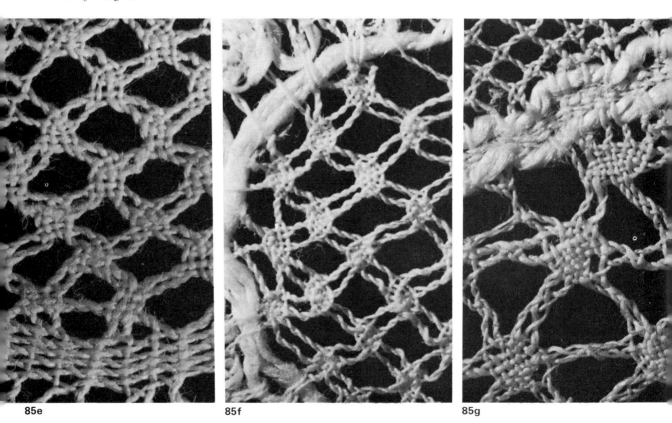

85e 85f 85g

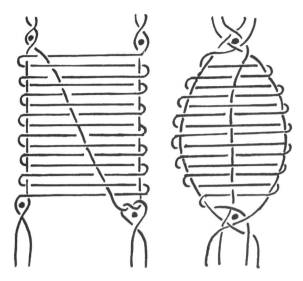

Fig. 86 *Sketches of the structure of square and oval point d'esprit.*

seventeenth-century and early-eighteenth century Flemish laces such as Mechlin, Binche, Valenciennes and point d'Angleterre.

Non-continuous laces frequently have more fillings than continuous ones. Since the filling stitches, like those of the ground, are attached to the motifs by sewings they could, at least in theory, all be made by different workers, each specializing in one stitch. Fig. 84 shows Milanese lace of the late seventeenth century. This small length contains no fewer than 20 different fillings. Fig. 85 shows other filling stitches found in various laces, but not being exclusive neither can they be conclusive in identification. No doubt in the future they will help a lot more than they do now.

Points d'esprit

A special group of decorative stitches known by the general term 'point d'esprit'. They are constructed by a kind of basket stitch (fig. 86), and are of two main forms:
A the square (points d'esprit carrées) known in Britain as tallies (east Midlands) and leadworks (Devon);
B the oval (points d'esprit ovales) known in Britain as leaves (Midlands).

Confusion can easily arise in translation, both because of the similarity of 'leaf' and 'lead'; and also because of the double meaning of 'leaf', as part of a floral sprig, and as an oval point d'esprit. The ideal universal lace language, when it is created, must free itself of such double entendres.

A 1 The square point d'esprit, suspended in the heart of a flower like a legless spider in a four-strand web, is characteristic equally of nineteenth-century Brussels, and of Honiton, laces (fig. 87).

2 In Honiton variations of the leadwork form important fillings, and can help to distinguish the lace from Brussels which, at the end of the nineteenth century, it very closely resembled (fig. 88).

3 In Bucks (east Midlands), Lille (north-east France) and Tonder (Denmark), little diapers of point d'esprit provide an attractive powdering to the ground (fig. 89). They more rarely appear as fillings, but in Bucks 'tallies in honeycomb' and 'clockwork with tallies' are quite characteristic (fig. 90).

4 They occur as a diamond-shaped grill or lattice filling in some of the Beds laces, especially those of the later nineteenth century which imitated Honiton designs, though not Honiton techniques, since Beds was continuous and Honiton non-continuous. These tallies fill the flower centres like so many stamens, but similar lattice-work may also form the ground of the lace, both in Beds and Honiton (fig. 69a & e, and see page 53).

5 In some Beds laces, especially those known as Beds Maltese (second half of the nineteenth century), and some eighteenth-century Flemish and Milanese laces, the square point d'esprit are curled above the surface like tiny buttons, prettily representing the hair of people or animals (fig. 91).

B 1 The oval point d'esprit is not found in Honiton, Bucks, Brussels, Lille or Tonder, but is found in the Beds, Le Puy, Hainault, and Cluny laces of the second half of the nineteenth century, and in Chinese copies of them. In Cluny the ovals most commonly radiate like

Fig. 87 *Honiton leadworks.*

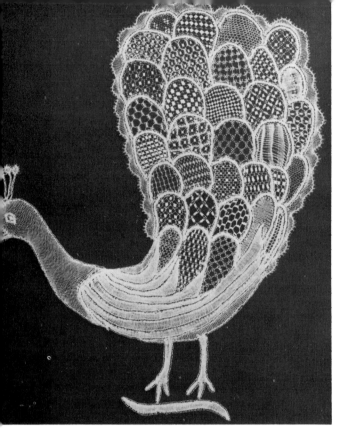

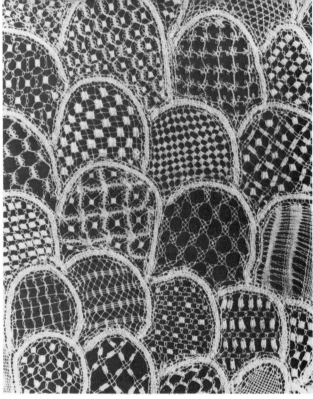

Fig. 88 **a** *A sampler of Honiton filling stitches;* **b** *detail;* **c** *key.*

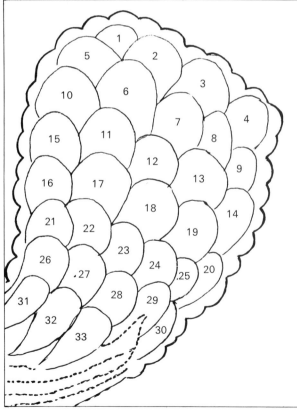

1 Spotted net
2 Strawberry (swing and a pin)
3 Chudleigh (variation)
4 Four pin with leadwork
5 Blossom with leadwork
6 Toad in the hole
7 Blossom
8 Link with leadwork
9 Four-pin bud
10 Link and leadwork (variation)
11 Devonshire cutwork
12 No pin
13 Diamond with leadwork
14 Toad in the hole (variation)
15 Snatches (snatch bar)
16 Cushion
17 Snatches with leadwork
18 Six-pin
19 Ladder trail
20 Net (trolley net)
21 Link and stitch (pin and a chain)
22 Italian
23 Link and leadwork
24 Taunton
25 Cushion and pin
26 No pin and link
27 Diamond
28 Brick
29 Boxes
30 Chudleigh twist
31 Link (pin and a stitch)
32 Cucumber (straight pin)
33 Four pin

90

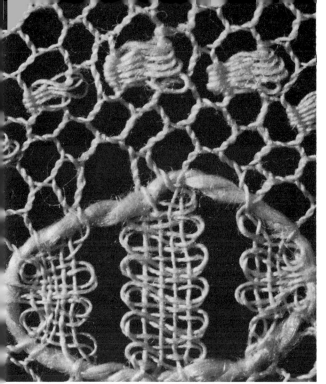

89 Fig. 89 *Lille with square point d'esprit in the ground.*

Fig. 90 *Bucks 'clothwork with tallies'.*

Fig. 91 **a** *Beds Maltese with leaves, and raised tallies.* **b** *Eighteenth-century Milanese, the raised point d'esprit adding interest to the symbols of the sacred heart, the cock and the cross;* **c** *detail* × 10.

91a

91b

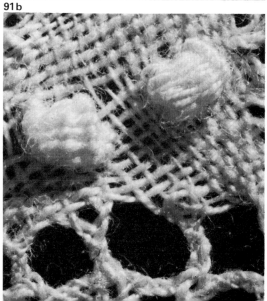

91c

Fig. 92 *Oval point d'esprit:* **a** *Cluny;* **b** *Le Puy – the lower border shows them arranged in rows.*

the spokes of a wheel, an arrangement found also in some torchon laces. In Le Puy they are frequently arranged in long rows like the pinnate fronds of a fern (fig. 92).

2 Raised leaves (sometimes known as 'raised wheatears'), attached flatly to the surface of the whole-stitch or halfstitch shapes, occur as a kind of appliqué decoration in some of the twentieth-century Beds, Le Puy and Hainault laces, especially where the design is otherwise rather uninteresting (fig. 93).

Picots

This is a general term for the little loops (also called purls or pearls) which protrude along the heading of a lace (fig. 87). They represent, in continuous laces, merely the points at which the threads have turned in order to work their way back towards the footing (fig. 45). In laces where the motifs are joined by bars (see pages 64–5), the little picots may hang along these strands like dewdrops on a wire fence. They may even be important enough to give their name to the definition of a lace, as in 'Flemish eighteenth-century bobbin lace with brides picotées' (fig. 94). Fig. 95(a) shows picots on braided bars which link also to oval point d'esprit to form a stout trelliswork. (b) shows a delicate use of picots in a dainty streamer-like filling. Note the immense difference in texture, itself an important feature in identification.

To summarize: Most laces have additional decorations, apart from the motifs and the ground. The decorations vary enormously in quantity and type, and if they are unique enough and consistent enough they may help to locate, or date, a lace.

The Stitches of the Grounds

The grounds of a lace comprise all the open parts which lie between the motifs. They enclose the motifs, in

Fig. 93 *Detail of Katherine of Aragon lace showing square and oval point d'esprit, one appliquéd to a wholestitch surface.*

Fig. 94 *An early eighteenth-century Flemish lace with brides picotées.*

95a

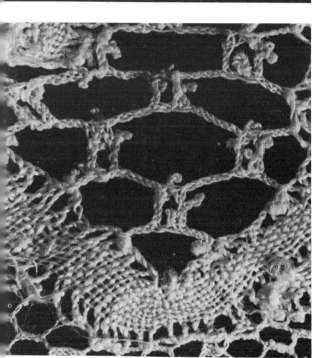

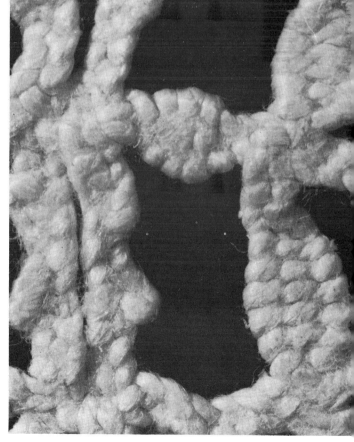

Fig. 95 **a** *Genoese lace c1600;* **b** *Eighteenth-century Devon 'point d'Angleterre' lace. Detail of decorative picots, both* × *10.*

95b

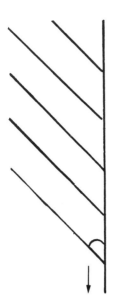

Fig. 96 *How the angle of working is measured.*

contradistinction to the fillings, which the motifs enclose.

Grounds are of prime importance in identifying the locality of laces, indeed some of the grounds are named after places. Some reference to geographical location will therefore be made here, though its full consideration is left to chapter 4.

We have seen already that the ground threads may be either continuous with those of the design motifs, or separate from them, i.e. non-continuous (see pages 30–3).

Apart from this, grounds may consist of fine, close regular meshes, or of variously distributed bars (brides, legs, bridges). Intermediate between the two, with a foot as it were in either camp, are a few laces with large irregular meshes made of bars, looking rather like crazy paving but with the solid blocks represented by holes and the lines between them by braided strands.

It follows that there are five basic groups of grounds:
1. Reseaux (meshworks) of continuous laces.
2. Reseaux of non-continuous laces.
3. Bars of continuous laces.
4. Bars of non-continuous laces.
5. Bars arranged as large meshes.
Laces with a ground of bars are sometimes called 'guipures'.

Group 1 *Reseaux of continuous laces*
There are quite a lot of these, distinguished in the main by the cross-twist sequences of which they are constructed. However, there is another extremely important variable, namely the angle of working. It has been

mentioned earlier (p. 23) that the active threads of nearly all bobbin laces pass across the passives in a diagonal manner. The angle is often a 45° one, but it can be as low as 40° or as high as 68°. Beyond that it jumps to 90° and then is no longer diagonal but straight.

When the pattern or pricking is constructed, this angle is measured along the footing of the lace (figs. 96, 61 & 6). The pricking is so called because of the tiny holes which are pierced in it ready to receive the pins during the working. In the area of the ground, the holes resolve themselves into a series of lines intersecting at the appropriate angle (fig. 97). The pricking provides in effect the skeleton around which the body of the lace is constructed. The fact that on the European continent continuous laces are worked with the footing to the left of the pillow, while in the east Midlands the footing is worked to the right – with that same independence of spirit which makes the British drive on the left – makes no significant difference in identification, since with few exceptions continuous laces are fully reversible.

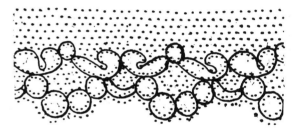

Fig. 97 *A pricking for Bucks daisy edging. The dots of the ground represent pinholes which run in diagonal lines at an angle to the footing.*

It has been suggested (Van Ruymbeke) that this contrary practice may have originated from the English tendency to copy continental European laces by taking rubbings. If paper is placed over the rough underside of a pricking, and smoothed with dark wax, the positions of the pinholes stand out sharply enough to provide a draft pattern – but the footing of the lace has been transposed from left to right. Try it yourself and see.

On the continent, less attention is given to the angles themselves than to the ratio of vertical to horizontal in the mesh shape. However, it comes to the same thing: a square divided parallel to the footing into 10 parts, and at right angles to it into six parts gives an angle of 60° (fig. 98). In either case, ready-made grids are obtainable, providing whatever angle or ratio may be desired.

As far as the cross-twist sequences are concerned, those quoted below do not pretend to provide in every case the full instructions for making the ground. They are intended only to give some idea of how even slight variations can result in quite different appearances. The

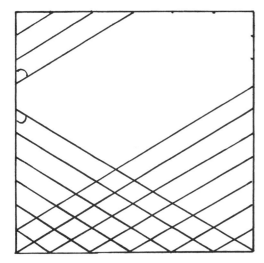

Fig. 98 *Construction of a grid with V10 H6 divisions, and a 60° angle.*

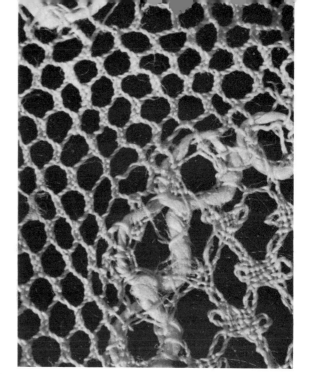

Fig. 99 *Mechlin ground:* **a** *from an eighteenth-century lace, arranged in the direction of working, × 10;* **b** *a sketch to show the technique.*

interaction of cross-twist sequences, and angles, allow a great range of possibilities, far more than can be coped with here. For example, for **vi** alone some authorities distinguish more than 20 variations (Jourde). In addition, the same sequence with a different angle can make quite a different looking ground – compare **vii** and **xiii**; while the speedy removal of the pins which temporarily fix the threads in position gives a greatly changed appearance compared with the pins being left in for some time, even when in both cases the angle and cross-twist sequence are precisely the same.

It is of course the look or finished appearance that one is dealing with in identification, rather than the detailed niceties of construction. Indeed grids and angles may, like X-rays, appear to make the flesh itself more obscure, and to be only confusing and irrelevant. However, apart from being the very stuff of the lace itself they have considerable importance in revealing at times unsuspected connections between one technique, or one lace, and another.

Faced with an actual piece of lace, the measurement of the angle may be far from easy. From the moment the lace is removed from the pillow, it suffers distortion, increased every time it is handled, worn or washed.

Whiting photographed and described 144 bobbin lace stitches, occurring either as grounds or fillings. All have their own names, indeed many have five or six different names, so that the compression of them here into 13 types, under 13 general names, has involved some stringent reduction. However, most of Whiting's grounds have not yet been tied consistently to specific laces, or else they are of such widespread occurrence as to be of little help in identification. Doubtless, as with

the filling stitches (see pages 40–6) further research will throw new light on where and when each variation occurred.

i Mechlin (Mechelen, Malines, Ice-ground). 40° angle. v8 H10 (fig. 99). This is made with two pairs of bobbins, and no pins are used. The working cannot be reduced to a simple cross-twist statement: four threads are braided three times parallel to the footing, the two pairs then separate, combine each with a pair from the next braid, make three plaits, and separate again. Such a ground is found only in Mechlin, and so is definitive. As far as design goes, late seventeenth- and early eighteenth-century Mechlin laces are indistinguishable from those of Binche and Valenciennes. A most unusual example of Mechlin combines this ground with a diamond-paned window effect set at a 45° angle (fig. 100).

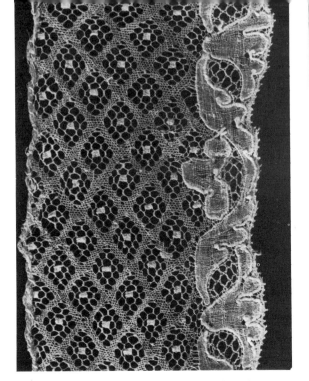

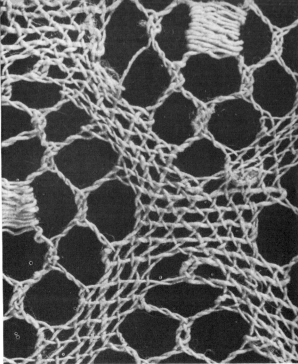

Fig. 100 *An unusual Mechlin worked at a 45° angle:* **a** *actual size;* **b** *detail.*

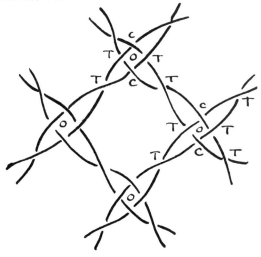

Fig. 101 *The working of torchon stitch.*

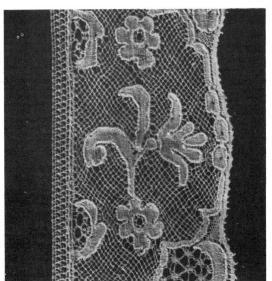

Fig. 102 *Late eighteenth-century Mechlin arranged in the direction in which it was worked. Slightly enlarged.*

ii Torchon (plain hole ground). 45° angle. V10 H10. The sequence CT-P-CT (or halfstitch-pin-halfstitch) is repeated throughout. This ground is characteristic of the late nineteenth- and twentieth-century torchon laces made throughout Europe and the Far East (fig. 101). Rarely it is found in late eighteenth-century Mechlin laces, distinguishable by their 40° angle, and floral instead of geometric designs (fig. 102). If two or three extra twists are added, the ground takes on a heavier look and is known as 'twisted halfstitch' (fig. 103).

iii Spanish ground (Maglia de Spagna, twisted hole ground, tulle double). 45° angle. V10 H10. CTT-P-CTT, repeat. This is very similar to **vii** but the pins are differently arranged, thus fixing the threads into another shape. It is also similar to **xiii**, but there the angle of working is 90° instead of 45° (fig. 104). A variation of Spanish ground is worked with an additional twist. It is typical of Spanish laces but is found occasionally in Bucks, Erzegebirge and Ipswich (Massachusetts) lace (fig. 148).

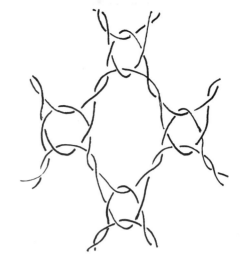

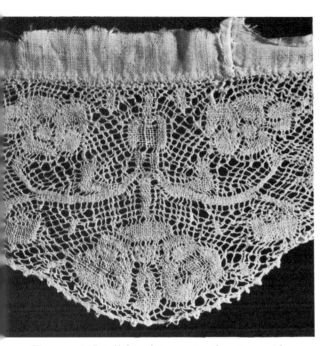

Fig. 103 *A 'Dutch' lace, late seventeenth century, with torchon ground. Actual size.*

Fig. 104 *Spanish mesh:* **a** *a sketch of the thread movements, in the position as worked;* **b** *a sample from a West Northants pattern book, 1820s;* **c** *a Spanish lace made of gold thread enriched with rose-coloured silk, nineteenth century.*

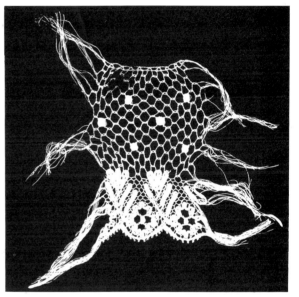

iv Snowball (boule de neige, fond de neige, partridge eye, oeil de perdrix). 45° angle. V10 H10. Superficially these small rotundities resemble spiders (fig. 105), but the thread movements which make them are quite different. They require six pairs of bobbins, and characteristically have six pinholes (fig. 106 and see fig. 83). Snowballs are found typically in Flemish laces, forming the distinctive ground of Binche and occasionally of Mechlin which, though its design may be identical, is distinguished by its outlining gimp (fig. 107).

v 'Plaited' ground (Beds). 45°. V10 H10. This is rare, and probably a plagiarism of the leadwork ground found in a few of the non-continuous Honiton laces of the mid-nineteenth century (fig. 69).

vi Five hole (Flanders, Antwerp, Krvisslagen, cinq trous, virgin ground, fond à la vierge, called in Le Puy fond mariage (Chaleyé), and in the east Midlands rose ground). 45° angle. V10 H10. There are many variations, depending on the number of pinholes per five-hole block, and the number of twists between the pins, for example Flanders (cinq trous) uses eight bobbins, one pin, and a wholestitch-halfstitch sequence; while virgin ground uses four bobbins, four pins, and halfstitch

Fig. 105 *Part of a baby bonnet made of spiders.*

Fig. 106 **a** *and* **b** *Details of two pieces of Binche c1700, to show a variety of snowballs.* × 10.

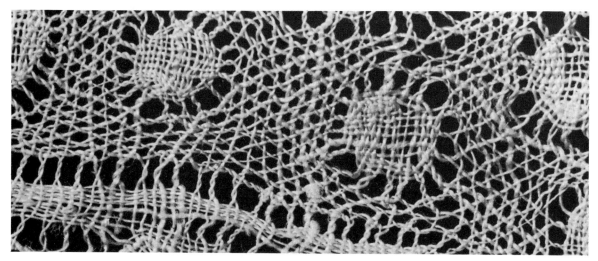

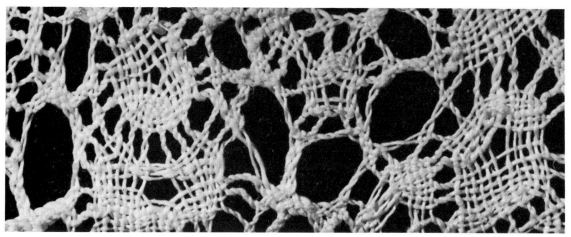

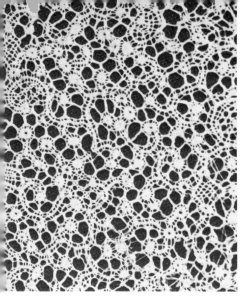
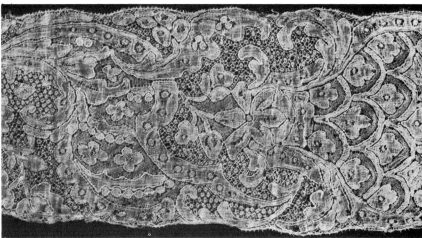

Fig. 107 *Snowballs forming the ground in* **a** *Binche;* **b** *Mechlin.*

only. English rose ground, using eight threads, four pins and halfstitch is illustrated in fig. 108(b). This ground occurs in laces from diverse times and areas (figs. 108, 109 & 110). Carlier distinguishes reseau de fantaisie, fond moucheté and fond epingle as very similar forms within this group.

vii Honeycomb (fond de mariage, point de rose, rosenground, spiegeltralie, and sometimes in Le Puy fond à la vierge (Jourde)). 45–65° angle. This is made by a repetition of CT-T-P followed by CT-T-P. When exactly the same stitch follows a pin as precedes it, this is referred to as 'closing the pin' or 'point d'epingle clos'. Honeycomb is rare as a ground (fig. 111). The cross-twist sequence is exactly the same as in **iii** but the pins are differently arranged, producing a more open mesh. It is also the same as **xiii** but at a different angle.

viii Square Valenciennes (Valenciennes à maille carrée). 50° angle. V10 H8. Two pairs of bobbins are used to make a braid which is attached to the adjacent one in a CT-P-CT manner before separating to form the next two braided sides (fig. 112). This ground was not made in Valenciennes itself after the Revolution of 1789, but it was copied in similar laces made at Ypres and elsewhere, and the original name was retained. Whiting distinguishes variations with 1 or 1½ braids (Honfleur), 2 or 2½ (Ghent), 3 or 3½ (Courtrai), 4 or 4½ (Bruges, Ypres, Alost), 5 or 5½ (Ypres, Alost). See also group **2 iii**.

ix Round Valenciennes (Valenciennes à mailles rondes). 50° angle. V10 H8. Carlier pinpoints this as one of the distinguishing features between true Valenciennes made in the town, and false Valenciennes made outside it. He says in addition that the false, or bastard, Valenciennes used only half the number of bobbins, and thicker thread, so that the designs appeared more loosely worked and were less sharply separated from the ground. Round Valenciennes is rare in continuous laces, but is found in some late seventeenth-century Flemish (fig. 113). See also group **2 ii**.

x Bucks point (Lille, fond simple). 52–68°, but commonly 52° or 58°. Basically the grid ratio is V14 H8 or V12 H7. The sequence is CT-T2-P (or CTTT-P, or halfstitch-twist twice-pin). It is not a distinctive ground, being common to Tonder (Danish), nineteenth-century Chantilly (French), and blonde (French and Spanish) as well as to Lille and Bucks (fig. 114). The ground can be made lighter by using only one twist, when it is known as 'fond clair', or heavier by using three twists. Each variation was imitated by the Heathcoat bobbinet machine.

xi Point de Paris (six-point star, wire ground, Kat stitch, fond chant). 60° angle. V10 H6. Pairs of threads merge to make a wholestitch with a pin in the middle – or sometimes below, they twist, separate, and combine with other pairs. There is a single form of point de Paris made with only three bobbins (one worker), and a double form made with six bobbins (two workers) (fig. 115). The name 'point de Paris' comes from its usage in lightweight laces of northern France, and Brittany. It occurs rarely in Bucks. A Belgian point de Paris is made at Turnhout. Fond chant was the ground of the eighteenth-century Chantilly lace (fig. 116) which ceased with the Revolution. Chantilly was revived by Napoleon 1 and made thereafter at Bayeux (Normandy), Grammont (Belgium) and in Saxony, though using a fond simple ground.

xii Fond d'armure (Spinnekop). 68° angle. This occurs, rarely, in eighteenth-century Mechlin laces, especially those made at Turnhout according to Morris and Hague (fig. 117).

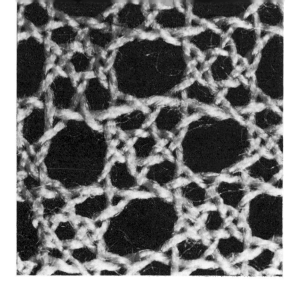

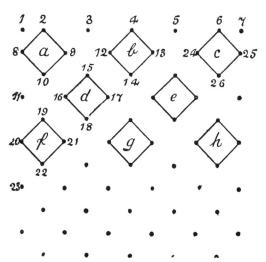

The manner in which the pattern is pricked when this stitch is to be worked is shown and it will be noticed that four holes mark the corner-set squares upon which the rest of the plaiting is founded. Four lines connect each of these holes, and a letter is set in the middle of each as a further guide to the worker.

To work the stitch, place a pin in each hole along the top of the pattern. Then on each of these pins hang one pair of bobbins. Make one half stitch with the second and third pairs, take out the pin from the hole marked 2, draw up the threads and put it in again between the two pairs into the same hole, then enclose it by working one half stitch. Make one half stitch with the first and second pairs, put a pin into the hole marked 8, enclose it as before, first opening out the threads so as to get their twist as close up against the pin as possible.

Work one half stitch with the fourth and fifth pairs, take out the pin from the hole marked 3, draw up the threads and put it in between the two middle of the four strands, enclose it in the usual way. Make one half stitch with the third and fourth pairs, place a pin in hole 9 and enclose it. Make one half stitch with the second and third pairs, place a pin in hole 10, enclose it, one half stitch with the third and fourth pairs, one half stitch with the first and second pairs, put a pin into hole 11, enclose it. Make a half stitch with the sixth and seventh pairs, put a pin into the hole marked 4 and enclose it, make one half stitch with the fifth and sixth pairs, putting a pin into hole 12, one half stitch with the seventh and eighth pairs, place a pin in hole 5 and enclose it.

Work one half stitch with the sixth and seventh pairs, put a pin into hole 13, enclose it, make one half stitch with the fifth and sixth pairs, put a pin into hole 14 and enclose it, work one half stitch with the sixth and seventh pairs, lay these two pairs aside, then make one half stitch with the fourth and fifth pairs, work one half stitch with the tenth and eleventh pairs, put a pin into the hole marked 6 and enclose it, one half stitch, put a pin at 24 and enclose it. Work one half stitch, put a pin at 25, enclose it, work one half stitch, put a pin at 26, enclose it, then work one half stitch with the tenth and eleventh pairs.

By this time the worker should have learnt the stitch sufficiently to enable her to proceed with it as far as is necessary without further repetition. It will have been noticed that for each square eight threads must be allowed. One half stitch is made first with the middle four threads, and a pin is placed in the top hole of the square, a half stitch is made with the four side threads at the left, a pin is set up and enclosed, a half stitch is made in a similar way with the four threads at the third and left-hand side, and a pin is set up and enclosed. Finally, a half stitch is made with the four middle threads, a pin is placed in the fourth hole of the square and enclosed with another half stitch.

This is double rose stitch briefly described, and it is well to practise making it, first with eight threads, then with sixteen, until the principle of the stitch is thoroughly understood.

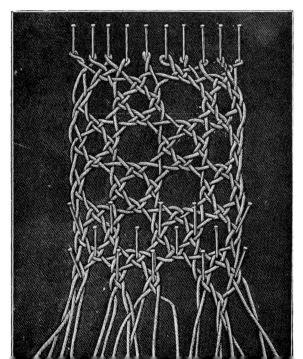

Fig 108 *Five hole ground:* **a** *detail* × *10;* **b** *pricking;* **c** *sketch, and directions for working English 'double rose ground'.*

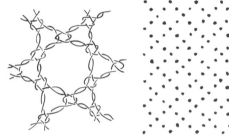

Fig. 109 *Forming the ground of late seventeenth-century Valenciennes.*

Fig. 110 *In a late nineteenth-century Yak (wool) lace.*

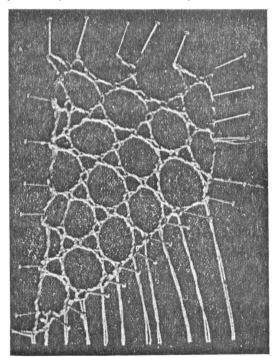

Fig. 111 *Honeycomb ground:* **a** *a sketch of the thread movements with directions;* **b** *pricking and* **c** *the finished product;* **d** *from a West Northants sample book, 1820s.*

Begin at the left-hand top corner. Pin up two couples at the first hole at the top and the left side. Work them together in half stitch, and one extra twist; put up the first pin and cover by working a half stitch and twist; then hang on two more couples on the next pin, which will be on a level, counting one for each hole, and a worker for the long row which contains double the number of holes. Take the worker, work it a half stitch, and twist with the next couple on the left, put up a pin, and cover it with the same stitch.

Take on your worker, and continue the same method until you reach the end of the line, when the last couple is left out. Start again at the right side, and work down the short row (one hole being unpricked between each). Take the worker through the next couple, work half stitch and twist, put up the pin, cover it with a half stitch and twist, and leave it. Take the next two couples and work the same way to the end of the line.

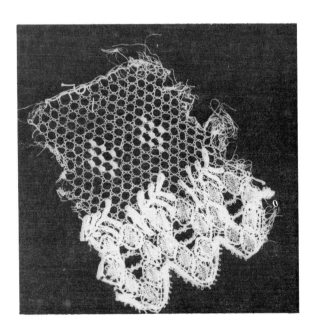

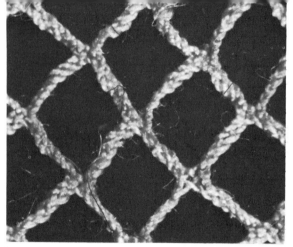

Fig. 112 *Square Valenciennes, nineteenth century,* × 10.

Fig. 113 *Round Valenciennes, continuous, from a seventeenth-century Flemish lace.* × 10.

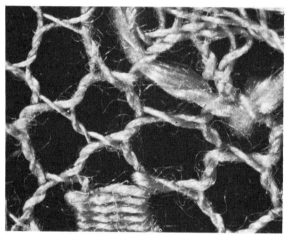

Fig. 114 *Bucks point ground,* × 10.

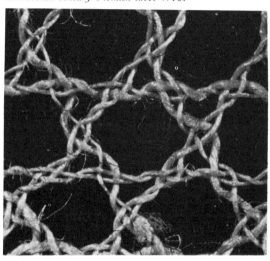

115a

Fig. 115 *Point de Paris:* **a** *detail* × 10; **b** *in Bucks;* **c** *in Belgian point de Paris, early twentieth century.*

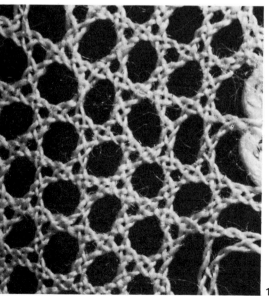

115b

115c

58

Fig. 116 *Eighteenth-century Chantilly, with fond chant.*

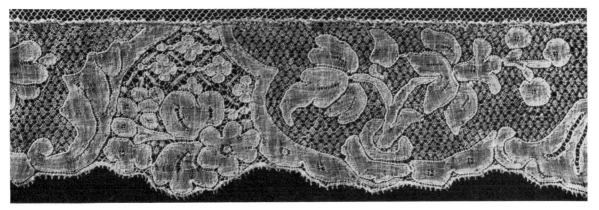

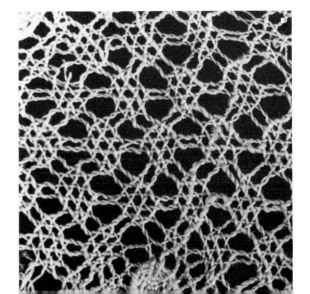

Fig. 117 *Fond d'armure:* **a** *Mechlin, first quarter of the eighteenth century;* **b** *detail,* × 10.

xiii Filet (90° torchon, wholestitch and twist). 90°. V10 H10. CTC-T3, repeat. The pin is placed in the middle of the wholestitch joint (fig. 118). With one twist only it becomes Bohemian (or gauze ground), in which the pins are rapidly removed so that the pinhole space is annihilated (Whiting). Also worked at a 90° angle is square tulle double, summarized CTT-P-CTT. All three types have approximately the appearance of a torchon ground worked vertically instead of diagonally. Identical meshes can be produced by the Barmen machine, though the footing is different.

Group 2 *Reseaux of non-continuous laces*

Only three forms occur at all commonly. Each involves braiding, or plaiting, of four threads.

i Droschel (drochel). This is found in the Brussels and Devon laces known as 'point d'Angleterre', from the late seventeenth to the early nineteenth century. When the separate motifs had been properly assembled, the droschel would be worked between them. In the Brussels form, the meshes were worked in narrow strips, sometimes only $\frac{1}{4}$-inch wide (fig. 119). These strips were laid parallel to the long axis of the lace, and joined by a special hooking stitch called 'point de raccroc'. Paulis calculated that, in examples at the Cinquantenaire, the width of the droschel strips varied on average between 13 and 15 meshes, so that each would require between 52 and 60 bobbins, i.e. four per mesh – hence the advantage of narrowness. The meshes were tiny, sometimes over 600 to a square inch, and every mesh took 32 movements of the bobbins to make. It was expensive costing £60 a square yard *c*1800. The two braided sides of each mesh ran parallel to the footing and Mme Paulis thus describes the method of joining them together: 'The two bands would be fixed to the cushion [pillow] side by side, separated by the width of one mesh. With two pairs of bobbins, the worker could fill in the space between them by constantly making hooked joinings [sewings] to the edge of the finished work. She would make a little braid, separate it into two strands of two threads each, attach them each twice at left and right, the first joining being made at the top, the other at the lower end of the middle part of the existing mesh. She would then make another little braid and pass on to the next mesh' (fig. 120). In Devon, on the other hand, the borders of the motifs seem to have been closely followed in taking the sewings. The result was that instead of neat, precise strips being constructed, the ground went all ways giving a light-hearted but somewhat vertiginous effect (fig. 121). The commercial manufacture of droschel disappeared in Belgium in the 1830s because of machine competition.

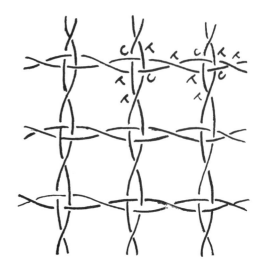

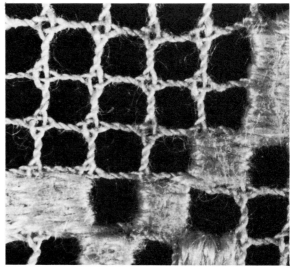

Fig. 118 *90° torchon-type:* **a** *the sequence with one twist (CTC-T-CTC-T);* **b** *a plain ground, made with two twists (CTC-T2 and repeat). The design has been darned on to it. Brazil, twentieth century.*

ii Round Valenciennes (round mesh, à mailles rondes). Paulis refers to this as the most ancient form of Brussels reseau. It occurs in late seventeenth- and eighteenth-century Flemish and also Milanese laces (fig. 122). She traces the evolution of the round mesh into the more delicately fragile droschel by the replacement of the shorter braided sides with a simple twist, and the lengthening of the two remaining braids in each mesh. According to Whiting, forms of round Valenciennes with 2-, 3-, 4-, or 5-braided sides have been identified, and may be related to distinct localities. See also group 1 ix.

Fig. 119 *Droschel:* **a** *strips joined by point de raccroc, and arranged to make a plain veil;* **b** *detail from the reverse side to show the stitch used in the attachment of appliqué work. The entire veil, 32 × 44 inches (81 × 112 cm) weighs 25 g (0.9 oz).*

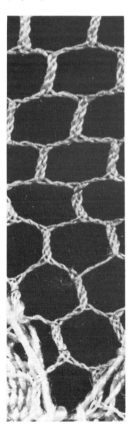

Fig. 120 *The point de raccroc technique (Paulis).*

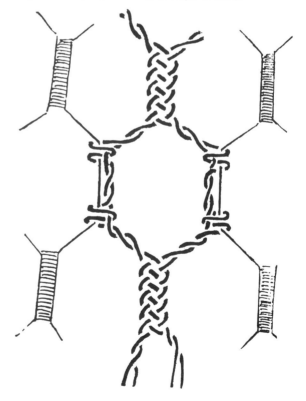

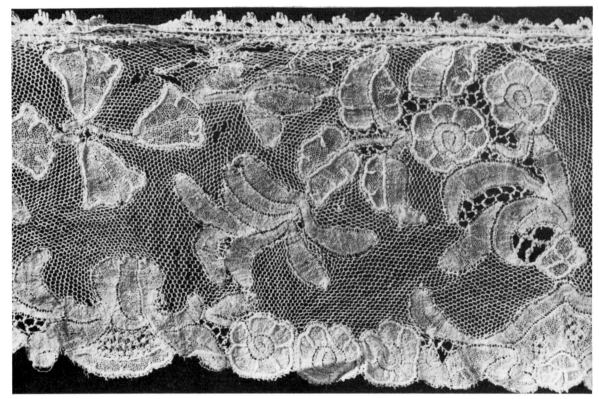

Fig. 121 *Droschel in an eighteenth-century Devon lace. The quality is as fine as in fig. 119, but the arrangement of the meshes is quite different.*

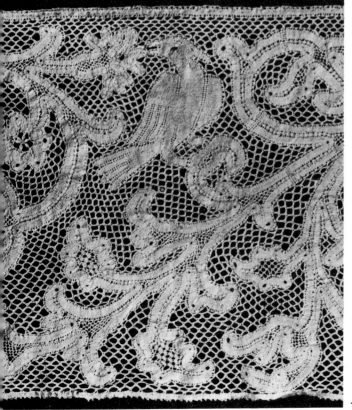

Fig. 122 *Round Valenciennes:* **a** *a Milanese lace of the mid-eighteenth century;* **b** *and* **c** *round Valenciennes and droschel, two sketches to show a possible technical transition from* **b** *into* **c** *(Paulis);* **d** *detail to show non-continuity,* ×10; **e** *Brabant Valenciennes, with raised work and torchon-type ground.*

122a

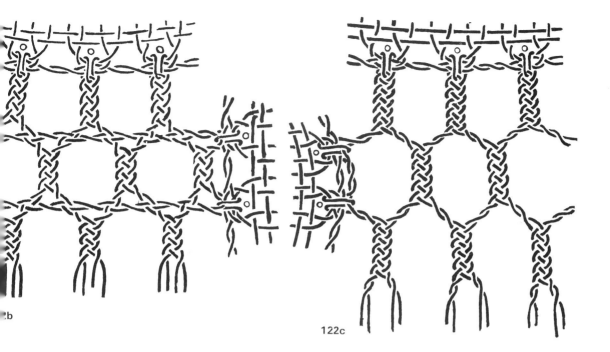

122b

122c

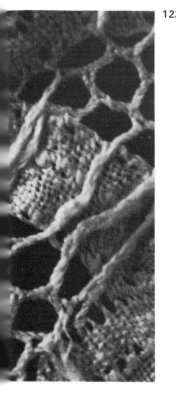

122d

122e

iii Square Valenciennes. The non-continuous use of this ground is restricted to a form of lace made around Ghent in the mid-nineteenth century which, apart from this feature, strongly resembles the traditional Valenciennes. The rare Brabant Valenciennes, or Valenciennes à relief (raised Valenciennes) may have this ground, or it may achieve a lighter appearance with a diamond-shaped mesh, twisted not braided, like a variation of group I ii (fig. 122e).

iv Leadwork ground. This is found occasionally in mid-nineteenth-century Honiton laces, and appears very similar to group I v, though the ground is not continuous, and has to be attached by sewings.

Group 3 *Bars of continuous laces*

This is not a frequent association, but is found traditionally in the Le Puy laces, revived in 1838 by Theodore Falcon; in Beds laces after about 1850 (45° angle); in the mid-nineteenth-century silk laces from Malta; and in the Cluny laces named, not after the town, but after some Genoese laces preserved at the Musée de Cluny in Paris, on which their designs were based (fig. 123).

Group 4 *Bars of non-continuous laces*

i Short, heavily braided and picoted bars, sometimes in a double form, are associated with Milanese lace, c1700–1750.

ii Lighter weight and picoted bars occur in late seventeenth- to early eighteenth-century Flemish (fig. 94).

iii Very short bars without picots are found in East European (Slavic) laces.

iv Snatchpin is a bobbin-plaited strand attached with needle and thread to the motifs in a zigzag manner. It is very labour-saving compared with methods which attach threads by innumerable sewings, then make the bars little by little with bobbins. It is characteristic of late nineteenth- or twentieth-century Bruges, and Honiton (fig. 124).

v In the last few years the non-continuous technique has been to some extent adopted in Le Puy and Beds as a labour-saving completion-hastening device.

Group 5 *Bars arranged as large meshes*

This type of ground is shared by some eighteenth-century Flemish and Milanese laces (fig. 125), and some nineteenth-century Le Puy, Beds, Russian and Bruges.

In sixteenth-century bobbin laces from Italy there was no ground as such, the lace being formed of braided strands which made twig-like patterns, not distinguishable into motif and ground.

Fig. 123 *Bars in continuous laces: a detail of fig. 69c, a Beds lace × 10.*

Fig. 124 *Bars in non-continuous laces:* a *Milanese c1700;* b *Flemish with brides picotées showing at the top right and left plaits of threads carried across the back of the work;* c *snatchpin in a Belgian lace, early twentieth century.*

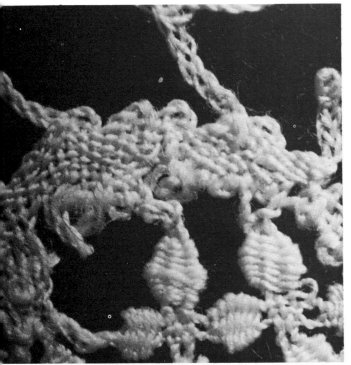

123

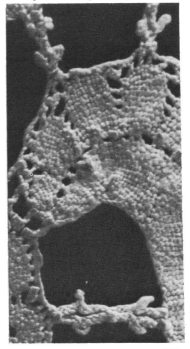

124a

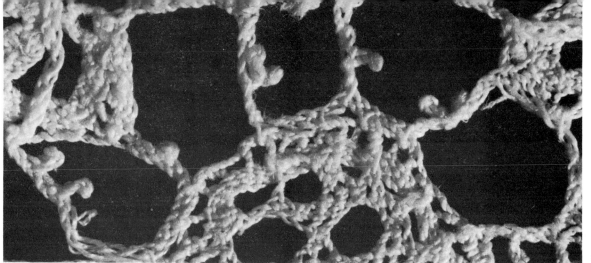

124b

124c

125a

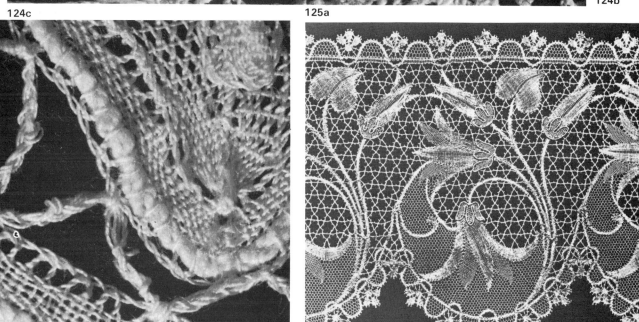

Fig. 125 *Bars arranged as meshes:* **a** *Le Puy, from a design by Chaleyé, c1906;* **b** *detail of a silk stole bought at Archangel,* USSR, *1899.*

125b

In some old laces from Sweden the extremely solid clothwork formed a background in which small geometrically arranged holes marked out a design (fig. 126) as in cutwork and hollie point.

Recording the Information

All the information acquired so far can be recorded most conveniently on index cards. Quite large ones would be preferable, printed with a constant set of sections in which data relevant to particular laces can be entered. Each lace must be allocated a provisional number such as 001, 002 etc. Though the initial order of laces and cards may then turn out to be rather haphazard, this is of no great importance: any subsequent rearrangement, or grouping, can simply refer to the appropriate numbers. Complete renumbering is also possible as the collection grows, but it will leave less scope for the addition of new pieces which might need an insertion point just where they would interfere most with the number sequence.

The cards would be best contained in individual polythene wallets so that accompanying photographs or documents could be enclosed with them. A consistent series of sections and sub-sections on the cards makes for ease of cross-referencing, and also for ease of comparison of individual pieces when to get the actual laces out of storage, spread them, and examine them, might not be at all convenient.

At this stage, the index cards can cover only the techniques for bobbin laces. Additions will therefore be made to them later, when information relevant to geography, dating and thread has been considered.

Fig. 126 *No ground:* **a** *sixteenth-century Italian plaited lace in coloured silk;* **b** *Scandinavian lace, eighteenth century – the extremely dense geometric border is of bobbin lace from Scania, Sweden.*

Suggestions for constructing similar sets of cards for needle laces will come at the end of chapter 8.

Index card layout
Reference number:
Photo or sketch of shape of piece, including dimensions
1 **Main technique:** woven (bobbin) – looped (needle) – other

Bobbin
2 Continuous – non-continuous

3 Outline – gimp thread – raised outline – none – central gimp

4 Motifs made of – wholestitch – halfstitch – mixed

5 Decorative fillings – number

6 Types of filling stitch – name(s) or photos

7 Point d'esprit – square – oval – none

8 Arrangement of point d'esprit:
Square – in reseau – as fillings or part fillings – as ground
Oval – wheels – rows – added to the surface

9 Picots – along heading – on bars – none

10 Ground – no separate ground – reseau: type (illustrate) – bars: type (illustrate)

FOUR

Determining the Place of Origin and Dating Bobbin Laces

Where?

To name a lace fully involves stating its basic technique, some centre with which it has a historical association, and a date. The previous chapter dealt with the variations of technique which occur in bobbin laces. Here, we deal with the naming of a location, which is a very different matter. In examining a technique, only a question – for example 'Is it continuous or non-continuous?', followed by an observation, and then by a positive or negative answer is needed. But the historical origin of a lace cannot be seen, it can only be deduced, and that from a number of quite different considerations. Evidence within the lace (design), and evidence external to the lace (portraits, inventories, wardrobe accounts, bills of sale, literature and provenanced museum collections), both need not only observation but also subjective assessments of relevance, and of value.

To begin with, it is known that bobbin and needle laces were European in origin. Not until the very late nineteenth or early twentieth century was lace making carried to India and the Far East by missionaries. It became there a flourishing industry, soon involved in a price war with the West. Torchon for example was made in Bombay and Ceylon, Bruges in Taiwan, and Valenciennes in the Congo. In the eighteenth century, English and French colonials in North America, and Spanish and Portuguese in South America, took their fashionable European laces with them, and imported more. But there no substantial bobbin or needle lace-making activity resulted.

There are thus a limited number of countries to consider: principally Italy, Flanders and France; in addition England, Spain, Eastern Europe, Germany, Malta and Denmark.

Evidence for location from technique

a The grounds of laces are particularly characteristic of specific localities, and for this reason many place names have already been mentioned in pages 51–64. This study no doubt made it obvious that the identification of locality was not going to be easy. Bucks can have four different grounds (group I ii, **vii, x, xi**); at the same time each of these grounds can appear in non-Bucks laces, for example French, German or Spanish.

b The non-continuous condition is characteristic of four areas: Flanders (Brussels and Bruges), Honiton, Milan and Eastern Europe; the continuous condition of all the others.

c Gimp thread outlines are found in all continuous laces except Binche and Valenciennes; raised work is truly characteristic only of the non-continuous Brussels and Honiton. Rarely, some three-dimensionality is found in Valenciennes, or in the superficial point d'esprit of Beds, Le Puy, Hainault, and others.

d Filling stitches can help to locate a lace (see pages 40–6).

e Footings are characteristic.

f Picots on bars or headings can also be distinctive.

These six helpful hints cut across each other in the most confusing manner. As a general rule one sufficiently detailed description can have only one place name attached to it; but the converse does not apply. Any geographical name will need several descriptions if all the laces it has ever produced are to be included.

Evidence for location from design

a Range of design. Each area (place name) has many different designs, some well over a thousand. Indeed it has been estimated that the now somewhat obscure centre of Neuchâtel, in Switzerland, produced 100,000 designs in the 80 years between 1750 and 1830 (Prof. Godet). A few are illustrated in figs. 127 to 129. The sheer diversity makes it difficult to isolate common characteristics for each place, and design thus compares unfavourably with the factual and relatively constant features of technique. Trying to identify a lace just by matching it with a photograph in which nothing but design can be clearly seen is a hazardous procedure, and not at all to be recommended (page 23).

b The free edge of a lace may help to place it. The early seventeenth-century Flemish and Genoese collar laces were scalloped in the Van Dyck manner; in Brussels and Honiton the heading followed the curves of the variously shaped flowers; nineteenth-century Lille and

Fig. 127 *Designs of Tønder lace.*

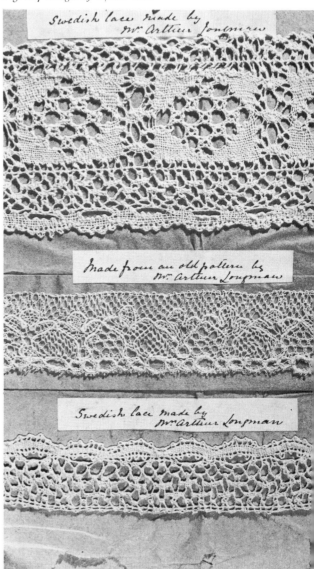

Swedish lace made by Mr Arthur Longman

Made from an old pattern by Mr Arthur Longman

Swedish lace made by Mr Arthur Longman

Fig. 128 *Designs of Swedish lace.*

mid-seventeenth-century Netherlands were often straight (fig. 71a). The 9-pin heading of Beds Maltese helps to distinguish it from Cluny which has a heavier less decorative border (fig. 130).

c Most countries have at various times produced 'trail' laces, that is laces where the design is formed by a wholestitch band which curls a snaky path within the lace. Examples are Palestrina (north-east Italy), Bruges Russian, Beds Russian, and the East European countries themselves, also Spain and some of the products of the Oneida Indians of North America. As a general rule, trail laces are non-continuous, but where they are made by a continuous technique the worker bobbins of the trail commonly remain the same throughout, while the passives change as threads are needed to maintain the connection with adjacent parts. In Cluny, however, where the trails tend to be straight lines linking circles together – like a road interrupted by frequent roundabouts – the trail is 'divided', something similar to a dual carriageway, a feature achieved by the passives remaining the same throughout while the worker bobbins enter or leave (fig. 131).

d Designs may approximate in different areas as a result of copying. Bucks and Tønder for example may

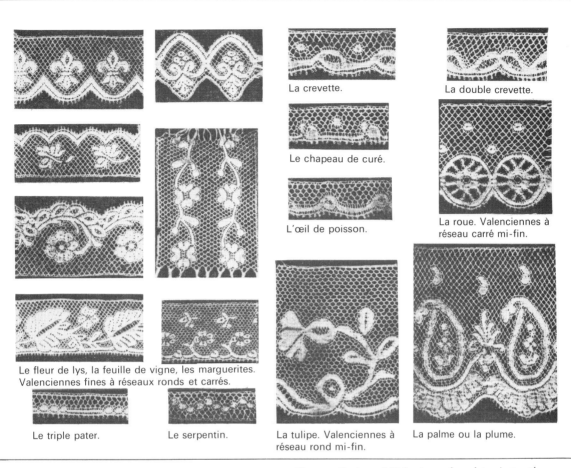

La crevette.

La double crevette.

Le chapeau de curé.

L'œil de poisson.

La roue. Valenciennes à réseau carré mi-fin.

Le fleur de lys, la feuille de vigne, les marguerites. Valenciennes fines à réseaux ronds et carrés.

Le triple pater.

Le serpentin.

La tulipe. Valenciennes à réseau rond mi-fin.

La palme ou la plume.

Fig. 129 *Designs of Valenciennes lace, late nineteenth century. The 'double crevette' (double shrimp) was made by fishermen's wives whose greetings to each other, 'As-tu fait ta crevette?' (Have you made your shrimp?), related not to the little crustacean but to the progress of their lace (Carlier).*

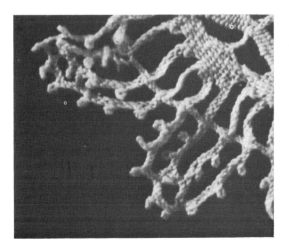

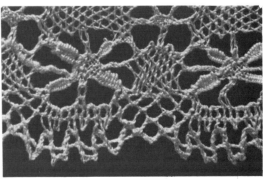

Fig. 130 *Headings:* **a** *Beds Maltese;* **b** *Cluny.*

131a

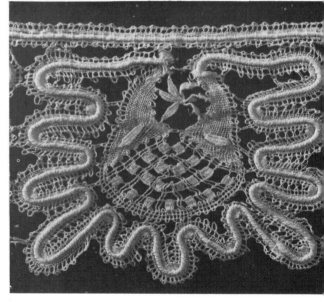

131b

131c

131d

131e

Fig. 131 *Trail laces:* **a** *Spanish, eighteenth century.* **b** *Katherine of Aragon.* **c** *Oneida Indians, Wisconsin, a derivative lace copied from an antique pattern in the Metropolitan Museum, New York.* **d** *Cluny.* **e** *detail of Beds Russian.* **f** *detail of Cluny divided trail.*

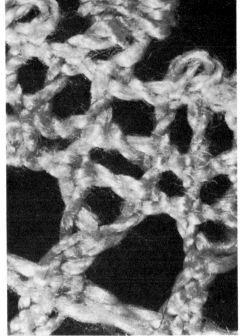

131f

imitate Lille techniques, or late-eighteenth-century Mechlin designs; in addition copies of Lille and Chantilly were made in Barcelona (Catalonia), and at Bayeux. In the 1880s Honiton imitated the commercially successful Brussels. Technical features may then come to the rescue, for example Mechlin has two twists between the gimp and the ground, Bucks two twists between wholestitch and gimp (fig. 132); while the fillings of Honiton (fig. 88) and the shapes of its roses are quite different from those of Brussels, however strikingly other design features may give a Brussels impression (fig. 132e & f).

e Some original but peculiar designs mark one type of lace from Devon in the late eighteenth century. They result perhaps from misinterpretation of Flemish patterns (fig. 133). The prickings mapping out the designs are like unfinished sketches formed only by a complex series of dots which, as in a puzzle book, must be correctly joined if the whole thing is to make any sense. The inking in of the thread courses (fig. 97), a process known as lining up (crayonage) has endless possibilities of error, and if errors are made the little forest of pins planted in the wrong holes becomes a confusing jungle in which the intricate thread contortions cannot find their way.

f Laces occasionally contain, in some feature of their design, direct clues as to their place of origin:

i In 1599 a bobbin lace coverlet was presented to the Archduke Albert of Brabant and his wife Isabella. 'Brabant' is worked in the lace (fig. 134a).

ii A Brazilian or Portuguese ribbon of lace bears the message: 'Recebo amiga este pinhor como um signal de meo amor' (Friend receive this pledge as a sign of my love) (fig. 134b).

iii Though not a bobbin lace but an embroidered net, the significance of the design in localizing this lace makes it relevant. The letters F.R. stand for 'Fernando Rey'; the motto 'Tanto Monta Monta Tanto' is a statement of the equality of power shared by Ferdinand and Isabella of fifteenth-century Spain; the two-headed eagle symbolizes the might of the Holy Roman Empire, which was the suzereignty of the Spanish and Austrian Habsburgs (fig. 135).

iv The two-headed eagle occurs in quite a variety of laces, and so usually needs other evidence to confirm the place of origin (fig. 136). Apart from the Roman Empire and its possessions, it is depicted in the arms of Germany and Russia, and also in those of the Duke of Marlborough as Prince of Mindelheim. In France, the imperial arms showed a single eagle 'rising and respecting to the sinister, grasping in both claws a thunderbolt or' (Eve). This eagle appears in French needle laces, but also in Brussels bobbin laces, ordered by Napoleon I.

v There is of course nothing at all to prevent a lace bearing the arms of one country being made in another and, after the passage of 300 years, the problem of the precise place of origin may be insoluble. A beautiful collar, preserved at The Art Institute of Chicago, bears the date 1661, the initials C.B., the name Carolus Rex, the Prince of Wales feathers, 'Baronet', and a teeming luxuriance of acorn and Tudor rose. It is thought to have been made as a gift from Charles II to his bride-to-be Catherine of Braganza, whom he finally married in May 1662. The design is a mystery. Though Charles was not crowned until 23 April 1661, he was regarded as king from the time of his father's death, and in the Court records 1661 was the twelfth year of his reign. He was thus entitled neither to the Prince of Wales feathers, nor to the Prince of Wales title, Baron of Renfrew, which would cease with his accession. Even if he were regarded as technically Prince of Wales until his coronation it would still not explain 'Baronet', a hereditary title created by the Earl of Salisbury in the times of James I, and sold at £1000 a time to raise money for various causes.

Locality by design might well put the lace into England, and into Devon because of its non-continuity. But there is no lace of that time, known to be English, to use for comparison. The fulsome praises of travellers do not begin until several years later; and Charles's ban on the importation of Flemish laces in late 1661 and 1662 would scarcely have been necessary had Devon lace been of sufficient quality to compete. Moreover Charles is said to have brought in Flemish workers to instruct the English, in 1662. Also, in 1660, England had for 10 years been under Cromwell's Commonwealth, which did little to encourage the making or wearing of lace; Charles himself was in Bruges after a 10-year sojourn on the European continent so that he would be much

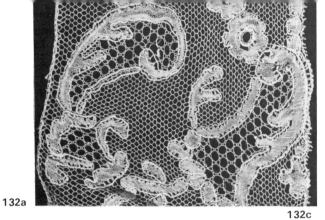

132a

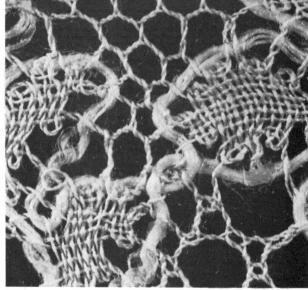

132c

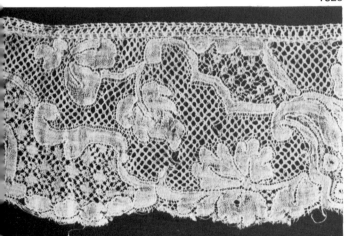

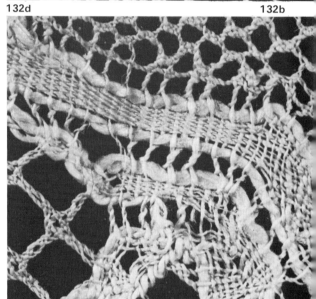

132d

132b

Fig. 132 **a** *Bucks showing twists within the gimp outline;* **b** *detail.* **c** *Mechlin showing twists outside the gimp outline;* **d** *detail;* **e** *A fine Honiton bobbin lace collar.* **f** *A Brussels collar of nineteenth-century point d'Angleterre, with bobbin motifs and a needle-made ground and fillings.*

132e

132f

Fig. 133 *A Devon confusion of design, eighteenth century.*

Fig. 134 **a** *Detail of the 1599 bed cover, Brabant.* **b** *A Portuguese love token.*

Fig. 135 *Embroidered net, Spanish, nineteenth century.*

Fig. 136 *The two-headed eagle in a Milanese lace.*

Fig. 137 a *Detail of the Catherine of Braganza collar: the Prince of Wales feathers, encircled with oak leaves and acorns, rest beneath a crown which bears the legend Carolus Rex (King Charles) – this represents an earlier English crown, melted down by Cromwell. Charles had to order a new one.* b *A lace of similar design attributed to Flanders and known as Dutch lace, c1660.*

Fig. 138 *An Australian fan leaf of embroidered net.*

more familiar with the lace manufactories there; the order for his coronation lace went to Flanders; and he and his family wore Flemish lace long after he had imposed his import restrictions.

It seems therefore inconceivable than an auspicious gift, to a bride who had been wooed even in his father's time, when Charles was only 14 years old, and Catherine seven, should not be similarly commissioned. Charles first landed at Dover in May 1660. The engagement was announced, and a proxy marriage completed in May 1661. The collar would certainly have taken several months to make, and may well have been ordered in Flanders, before Charles's repatriation. The insignia apart, it bears a close resemblance to a kind of Flemish lace thought to have been made in Antwerp, and known as 'Dutch' (fig. 137).

Even with all these considerations taken into account, it is obvious that one ends only with probabilities, not certainties. This is as well to remember: once the factual world of technique is left behind, the placing and dating of a lace must always involve some degree of speculation.

Fig. 139 *Spanish, nineteenth century.*

140a

140b

Fig. 140 *Pattern books:* **a** *Le Pompe, Venice;* **b** *by Parasole, Rome.*

vi Fig. 138 shows a fan leaf designed by an Australian, Miss Patty Moult. It was called by her 'kangaroo-apple kangaroo' and was shown at the Tasmanian Lace Exhibition of 1910.

vii Colour can be regarded as an aspect of design. It is especially characteristic of Slavic, Spanish and Sardinian laces, and occurs sometimes in Sweden. Black silk, and gold thread, occur in many other countries as well. Even east Devon ventured briefly into colour with Colyton chromatic; while the east Midlands produced over a short period a range of coloured yaks. But as a characteristic locality feature, only the bright red and blue of Russia; the crimson, pink and pale azure silks of Spain; and the ochre and green of some Austrian laces, can be called distinctive (fig. 139).

Evidence for location from documents
There is a great deal of this evidence, establishing for individual towns and countries a fascinating history of the journeyings, successes and misfortunes of their

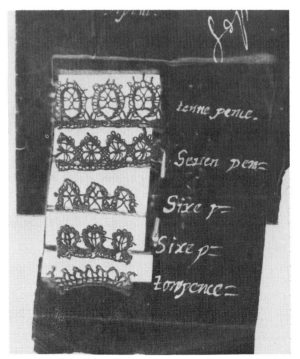

Fig. 141 *The five samples from the Isham letter.*

laces. However, the references are almost never illustrated and the laces seldom even described, so that in fact they give little help in identifying particular pieces.

a A Ghent document of 1591 prohibited the making of 'spellewercke' (pin work, or bobbin lace).

b In the many pattern books of the sixteenth and early seventeenth centuries, the designs were printed as woodcuts. They are regarded as characteristic of the laces of the country or city where the book was published (fig. 140). The production of such books ceased about 1630, as the lace became more complex and its production more commercial and competitive.

c A letter written by Elizabeth Isham *c*1625 encloses five samples of bobbin lace, priced, and presumably made in Northampton. It reads: 'Deare father, I glad to heare of your health which I pray God to continue. I receiv'd not your letter by Howcot nither can I heare of John Ashwell nor what he hath done with the mony. I have sent heare paturnes of lace and the prises of them, they have there bandes but narrow. We are heare all in health and doe thank you for your pigeon pie, and so remembering my duty to you, and my love to my Sister, I rest, Your obedient daughter . . .' (fig. 141). A band was a collar, slightly raised off the shoulders.

d Records of Court proceedings in Maryland in 1658 relate to the theft by John and Mary Williams of 'one fflaunder [Flanders] lac'd dressing, 3 fflaunders Lac'd quoyfes [coifs], one fflaunder Lac'd pinner [apron?],

one fflaunder Lac'd gorghett [gorget] and one bastard fflaunder lac'd holland smock' from the house of one Simon Ouerzee. In 1712 and 1745 it was recorded that the city of Lima (Peru) had no fewer than 45 counts and marquises and that 'no woman of rank would condescend to wear any other lace than that of Flanders' (Morris and Hague). But such records have really little significance in identification without some accompanying visual image, a portrait, or a piece of lace.

e A west Northamptonshire sample book carries a date for 1827. The actual samples of lace are numbered, and opposed by entries of the names of makers from whom the lace has been ordered. Similar sample books of Tonder lace are preserved in Denmark; and of the laces of Sluis, Holland, in Amsterdam (Wardle).

f In the nineteenth century preliminary drawings, signed by the designer, are known, for example those by Thomas Lester, now at the Cecil Higgins Art Gallery, Bedford. The Impressionist painter, Chaleyé, of Le Puy (1878–1960) produced some compelling designs, executed by the manufacturer Oudin, who employed many lace makers (figs. 125a, 152).

g Exhibition catalogues, if illustrated, are also extremely helpful, for example that produced by Peter Robinson of Oxford Street on the occasion of the International Health Exhibition of 1884 (fig. 142).

h Modern publicity leaflets throw light on the productions of less well-known lace-making centres, for example that of Offida in central Italy (fig. 143).

To summarize: Lace names are group, or generic, names representing the historic sites for the making of that kind of lace, but not necessarily the present site, or even that of the recent past. In relation to a particular piece of lace, the geographic name is determined by reference to various points of technique, design, thread and texture, supplemented by documentary evidence wherever possible.

When?

This question is just as problematical, and the answers just as speculative as in the case of determining the place of origin. In both, the situation is complicated by contemporary, and later, copyings of techniques and designs (see chapter 8). There is no entirely foolproof way of telling the age of a lace, only a number of pointers.

Evidence for dating from technique

a Amount of ground. The general sequence is firstly no ground – either because there are no separate entities of design (fig. 126), or because the ground is crowded out by the design's massive proportions. During the seventeenth century the ground gradually forced the motifs

Duke of Buckingham and Chandos, with the view of drawing attention to the beauty of the work, is exhibiting in the conservatory at the I. H. E. some superb specimens of Lace manufactured at various dates under the supervision of Mr. VICCARS, formerly of Padbury, near Buckingham, worked chiefly from designs by Messrs. ABRAHAM, father and son; amongst the most noticeable are a grand court train, 5¼ yards long and 38 inches in depth, with the other appendages necessary for completing the suite, and also a scarf of beautiful design and finished workmanship. His Grace has also brought two skilled workers from the vicinity of Buckingham to show the mode of manufacture, who are now working for Mr. PETER ROBINSON, of Oxford Street and Regent Street, who has commissioned Mr. VICCARS to manufacture a large number of specimens of the art, which can be ordered at either of his establishments, or at the "Buckingham" Lace stall in the Conservatory in the International Health Exhibition.

The distinguishing feature of "Buckingham" Lace is, that the worker makes both the pattern and the net or ground simultaneously, increasing

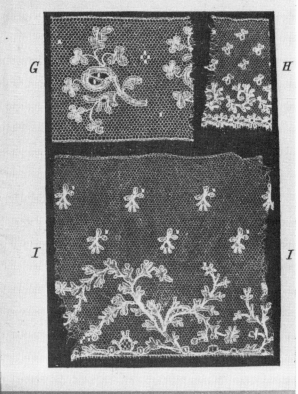

Fig. 142 *A page from Peter Robinson's promotion of Bucks lace making, 1884, International Health Exhibition.*

apart until it occupied about half the total space and, by the end of the eighteenth century, had taken over, the design being relegated to a small border of symbolic flower heads and a repetitive powdering of dots or drifting scales. In the nineteenth-century revivals the ground occupied, on average, 50 per cent or more of the lace (fig. 144).

b Type of ground. There seems no doubt that bars antedated reseaux, and the seventeenth century shows a sequence of no clear ground, bars, reseaux. Reseaux continued through the eighteenth century, completely displaced bars by the middle, and dominated lace structure until the mid-nineteenth century when bars reappeared and the two forms of ground co-existed. Some anachronistic ecclesiastical laces never transferred to reseaux – bars were much better suited to the impact-from-a-distance needs of large-scale alb flounces and altar cloths (fig. 145).

c Continuity and non-continuity. Mme Paulis in her reconstruction of the bobbin laces illustrated in the pattern book *Le Pompe*, first published in 1557 (fig. 146), was able to distinguish two types of bobbin laces: the skeletal kind made of braided threads (fig. 126a), simple to look at, but with technically complex intersections; and a more substantial form in which the pillow

Fig. 143 *The cover of a leaflet publicizing Offida laces, 1980.*

mostra del merletto a tombolo offidano

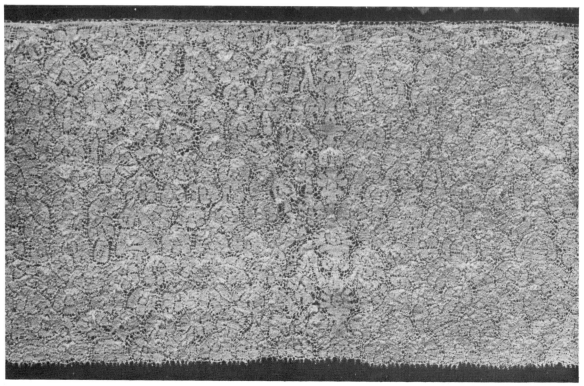

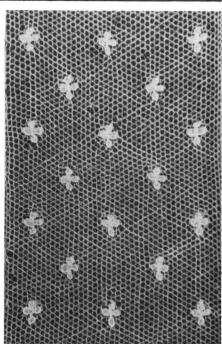

Fig. 144 a *Almost no ground, a very dense Flemish lace of the seventeenth century.* b *About 50% ground, Devon (Bath Brussels), second half of the eighteenth century.* c *Minimal, spindly design, point de Paris lace from north France, c1800.*

145a

145b

145c

145d

Fig. 145 **a** *No clear distinction between motif and ground. Detail of the collar of King Gustavus* II *Adolphus of Sweden, first quarter seventeenth century.* **b** *Bars: a Flemish lace, late seventeenth century.* **c** *Reseau: in Flemish or Milanese flouncing, mid-eighteenth century.* **d** *Bars in the second half nineteenth century, Bruges.*

146a

146b

Fig. 146 **a** *Page 26 of Le Pompe;* **b** *The execution of the lower, non-continuous, pattern by Mme Paulis.*

147a

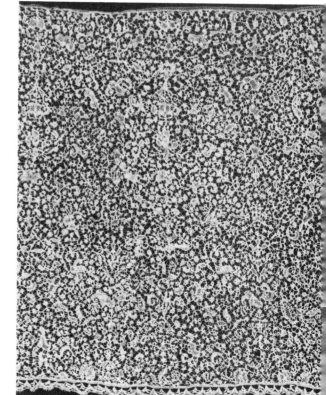

147c

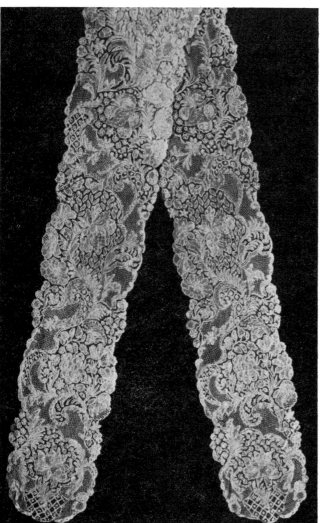

147b

147d

147e

147f

147h

147g

Fig. 147 *Design sequence.* **a** *Geometric: Venetian pattern,
sixteenth century.* **b** *Baroque: the luscious and extravagant
blooms seem too ebullient for the frail texture, Brussels bobbin
lace (point d'Angleterre à brides) c1700.* **c** *Rococo: a busy
Flemish bobbin lace with brides picotées c1725.* **d** *Stylized:
Valenciennes lappets c1750.* **e** *Florid: Brussels mixed lace
mid-nineteenth century.* **f** *Naturalistic: part of a wedding veil
with bobbin flowers appliquéd, nineteenth century.* **g** *Art
Nouveau: an original design for Honiton lace by Lydia C.
Hammett, 1906.* **h** *Anonymous: the symbols of the Passion in
this well-executed piece give no clue to its identity, but
technique and texture place it at Bayeux, early twentieth
century.*

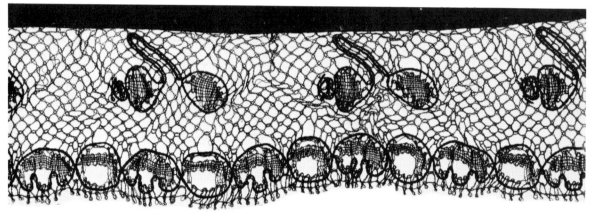

Fig. 148 *Ipswich (Mass.) lace late eighteenth century.*

would have to be turned so that the thread could follow the curving course of the design, the worker bobbins changed at intervals to create little holes as in Cluny's divided trail (page 68), and sewings taken to link the parts together, that is the lace was non-continuous (fig. 146). Thus both continuous and non-continuous techniques were in use as early as the mid-sixteenth century, providing no time sequence to help with dating.

d Types of stitch might help to date a lace, but further research is needed.

Evidence for dating from design
Designs, like fashions, change over the years, so that certain forms are characteristic of certain periods. Each is in harmony with the spirit of the time which breathes into it a vitality and appropriateness. When the work is copied at a later date, this harmony is lost: the natural expression of quite different attitudes and personalities is being forced into an unnatural mould.

The prevailing mode is mirrored in all art forms, whether architecture, painting, sculpture or textiles. For lace, the following sequence, though not to be interpreted too rigidly, is helpful:

Geometric, sometimes called Gothic, sixteenth to early seventeenth century; Baroque, mainly floral, mid-seventeenth to early eighteenth; Rococo, crowded, sometimes riotously, sometimes with an architectural symmetry, late seventeenth to early eighteenth century; Stylized, with a short repeat and simplified design, verging into the Neo-Classical, 1725 to 1800; Florid, ornate or Neo-Baroque, 1830 to 1850; Naturalistic, with a growing rash of talented designers, second half of the nineteenth century; Art Nouveau, 1880 to 1910; and what can only be called Anonymity because of ubiquitous pirating, 1910 and after (fig. 147). Modern laces are geographically non-distinctive: old methods are broken down into kaleidoscopic images making use of everything in the ancient forms.

Figures of people and animals may occur occasionally in the bobbin laces of Milan and Flanders, and even more rarely in those of Bayeux. Apart from birds and butterflies, they do not appear in English laces until after 1900.

Evidence for dating from documents etc.
a Portraits, and records of actual laces commissioned from specific designers reinforce the sequence outlined above. Portraits give little help with the locality of a lace, but they do prove the existence and wearing of a particular lace type at a particular time (fig. 149).
b Pattern books were mostly dated, and though not many of the early ones were specifically for bobbin laces, they do help (fig. 140a).
c The examples of evidence for location from documents, quoted in the previous section, are mostly dated, and so at the same time provide evidence of age. Mechlin is first recorded in 1657; and point d'Angleterre around 1662. Quotations by Morris and Hague indicate the popularity of Flemish lace in Spain and in Boston in 1704; the persistence of gold and silver lace in 1712; and the innovation of blonde lace in 1768. Records at Ipswich, Massachusetts, including actual lace samples and the names of the makers, establish a bobbin lace industry there in the late eighteenth century. In the nineteenth century records are much more prolific, and doubtless less open to misinterpretation. Von Henneberg states that the very last piece of 'real old lace' made in the town of Valenciennes was in 1840, for the Duchesse de Nemours. The work was organized by Mlle Glairo, then aged 60, with a number of 80-year-old helpers, who would have been in their thirties at the time of the Revolution. The revival of Maltese lace (1833); the innovation of Ghent Valenciennes (1852); the branching off of east Midlands laces into Beds guipures (post 1850); the establishment of the Lefebure factories at Bayeux (c1829); and innumerable

others, all help to date events, and to indicate the possibilities; while photographs, after 1870, were available to elucidate the documentary records. Statistics, for many areas, establish an industry as failing or flourishing. For example, in 1851 there were 369 lace schools in east Flanders alone; in 1914 there were 106; in 1924, only 26 in the whole of Belgium.

d The familiar problem of knowing that a lace existed, but not knowing what it looked like, applies perhaps most particularly to the English bobbin laces of the late seventeenth and early eighteenth centuries. Glowingly praised by historians and travellers, their actual appearance remains a mystery. Defoe, in 1724, says in his *Tour through the Whole Island of Great Britain*, 'From hence [Ampthill] thro' the whole south part of this county, as far as the border of Bucks and Herts, the people are taken up with the manufacture of bone-lace, in which they are wonderfully encreas'd and improv'd within these few years past'.

e Loss of records. The poorer houses, where lace makers might have lived, were often wooden, or at least contained much wood in their construction, and fires were frequent. Honiton alone had no fewer than six severe fires between 1672 and 1767, which must have swept away both lace and the records of it.

Evidence for dating from the thread
The threads used in lace making will be considered more fully in the next chapter. They have a limited relevance to dating:

a Type of fibre. Laces up to the 1830s were made of precious metal, silk, or 'thread' (i.e. flax). Wool was used only for burial, and none has survived. In the 1830s cotton began to be used for hand-made laces. Its feel is quite different from linen: it is warmer, softer and lighter; it does not drape from the hand with the cold, supple inelasticity of a snake.

b Diameter of the threads (see table on page 89). Thickish thread was characteristic of the sixteenth-century laces, but also of many peasant and ecclesiastical laces thereafter, up to the twentieth century. Between approximately 1650 and 1750, exceptionally fine thread was used to make the almost weightless Flemish laces: the Mechlin lappet illustrated in fig. 107(b) measures 610 cm by 40 cm, and weighs only 3.59 g (0.1 oz). Such thread was used also for the early Venetian needle laces which, though heavily rich with their designs of vast raised flowers, yet contained buttonhole stitches so minute that more than 6000 could be crowded into one square inch (page 111).

c Lustre. The same fine thread, through slow hand retting in carefully selected river waters, retained its natural waxes, so easily removed by any harshness of treatment. They thus have a softly polished look, lost in

Fig. 149 *'Countess Samoilova and Her Foster Daughter' by Karl Briullov, c1832. A corn-coloured silk blonde trims a dress of bright blue satin.*

later laces, and quite different from the cold ironing with an aficot (see diagram on page 168) which attempted to imitate it, but produced only an unpleasant shine, and crushed stitches.

d Spin. The precise direction, angle, tightness and ply of the spin may be relevant to the dating, or placing, of antique laces, but in this respect they have not yet been analyzed in sufficient detail. Machine-spun threads, available from the last quarter of the eighteenth century, were tighter, and had to be thicker to survive the tensions imposed on them by the machine. Indeed the brittleness of deformed flax fibres (diagram on page 171), and their proclivity to fracture, encouraged the trend in favour of the less expensive cotton.

e Texture. The tighter twist of the machine spun threads gives a harsher texture to laces made with it. Cotton too was often given extra substance by the use of starch or gum. But too much reliance should not be placed on this feature: starch was used also on linen laces after 1570, and stiffening gums were used in the eighteenth, nineteenth and twentieth centuries.

FIVE
A Note on Threads

Type of fibre

A thread is 'a fine cord composed of fibres or filaments of flax, cotton, wool, silk etc. spun to a considerable length . . . also similar products from glass, asbestos, or ductile metal etc.' (*Oxford English Dictionary*). All of these have at various times been used to make lace. Other vegetable fibres such as nettle, ramie, sweet pea, solomon's seal, pineapple and aloe are not dissimilar to flax, though they lack for the most part its prime qualities, or are more difficult to extract. Nettles in particular have strong lustrous fibres. They were used

Fig. 150 *Point d'Espagne, seventeenth century.*

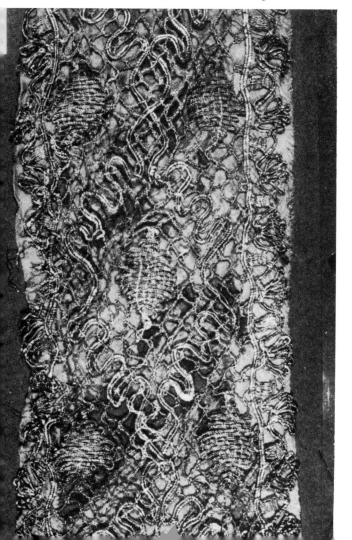

in the Bronze Age for binding axe heads; nitill (nettle cloth) appears in the Customs House accounts of 1550 (Edwards and Nevinson); and textiles of nettle cloth were collected by Captain Cook in the East Indies, *c*1770. Ramie is a member of the nettle family. Its fibre is very resistant to rotting, and to insect attack.

The use of gold, silver and cliquant (an alloy with base metal) for braids considerably antedated the fashion for lace. Its use was extravagant, and it was the sumptuary edicts directed against its wearing which prompted the switch to flax thread and so, perhaps initially to speed things up, to the making of holes, and lace. Some of the sixteenth- and early seventeenth-century gold laces known as point d'Espagne (Spanish point) were made in the Auvergne (Le Puy) area of central France as well as in Spain itself (fig. 150). The gold was not so much drawn into a fine wire as beaten into a thin foil which was then cut into long slivers and wound in the first instance around parchment, then at a later date around yellow silk. The parchment form, though openwork, was only dubiously a textile. The 22 ct gold foil covering the intertwined parchment formed a fabric which, though heavy and stiff, was of extreme richness. The work was difficult: the cut gold foil could slice into the fingers, or spiral tightly on itself, making it difficult to handle. Sometimes very large bobbins were used, to provide adequate weight and tension. The winding of the gold onto a core of yellow silk produced a greater flexibility, and something more like a textile. This technique was used in the gold laces of South America in the nineteenth century (fig. 151).

Scarcely one piece of the early precious metal laces survived the ravellings (unwinding the gold for its scrap value) of later years, when Court ladies and gentlemen were chronically in debt over their wild extravagances on linen lace. From the point of view of identification, gold laces of the seventeenth and eighteenth century are usually attributed to France or Spain (fig. 139b). Late nineteenth century ones were made in Le Puy and Brazil (fig. 152) and, on a small scale, in Ireland, Germany and the east Midlands.

The natural fibres of flax, cotton, silk and wool are known from antiquity. Linen is recorded in Egypt in

7000 BC, silk in China in 5000 BC, wool in Israel 896 BC, and cotton in India 450 BC when it was seen for the first time by the Greek historian Herodotus who thus described the unknown in terms of the known: 'The wild trees of that country bear fleeces as their fruit, surpassing those of the sheep in beauty and excellence; and the Indians use cloth made from this tree wool' (Murphy).

As far as locality is concerned, the use of flax and cotton was too widespread to help in identification and wool also, though it was far less popular, was not characteristic of any particular place. Silk laces, on the other hand, were associated commercially only with Spain (sixteenth to nineteenth century), Malta (post 1833), and northern France (mainly Chantilly and Bayeux, mid-eighteenth to early twentieth century). However, silk does also occur in most other countries, to a lesser extent. Aloe, of little importance for wear, is associated with Portugal and its possessions (fig. 153). The type of fibre is therefore no great help in placing a lace.

The relation of fibres to dating has been discussed at the end of chapter 4.

In needle laces, linen thread was used more than any other, mainly because of the constant friction as the buttonhole stitch loops were pulled through each other. This causes the short fibres of cotton to fluff out from the spun thread, giving a cloudy appearance; while the sharp edge of gold foil, and the microscopic scales of wool fibres, would both catch repeatedly, making any evenness of texture impossible (see table on page 88). See also pages 170–1.

Spinning

Fibres, as they come from the plant or animal, are insufficiently long, or strong, for lace making. Spinning is the process which corrects this. It consists in effect of twisting groups of fibres in such a way that they cling together into a smooth strand. The twist may be either clockwise or anticlockwise, the former being referred to as s, the latter as z, from the direction of their central stroke. If greater thickness is required, a number of these single strands can be spun together, a process known as 'plying'. This second twist is usually in a contrary direction to the first, and so has the effect of tightening the thread; a secondary twist in the same direction would produce a loose yarn. The spinning of two singles together forms a two-ply thread, of three singles a three-ply, and so on. Singles are most commonly found in antique laces. Only the gimp threads which are intentionally much thicker, or some of the heavier peasant laces, are plyed (fig. 154). The twists of the finer threads are not easy to see, and usually need more than a × 10 magnification. Information

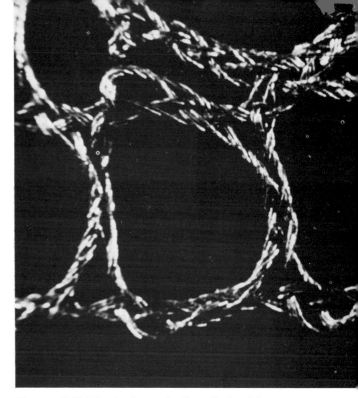

Fig. 151 *Gold foil twisted around yellow silk, detail from a South American bobbin lace.*

Fig. 152 *A lace of gold thread and polychrome silk, designed by Johannes Chaleyé of Le Puy, which won first prize at the International Exposition in Brussels in 1910.*

153a

153b

153c

153d

153e

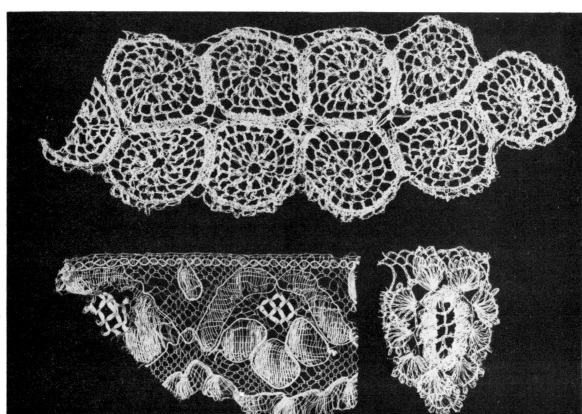

Fig. 153 *Silk laces:* **a** *Spain;* **b** *Malta;* **c** *Caen;* **d** *Tientsin;* **e** *fragments of lace made from Aloe fibre, Paraguay;* **f** *a cap knitted from Solomon's seal fibre, c1840. All nineteenth century.*

153f

154a

S twist

Z twist

Fig. 154 **a** *Sketches to show S and Z twists.* **b** *Ply S. 2 gimp.* **c** *Ply Z. 2 gimp.*

154b

154c

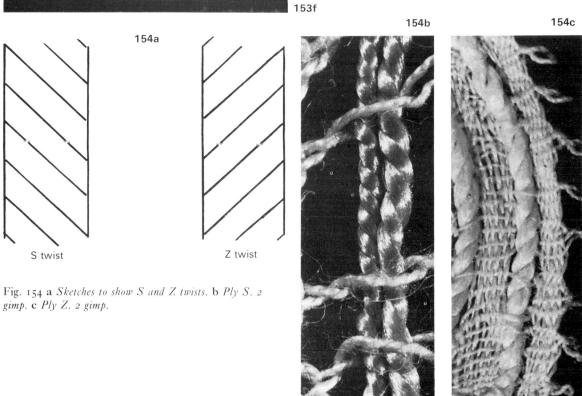

regarding the spin is recorded in the following manner:

Single = first spinning; Ply = second spinning;
$\#$ = number of ply.
For example: Single s, Ply s, $\#$ 2
Single z, Ply s, $\#$ 2   Modern threads for lace making, whether linen or
Single s (not plyed)   cotton, are usually 2-ply.

A Summary of the Qualities of the Four Main Natural Fibres Used in Lace.

	Flax	Cotton	Silk	Wool
Source	Bast fibres of flax stem and root	Hairs of cotton boll attached to seeds	Cocoon of silk moth	Hair of sheep
Length	Staple, 1 in. (2.5 cm) fibres joined in 3 ft strands	Staple, up to $2\frac{1}{2}$ in	Filament, up to 2 miles	Staple, up to 15 in.
Physical characteristics	Cool, heavy, supple, some lustre	Warm, light, slightly elastic	Soft, lustrous, smooth	Scaly, resilient
Chemical nature	Cellulose and lignin	Pure cellulose	Protein (fibroin)	Protein (keratin)
Tests	The lignin stains with methyl orange, and with phloroglucin (red). Burns readily leaving little ash.	Does not stain.	Does not stain. Burning: goes out if flame removed, and each fibre forms a black charcoal knob. Frizzles, and gives off an acrid smell.	

Appearance

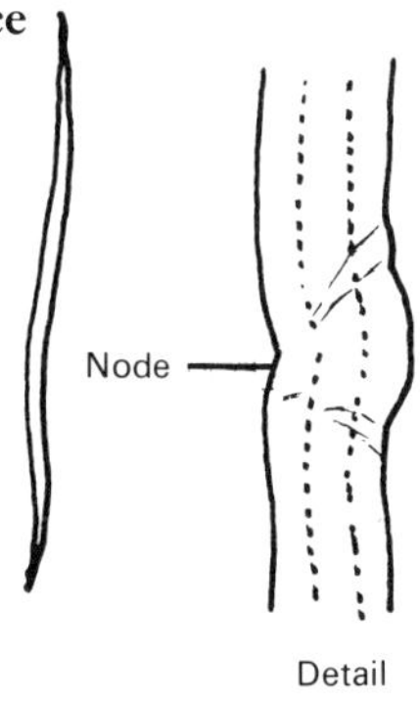

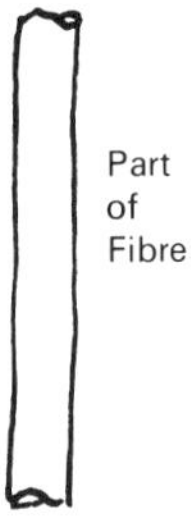

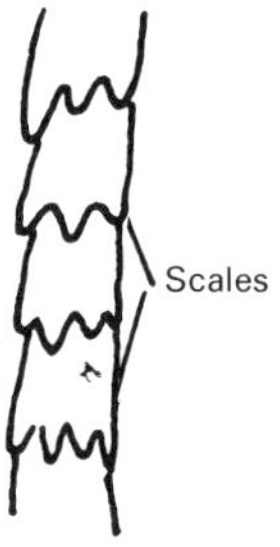

Acid versus alkali effect	Harmed by acid which digests the molecules into soluble particles, ultimately glucose		Harmed by alkalis which denature (i.e. change the nature of) the molecules	
Relation to laces	Bobbin and needle	Mainly bobbin, post 1830. Lace softer and less crisp.	Mainly bobbin. Takes black dyes well.	Bobbin only. Burial, 17th century; Yak 19th century.

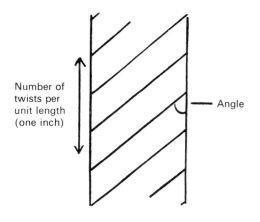

Number of twists per unit length (one inch)

— Angle

Fig. 155 *A sketch to show the calculation of tightness, and angle, of spin.*

Other details of spinning, such as the tightness and the angle (fig. 155) should also be considered. To date, their relevance to identification is uncertain since not nearly enough have been investigated for any date or locality pattern to emerge. But to assemble the necessary information, nothing is needed except time and infinite patience.

Number of fibres per thread, diameter of thread, weight of lace

All these features are related to the quality of thread used in specific laces. The number of fibres per thread can be counted by a mild macerating technique; the diameter by reference to a micrometer eyepiece; and the weight using an electronic balance. Only four pieces of lace were investigated in this way so that no statistically valid averages are possible, but the examples were quite typical of their time and place. Three other types of lace were weighed, and for all pieces the actual weight was reduced to that of a standard area, 150 sq.cm.

The Comparative Fibre Dimensions and Weights of Laces

Type of lace	Spin	Diameter of thread	Number of fibres per thread	Diameter of fibres	Weight of lace per 150 sq. cm	Average thread count (wholestitch area) per inch
Binche late 17th C	S	60 μ (0.06 mm)	28	2 μ	1.14 g	104 × 104
Valenciennes late 17th C First piece* Second piece	S	90 μ (0.09 mm)	55 —	1.6 μ —	— 0.886 g	104 × 112 128 × 136
Devon 18th C	S	50 μ (0.05 mm)	32	1.56μ	0.99 g	88 × 88
Flemish collar lace early 17th C	S Ply Z 2	240 μ (0.24 mm)	150	1.6 μ	2.13 g	64 × 64
Point d'Angleterre early 18th C					1.15 g	112 × 120
Mechlin (fig. 108b) *c.*1700					1.1 g	112 × 120
Needle lace: **Reseau Venise** early 18th C					1.2 g	16 stitches and 10 rows average per $\frac{1}{8}$ in. square = 10,240 per sq. in.

* Note: The piece of Valenciennes first investigated was found to have some extraneous thread along the footing which would falsify the weight. A second piece was weighed and counted.

It will be noted that heaviness of texture does not necessarily mean coarseness of fibre, only that far more fibres were combined when the thread was spun. The total weight of a pair of lappets (Mechlin 7.18 g, each lappet approximately 61 × 8 cm); Brussels bobbin, or point d'Angleterre (9.02 g, each lappet with sloping and scalloped sides but on average 59 × 10 cm) indicates that 89 pairs of such Mechlin lappets, or 71 of similar point d'Angleterre ones could be made from one pound of flax thread (640 g), so that its highest price (£240 per pound, at one time) seems not so excessive.

The total cost of thread for this pair of Mechlin lappets would then be £2.70, and for the point d'Angleterre £3.38, which was still, between 200 and 300 years ago, far from cheap. One might speculate on the colossal number of lappets and other lace seized by the Customs men: each smuggler dog, for example, is said to have been wrapped with 26 lb (12 kg) of lace, equivalent in weight to about 1500 pairs of Flemish lappets.

The relevance of this and other numerical data to establishing the age and location of a lace has yet to be firmly determined. The ethereal flax thread was legitimately exported as well as smuggled, and may be found in any country. Datewise it is restricted to approximately the hundred years between 1650 and 1750 (see table p. 89 and fig. 156).

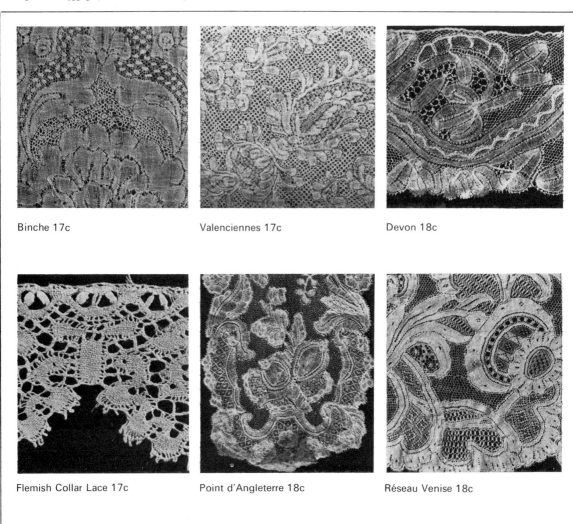

Binche 17c

Valenciennes 17c

Devon 18c

Flemish Collar Lace 17c

Point d'Angleterre 18c

Réseau Venise 18c

Fig. 156 *The laces measured in the table.*

Thread count (bobbin lace) and stitch count (needle lace)

This, combined with thread diameter, is a useful indication of the looseness or tightness of working of a lace. A thread counter (fig. 27) is used. The only care needed is to arrange the lace so that the threads, or lines of stitches, are strictly parallel to the graduated sides; and the only skill, an ability to count.

Index cards

A further section can now be added to the index cards begun on page 66. Spaces for answers would of course be left:

11 Suggested locality name (chapter 4)
    Technical evidence to support this
    Other evidence, e.g. documents, hearsay

12 Suggested date (chapter 4)
    Technical evidence to support this
    Evidence of design
    Evidence of documents etc.

13 Evidence of thread (this chapter)
    Type of thread
    Diameter of thread, and of fibre
    Thread count, or buttonhole stitch count
    Weight, and area
    Single   Ply
    Texture: soft/hard;   loose/tight;   light/heavy;
    cold/warm

SIX

The Technique of Needle Laces

The Stitches of the Motifs

Needle laces are defined as those made up of buttonhole stitches. The transition form between the earliest needle laces in which the stitches were made over a pattern (punto in aria) instead of on a fabric, is called 'reticella', or 'little net' (fig. 157). Blocks were cut out of a cloth to make empty squares (hence the name) inside which decorations were created by filling them in with buttonhole stitches, something in the manner of a church window filled with patterns of coloured glass.

In some ways needle laces are a good deal simpler than bobbin. They have fewer than 90 stitch variations compared with several hundred; they are all non-continuous, except for hollie point which has no distinction into ground and motif so that considerations of continuous or non-continuous are irrelevant; and their reseau types are few. They also took longer to make, required perhaps more concentration, certainly incurred more strain on the eyes, were more expensive, and fewer centres made them. The finest were very splendid.

The basic detached buttonhole stitch (point de

Fig. 157 *A length of reticella showing the linen fabric within which it is worked, and the square net of warp and weft threads which gives it its name.*

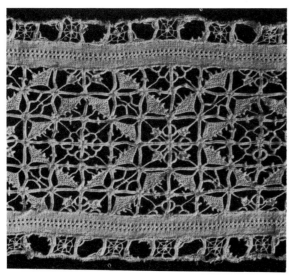

feston, point noné, punto a occhiello, punto a festone, fig. 29) worked from left to right and then back from right to left, or vice versa, occurs only rarely, as a filling. The stitch most consistently used for the motifs is either the detached buttonhole stitch with a straight return, or the knotted buttonhole stitch (point noué).

The detached buttonhole stitch may be worked in either a closed, or an open, manner (fig. 158). In both (a) and (b) the loops pass in one direction, then the thread is carried back straight, below the loops, and caught to them by the stitches of the following row.

The direction of the alternate rows of looping may be either from right to left, or from left to right, whichever is more convenient for the maker. They may also proceed, within each shape, from the bottom up, with the needle pointing away from the maker, or from the top down with the needle pointing towards her. For a right-handed person the direction right to left is easier when the needle is pointed away, while left to right is easier when the needle is pointed towards, since each allows the left thumb to hold down the loop, while the right hand manipulates the needle and thread. When the work is completed, it is no longer possible to determine which method has been chosen, since left to right worked towards looks precisely the same as right to left worked away from – and mutatis mutandis.

The knotted stitch produces a considerably firmer texture and is on the whole associated with older – seventeenth- and eighteenth-century – laces, made of thickish thread. There are at least three distinct techniques which produce the knotted buttonhole stitch appearance, but in the most closely worked laces it is extremely difficult to analyze the precise course of the threads (fig. 159). Fig. 160 demonstrates the three possible techniques. Each can be worked left-right, right-left. Sometimes the loops are worked in one direction only, and the thread is then returned either by bringing it straight back just below the loops of the previous row (straight return), or by twisting it one or more times around each loop (whipped return). The position of the knot at the top or at the lower end of the bar may be significant, though the actual technique of making it is the same.

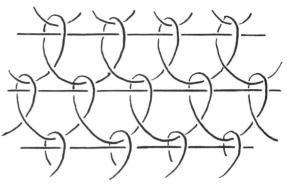

Fig. 158 *Detached buttonhole stitch with a straight return:* **a** *open;* **b** *closed;* **c** *a sketch of the stitch common to both* **a** *and* **b**.

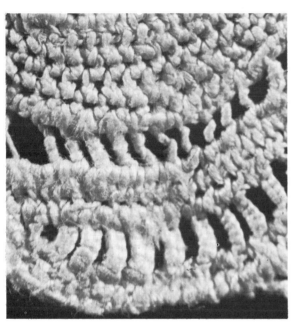

Fig. 159 **a** *Netherlands, knotted buttonhole stitch worked LR, RL,* ×*10.* **b** *Cretan lace, seventeenth century;* **c** *detail, showing extremely close texture,* ×*10.*

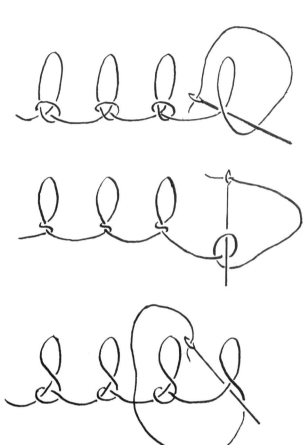

Fig. 161 *An early seventeenth-century knotted lace,* × 10. *The appearance is quite different from buttonhole stitch.*

Fig. 160 *The technique of three forms of knotted buttonhole stitch.* **b** *is not really worked with a knot, but with a tight twist located at the lower end of the bar, but in closely worked laces it appears knotted.*

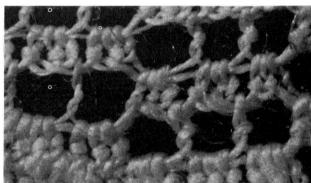

Fig. 162 *Hollie point,* × 10. *Some of the stitches can be seen quite clearly to be of type 160b.*

In fig. 159(a) (Netherlands), the alternating slope of the knots suggests that the stitch is worked left-right, right-left. Such a stitch is called 'punto avorio' by Margaret Taylor Johnstone. She also calls it 'punto greco', 'punto saraceno', and 'puncetto' though the knotting of the latter is quite different (fig. 161). She also equates it with punto a mezzo mandolino (stitch of half an almond shape) mentioned in the pattern book of Parasole *Specchio della Virtuosa Donne*, 1595 and 1616. This example is given simply as a reminder that there is no general agreement on the naming of buttonhole stitches. Dillmont's method of numbering some 40 varieties has much to recommend it, even though numbers call up visual images less readily than words. Figs. 158(a) and (b) correspond to Dillmont's 18th and 19th stitches and fig. 160(a) to her 33rd.

In the English needle lace hollie point, of the seventeenth and eighteenth centuries, the stitches are sufficiently separated for the return thread to be seen,

and the consistent slope of the knots confirms that the loops were worked in one direction only (fig. 162).

The following laces have their main motifs of type 158(a): point de gaze, Argentan and Alençon, eighteenth and nineteenth centuries. 158b is found in: Venetian raised point, reseau Venise, coralline and Burano, seventeenth to nineteenth century (fig. 163). The motifs are formed of knotted buttonhole stitch in: English needle lace, Netherlands and Cretan, all of the seventeenth century (figs. 162, 158c & 159). This stitch was also found to occur, rather unexpectedly, in a piece generally regarded as Venetian point plat which to some extent closely resembles a finely made English needlepoint. Whether this stitch, uncharacteristic of Venetian laces, indicates that that piece is in fact English

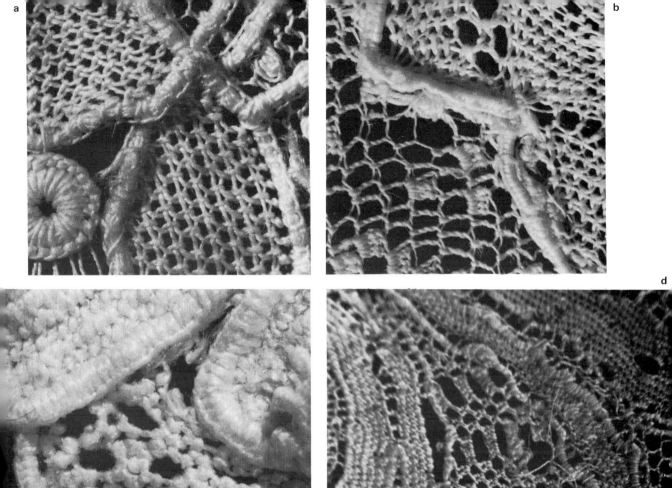

could only be determined by the examination of a vastly larger number of examples.

To summarize: The stitches used for the motifs of needle laces fall into two major categories:

1 Detached buttonhole stitch with a straight return. **a** open texture; **b** close texture.

2 Knotted buttonhole stitch. **a** LR, RL; **b** one direction looping with a straight or whipped return.

These motif stitches appear to be restricted in their use both geographically and temporally. This correlation may, when more data are available, prove extremely helpful in identification.

The Stitches of the Decorative Fillings

As yet no extensive matching up of types of stitch and types of lace has been achieved, but research is proceeding apace, and when sufficient information has been collated it may well be found that the occurrence

Fig. 163 **a** *Point de gaze;* **b** *Argentan;* **c** *Venetian gros point;* **d** *Reseau Venise. All* × *10. The motif parts of* **a** *and* **b** *show the open form of detached buttonhole stitch with straight return, and the motif parts of* **c** *and* **d** *the close form.*

of certain stitches will provide reliable evidence for identification.

Meanwhile confusion over the naming of stitches is extreme. For one thing the French word 'point' and the Italian and Spanish 'punto' mean, literally, a stitch. But in addition these terms were, and to some extent still are, used for completed laces. So when the following appear in historical records – 'point d'Espagne', 'point de Raguse', 'punto avorio', 'punti di greco', even 'hollie point' – we have no way of knowing whether a lace, or an embroidery stitch, is intended.

If the presence of a particular buttonhole stitch, such as Spanish stitch, meant that the lace had been made in Spain, it would be joyful indeed. But at the present state

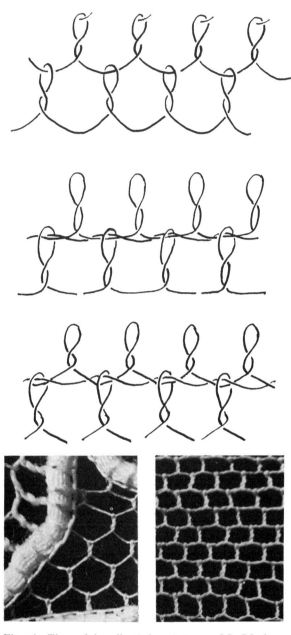

Fig. 164 *Three of the tulle stitch variations:* **a** *LR, RL;* **b** *with whipped return tightened to make a square mesh;* **c** *with the whipped return left slack to give a hexagonal mesh. The number of twists per bar can also vary in each.* **d** *LR, RL mesh in point de gaze;* **e** *mesh* **b** *in Alençon.*

of our knowledge it seems extremely unlikely. Dillmont names her 22nd lace stitch and its variations 'point d'Espagne'. It may be worked LR and then RL; in one direction only with a whipped return, then the meshes drawn into a squarish shape by tightening the return thread; or with a double whipped return (29th stitch)

when it has a hexagonal mesh and she calls it 'Greek stitch' (fig. 164).

The presence of 'Ragusa stitch' according to Margaret Taylor Johnstone points to laces made in seventeenth-century Ragusa (now Dubrovnik). Two of the laces which she attributed to Ragusa are shown in figs. 165 and 166. She describes the stitches as 'Dillmont's point noué', except that they are paired on long loops, and worked left-right, right-left. Her directions for this stitch are to make a loose loop, and then a tighter loop, of stitch A (page 17), then make a buttonhole loop into the first loop and draw up fairly firmly (fig. 166b).

Fillings of different laces may vary in type of stitch, in the number of stitch variations, and in the amount of space which the fillings occupy. There is also a distinction between what might be called 'pure stitches' and 'characteristic stitch formations'. Figs. 167–169 show some of the filling stitches of reseau Venise, Argentan, Alençon and Youghal.

Outlines, Picots and the Third Dimension

All needle laces have an outline to their motifs because of the way they were made. When the work begins, the pattern is drawn on card or parchment, then outlined with a couched thread caught down to it, and filled in with buttonhole stitches. The pattern is later removed by cutting through the couching stitches from the reverse side. If the lace is left like this, and there is no further raising, it is regarded as a flat needle lace (fig. 170).

Completely flat needle laces include punto in aria; the Venetian laces point plat, coralline and reseau Venise; English needle lace and hollie point; Netherlands, and some point de France. But raising began early, and in general is far more extensive and intensive than in bobbin laces. Even the transitional reticellas of the late sixteenth and early seventeenth centuries decorated their animal representations with raised work, often in the form of tiny blunt spikes which gave a furry look of depth to the manes of lions, the feathers of eagles, the quills of the porcupines, or the hairs of a hound (fig. 171). Such picots were made either by winding a thread eight or nine times around a needle and then drawing the needle through; by making a simple loop; or by making a loop and then covering it with a row of buttonhole stitches (fig. 172).

It seems likely that these sixteenth-century adventures into the third dimension were the immediate forerunners of the great raising in height of some of the most superb laces of the mid-seventeenth century. The flat outlines do not seem gradually to have bolstered outwards into swollen curves; the ballooning on the contrary was sudden and extreme. It was the sub-

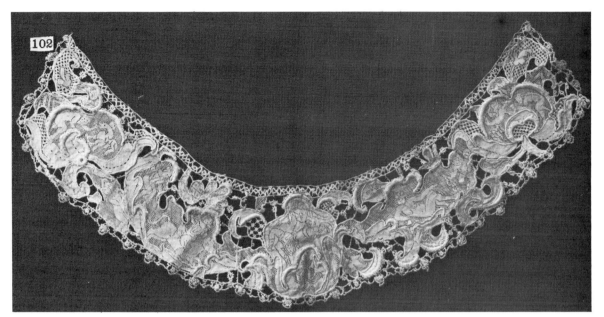

Fig. 165 *A needle lace collar, the exquisitely fine medallions with pictorial insets of Leda and the Swan, Cupid and Psyche, and Europa and the Bull. Seventeenth century. $2\frac{1}{4} \times 13$ inches.*

Direction of working

Fig. 166 a *A lace strongly resembling in texture that of the Netherlands, except for the Byzantine element of the crowned Madonna with the infant Christ. $3\frac{1}{4} \times 39$ inches.* b *Ragusa stitch, or knot stitch, untightened to show method of working.*

sequent shrinking downwards which was gradual, spreading over nearly 50 years. Such outlines would have been added after the preliminary flat work was completed. They took several forms, which are helpful in identification:

a Thick padding, of the so-called gros (large) point of the mid-seventeenth century. A core of coarse thread, tow or wool, was laid along the outlines of the large acanthus, lily, or other stylized flowers, and then held in place with close buttonhole stitching (fig. 173). Additional decoration was produced by looped, spiked and fringed picots, which sprouted from the bulge like so

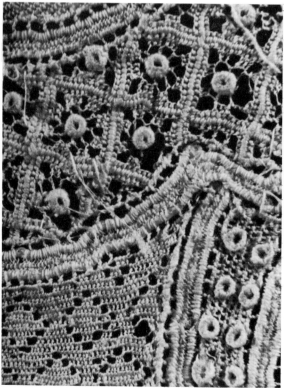

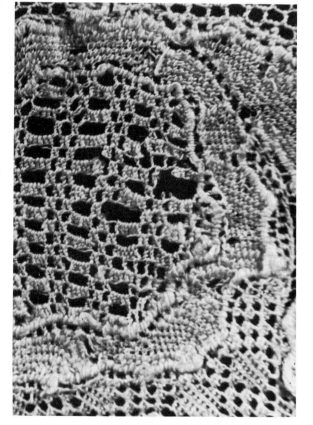

Fig. 167 **a** *Reseau Venise showing at least 14 different fillings.* **b** *and* **c** *Five of the filling stitches,* ×10.

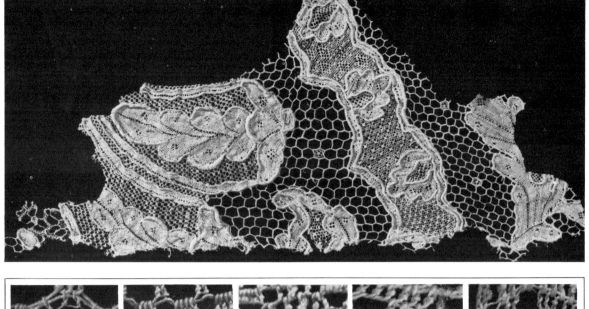

many seedling plants uncurling their richly varied foliage (fig. 174).

b A smaller design with lower padding, more intricately decorated, is characteristic of Venetian rose (raised) point of the second half of the seventeenth century (fig. 175). This culminated in the miniscule spangled effect of point de neige, like snow crystals settling on an over-decorated Christmas tree (fig. 176).

c Low rim-like outlines, closely oversewn with buttonhole stitches, but with little or no additional decoration, are characteristic of Argentan and Alençon, French needle laces of the eighteenth and nineteenth centuries (fig. 177a). Legend has it that such outlines were built over horsehair, but examination of a large number of cut ends of cordonnets has discovered only cords of tightly twisted thread. No horsehair has been seen, except in one rather clumsily made and non-commercial fragment which incorporated net to imitate the petit reseau (page 107) of traditional Alençon, and was almost certainly twentieth-century (fig. 177b); and in one piece of Belgian lace known to date from about 1900, in which the scalloped heading was stiffened by horsehair held by spaced buttonhole stitching. Nor has any eighteenth-century documentary evidence been forthcoming which unequivocally supports this belief. Lefebure (1888) introduces a fine ambiguity of reference between cordonnet and picots. 'This method is still used in the making of fine point d'Alençon. . . .' Grammatically, however, 'this method' refers to the use of horsehair to impart a 'finished crispness' to 'tiny loops or picots'. The *Dictionnaire du Citoyen* (Paris,

Fig. 168 **a** *Argentan, first half eighteenth century, a fragment; and* **b** *five characteristic filling stitches,* × 10.

1761) makes a slightly clearer statement: 'Alençon's chief defect consists in the cordonnet which shrinks when put in water. The horsehair edge *also* draws up the ground.' This implies that the horsehair edge is not the same as the cordonnet. Whatever the true story of the cordonnet may be, there is no doubt that horsehair was used to support the border of picots which projected from it. The hair was either withdrawn as each stitch was completed, or left in the lace, a technique still used in Alençon in the 1980s.

d Other forms of outline are the slightly raised, and spasmodic cordonnets of the early point de France, a more Rococo form not yet systematized into the tamer laces of Alençon and Argentan, but also closely oversewn with buttonhole stitches (fig. 195a).

e In Belgian laces there are spaces between the buttonhole stitches which hold down the separate strands of thread (fig. 178).

f A further simplification is in late nineteenth-century Burano laces where the raised outline is not formed of distinct strands but of a plyed gimp thread, couched down rather than buttonhole stitched over (fig. 179).

Raising gives a right and wrong, or upper and reverse, side to the lace. The method of construction of needle laces, by individual needle movements, in non-continuous fragments, imposes no constraint on the design, or on the size of the pieces constructed.

The use of picots in relation to grounds will be considered in the next section.

169a

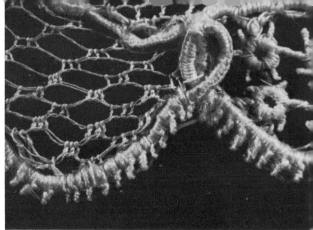

169b

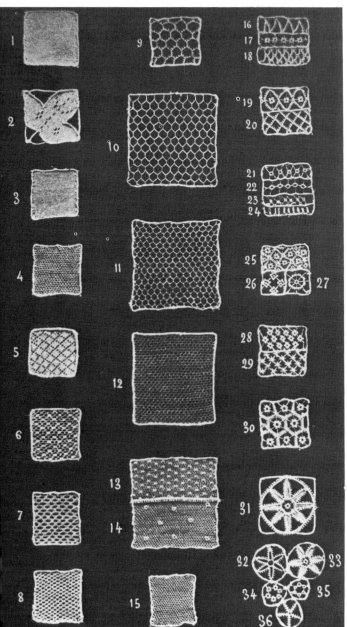

1 Fond or entoilage
2 Portes
3 Gaze serrée or ordinaire
4 Gaze claire
5 Quadrilles
6 Point d'Argentan
7 Point mignon
8 Point à trou
9 Brides à picots or dentelure
10 Bride bouclée (buttonholed plain)
11 Grand réseau (bride tortille)
12 Réseau ordinaire
13 Réseau mouche
14 Réseau avec bobine
15 Petit réseau
16 Venises
17 O à nez en queue
18 Écailles
19 Mosaïques
20 Rateaux
21 O en chainettes
22 O bouclés en queue
23 Mouches
24 Rangs blancs
25 O encadrés
26 Boulettes
27 O à 8 pattes
28 O à nez en chainettes
29 X en chainettes
30 • Pavés avec cannetille
31 St. Esprit avec rangs clairs
32 St. Esprit à six branches
33 St. Esprit avec gaze ordinaire
34 Couronne d'Or à nez
35 Couronne d'Or bouclés
36 Étoile à double nez

Fig. 169 a *and* b *Three characteristic fillings of Alençon,
second half eighteenth century.* c *Alençon stitches (Morris
and Hague);* d *and* e *Two fillings of Youghal, late
nineteenth century.* b, d *and* e × *10.*

169c

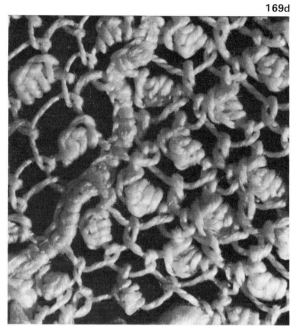

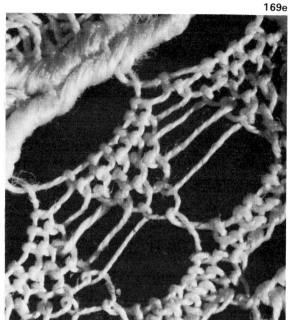

170

171

Fig. 170 *The flat structural outline which is a* sine qua non *of all needle laces, here left in its primal state. Reseau Venise, first quarter eighteenth century. The shapes are filled in with a variety of buttonhole stitches.* × 10.

Fig. 171 *A form of reticella, showing picots raised to give depth and emphasis. The arms of the Poeta-Mangioli families. Aemilia Ars, twentieth century, after Passarotti, 1591.*

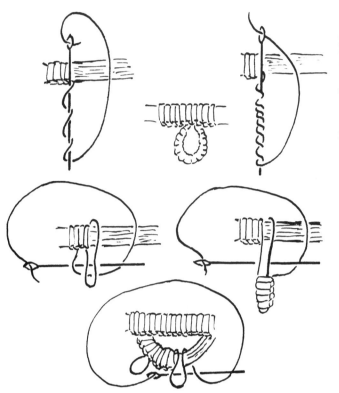

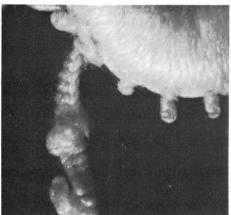

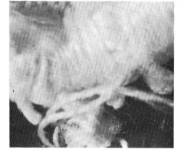

Fig. 172 *Several techniques for making picots.* **a** *Simple;* **b** *Bullion, converted into* **c** *by pulling the twists back to the cord;* **d** *looped, with one or two buttonhole stitches;* **e** *Venetian;* **f** *Buttonhole bar with picots.*

Fig. 173 *The packed threads laid around the outline to pad the cordonnet are visible where the covering buttonhole stitches have broken. Venetian gros point, seventeenth century.*

174a

Fig. 174 *The raised and picot-decorated cordonnets of* **a** *Venetian gros point;* **b** *Spanish,* × 2.

Fig. 175 *Venetian rose point (slightly reduced).*

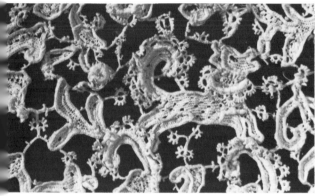

Fig. 176 *Venetian point de neige (× 2), late seventeenth or first years of eighteenth century.*

Fig. 177 **a** *A typical cordonnet of Alençon, the two broken ends indicated by arrows show only tufts of thread emerging. Horsehair, however, supports the picots. Nineteenth century.* **b** *A cordonnet worked over horsehair, probably twentieth century. The buttonhole stitches are not very close, and the hair is visible between them in places.*

177a

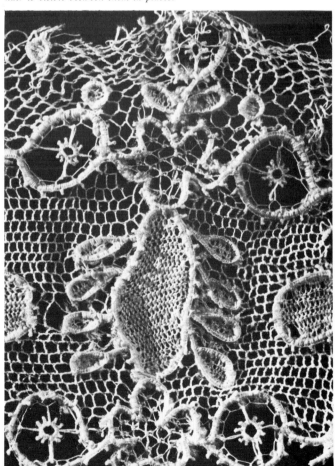

177b

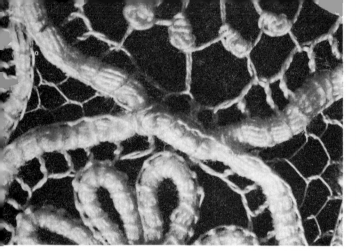

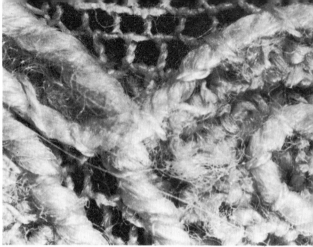

Fig. 178 *The strands of thread of the cordonnet held by spaced buttonhole stitching, point de gaze, second half nineteenth century.*

Fig. 179 *The S-plyed gimp thread is couched to the border of the flat motifs. Note the very closely worked detached buttonhole stitch within them. Burano, late nineteenth century.*

Fig. 180 *No clear distinction between ground and design. Punto in aria, sixteenth century, needle lace with some braided strands.*

The Stitches of the Grounds

Historically the proportion of solid to open part of the lace follows much the same sequence for needle as for bobbin laces:

a The earliest punto in aria had no structural distinction between ground and motif (fig. 180).

b In early Venetian forms the huge Baroque blooms encroached on each other almost obliterating the space between them. In Netherlands forms, the narrow open straits were crossed by short bars (fig. 181).

c As the bars linking the motifs grew longer they were buttonhole stitched over and, in the richer forms, heavily picoted until the picots formed almost a subsidiary design (fig. 182).

d Near the end of the seventeenth century, as the motifs drifted apart, the bars became organized into a large picoted meshwork (fig. 183).

e There is apparently no record of needle reseaux before 1711. In Argentan laces the reseau was firm and regular, forming a kind of diminutive of the mesh of bars (Fr, brides), indeed it is sometimes known as 'brides bouclées'. The picots, characteristic of group (d) were shed, but the oversewing by buttonhole stitching retained. According to Boulard there might be as many as 90 to 120 stitches around each mesh, but 60 might be regarded as a more usual number (fig. 184).

f As the designs became more delicate, and the laces more fragile-looking, the meshes dwindled in size. It is at this point that complications of technique and identification arise. In most forms the mesh was worked in one direction only and the returning thread was not straight but whipped around the lower part of the loops already formed. Several variations are found:

Fig. 181 *Almost no ground;* **a** *Venetian;* **b** *Netherlands with a design of two-headed eagles. Both second half seventeenth century.*

Fig. 182 *Richly picoted bars. Venetian, late seventeenth century.*

183a

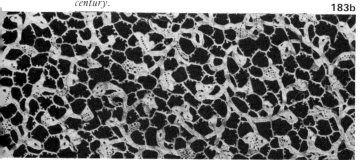
183b

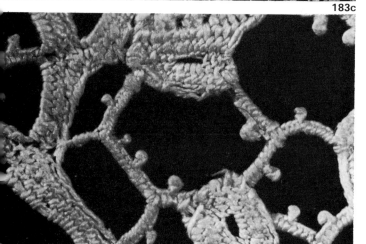
183c

Fig. 183 *Bars forming a picoted meshwork:* **a** *point de France;* **b** *coralline;* **c** *detail of* **b** × 10. *Late seventeenth century.*

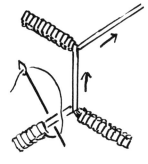

Fig. 184 **a** *The making of brides bouclées, the arrows show the direction of working.* **b** *Argentan, mid-eighteenth century.*

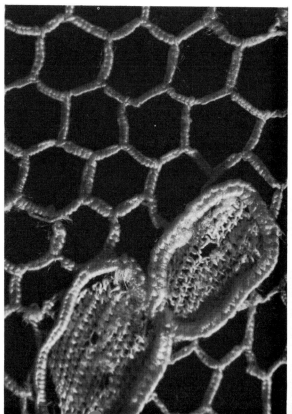

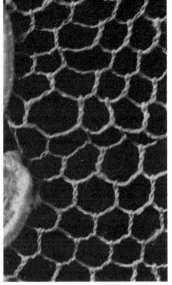
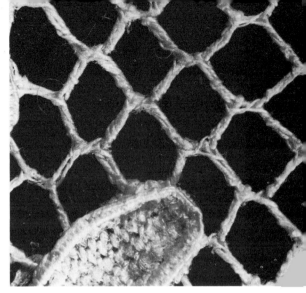

Fig. 185 **a** *Square meshes in Burano.* **b** *Hexagonal meshes in Alençon.* **c** *Brides tortillées in Alençon, nineteenth century.* **d** *From the top, reseau ordinaire, brides tortillées, brides bouclées.*

i The return thread is pulled very tight, giving the meshes a square or rectangular appearance (figs. 164b & e, & 185a);

ii The return thread is left slack so that a more delicate hexagonal mesh appears. Both (i) and (ii) correspond to Dillmont's 23rd lace stitch, and are sometimes called 'reseau ordinaire', or 'petit reseau' when they occur on a small scale as a filling.

iii The loops are left slack as in (ii), and the returning thread is wound not twice but four times around each so that the mesh is more sharply hexagonal (figs. 177a & 185b). This is Dillmont's 29th stitch, which she calls 'Greek stitch'.

iv A thread was twisted the whole way around every mesh, giving the lace from a short distance the appearance of an Argentan ground. Argentan was a more expensive lace, and there seems no doubt that the object of this exercise was to deceive. This form is called 'brides tortillées' (fig. 185c).

v In addition, the meshes of group (f) may be constructed either crosswise or lengthwise of the lace (fig. 186).

g In point de gaze, the 'gauze' relates to an even finer mesh made from left to right and then back from right to left, giving it the appearance of a single twist in one row and a double in the next (fig. 187).

h A somewhat coarse mesh of bars, of curved rather than strictly hexagonal form, and graced with picots, was used for some Irish laces of the later nineteenth century (fig. 188).

i Reseau rosacé may be regarded as a filling stitch expanded into a ground in a lace known as Argentella, perhaps named from the little town of Argentelles, not

Fig. 186 *Flat laces with the meshes constructed,* **a** *crosswise of the lace;* **b** *lengthwise of the lace. Both reseau Venise (?), early eighteenth century.*

Fig. 187 *Point de gaze ground,* **a** *photograph and* **b** *sketch.*

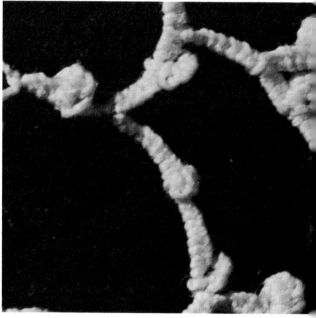

Fig. 188 **a** *Youghal lace, second half nineteenth century;* **b** *detail of the ground* × 10.

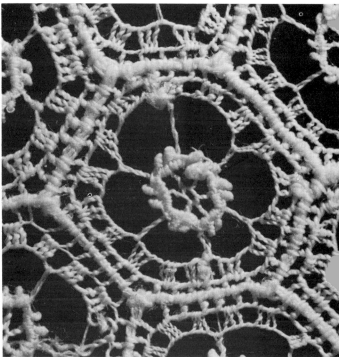

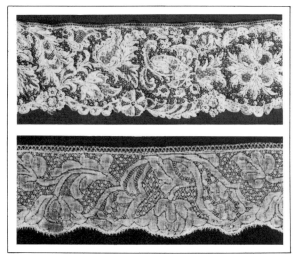

Fig. 189 **a** *Argentella;* **b** *detail of the ground* ×10. **c** *Distance views of Argentella and Binche showing the similarity of appearance of their grounds.*

far from Argentan in Normandy. The peculiar arrangement of bees-comb hexagons each with its central grub is sometimes referred to as oeil de perdrix, as if to suggest that it was copying by a needle technique the pierced snowballs of the seventeenth-century bobbin Binche (fig. 189). The precise detail of the hexagon contents varies, but the general impression is always the same.

SEVEN

Determining the Place of Origin and Dating Needle Laces

Where?

The attribution of needle laces to centres in France, England and the Venetian Republic is, in the main, fairly straightforward, since they have marked distinguishing characteristics. However, various problems arise at the end of the seventeenth and beginning of the eighteenth century (page 113–17).

Evidence for location from technique

a Grounds: Elaborately picoted bars, sometimes like starry constellations, are characteristic of Venice, and of the best English needle laces, both from the second half of the seventeenth century.

A ground of meshed bars with picots is found in the French laces, point de France and point de Sedan, also of the later seventeenth century; in Venetian coralline which copied point de France; and in nineteenth-century Irish laces such as Youghal which were also initially imitative.

Reseau grounds are found in eighteenth- and nineteenth-century French and Burano laces; in Belgian needle laces, and in the mixed nineteenth-century form known as 'point d'Angleterre'.

Fig. 190 *A copy of seventeenth-century Venetian made in Burano, late nineteenth century. Carlier (1903) described this lace as like a chiselled ivory, 'the plentifully flowered branches unrolling and curling back with a capricious sinuosity, like a dream of the Orient'.*

Plain or fairly plain bars usually indicate nineteenth- and twentieth-century copies of Venetian laces, for example in Burano, at Bayeux, at Kenmare and Inishmacsaint in Ireland, in Belgium as 'point de Venise', and in China (fig. 190).

Details of these grounds are given in the previous chapter.

b Markedly raised outlines are characteristic of Venice and Spain; superficial outlining cords of France, Belgium and Burano, in a series from close to open overstitching. English laces were flat, as were some forms of Venetian and of point de France at the beginning of the eighteenth century (see pages 96–9). Some Netherlands' laces are flat, some have narrow raised rims making them look as if the crowded motifs are struggling for elbow room (fig. 191).

c Filling stitches of large quantity and richly varied types are common to the French point de Sedan, and the Burano reseau Venise, though the former has a ground of meshed bars, and the latter a reseau (fig. 192). Altogether some 90 stitches are known, but they have yet to be attributed to specific localities. A few are illustrated in figs. 167 to 169. The situation is in fact quite complicated: Argentella, originally about 1860 attributed to Burano, was wrested from it by Dupont Auberville on the grounds that the reseau rosacé had been found in laces which were undeniably French. Yet

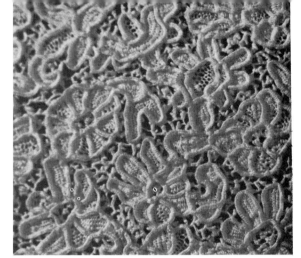

Fig. 191 **a** *The cramped appearance of Netherlands needle lace with a raised cordonnet;* **b** *detail.*

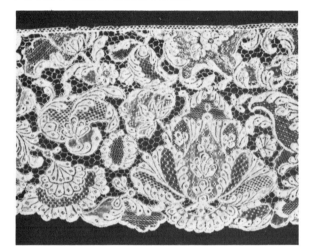
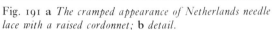

Fig. 192 *The great variety of filling stitches characteristic of* **a** *point de Sedan;* **b** *reseau Venise. Both early eighteenth century.*

variations of this stitch do occur in the putatively Italian reseau Venise (figs. 193a, b & c).

d The number of stitches per unit area has potentially great significance (see page 113 and table on page 89). The following figures were based on an average of counts in $\frac{1}{8}$-inch square areas, from which 1-inch square totals were calculated.

Lace	Stitches per sq.in.
Venetian gros point, 17th C	6300
Reseau Venise, beginning 18th C	10,000
English needle lace, 17th C	2000
Hollie point, early 18th C	3000
Alençon, early 18th C	4500
Burano, 1930s	1700
Singapore needle lace, 1982	380
19th C Viennese copies of 17th C Venetian gros point	2000–4000

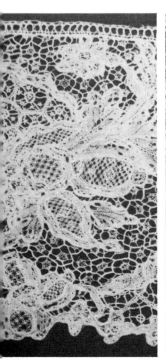

Fig. 193 *The rosacé stitch:* **a** *as a ground in Argentella;* **b** *as a filling in traditional reseau Venise;* **c** *as a filling in Alençon. Number of stitches:* **d** *Venetian 'fleurs volants', seventeenth century;* **e** *Viennese copy,* c1900.

Such counts can be of great importance in distinguishing genuine seventeenth-century laces from their nineteenth-century imitations, which are often almost identical in design. The difference in texture between the Venetian fleures volantes and the Viennese copy is visible in the photographs (fig. 193d & e), which show them at the same magnification. In both, the tiers of raised work are joined at only one point to the basal motif so that they can be lifted like separate petals. The results above provide a useful, if rather incomplete, comparison. Since there are often considerable variations between different motifs of the same lace, a random sampling method would be needed to give entirely reliable stitch counts.

e The stitch count is necessarily linked with both the fineness or coarseness of the thread, and the closeness or looseness of the work.

Evidence for location from design
The range of designs is far smaller in needle than in bobbin laces, and broad generalizations are possible.
a An Islamic form of punto in aria, with sinuous curves interlacing like a wrought-iron screen is associated with an Eastern influence which affected Venetian art more profoundly than that of northern Europe (fig. 194).
b The Venetian raised laces delight in sumptuously idealized designs of flowers and scrolls which curl and swell into exuberant blooms (fig. 174).
c A constructional discipline at once intricately formal and rigidly symmetrical is characteristic of point de France in the second half of the seventeenth century. It appears to have influenced a subdued Venice whose later point de neige, point plat and coralline show a diminution and amorphization of Venetian motifs into symmetrical or scattered fragments, both alien to the generous yet conventional forms of Italian art (fig. 195).
d Spanish laces, which may or may not have been commissioned from Venice, are characterized by an obtrusive opulence of appearance, as if pinked, padded, puffed, pouched, slashed and encrusted with pearls in the manner of the Spanish farthingales introduced into Tudor courts in the late sixteenth century (fig. 174b).
e Flemish needle laces are known from the mid-eighteenth century, but their earlier form, and even existence, are controversial. One might expect them to be representational, bearing in mind the stylized portrayals of garden blooms which render the bobbin laces of that country so entrancing.
f English needle laces, connected by more or less decorated bars, tend to be clumsy, angular and gauche. The more pictorial forms such as hollie point, or the little raised-work pictures, are intended to tell a story (fig. 196).

Fig. 194 *An Islamic design in punto in aria. Probably Venetian, early seventeenth century.*

g The occurrence of specific representations which might help with placing are not particularly common. The two-headed eagle has been discussed on page 71. Fig. 197(a) shows a dolphin in a somewhat damaged piece of needle lace of seventeenth-century Venetian type. Its significance is uncertain. It could have been commissioned by the noble Delfini family of Bologna, or the dolphin may symbolize the Dauphin, eldest son of the king of France, and it may have been destined for that country or even, conceivably, have been made there.
h A border of finely made needle lace tells in pictorial cartoon the story of Judith and Holofernes, while a legend above in antique Portuguese describes how she cut off his head in the night as he slept and placed it on the tower of the city, i.e. Jerusalem. Undoubtedly the piece was commissioned for Portugal, but there can be no certainty that it was made there (fig. 197b).

Evidence for location from documents
Of the major countries concerned with the making of needle laces, only France has full and reliable documentation, from the time of the setting up of the industry by Louis XIV and Colbert in 1665 to the present day. Venetian references are woefully lacking, which is a pity because the major problems of localization in fact relate to just what laces, and when, Venice did or did not produce. Flemish records of the seventeenth and eighteenth centuries are vague and subject to differing interpretations, and the Brussels archives were destroyed by fire in 1731. English records are near non-existent, except for rare provenanced pieces: it seems likely that the laces were made by nuns, not for export like those of Venice and Flanders, and not on an impressively organized scale like those of France.

It is small wonder that there are differences of

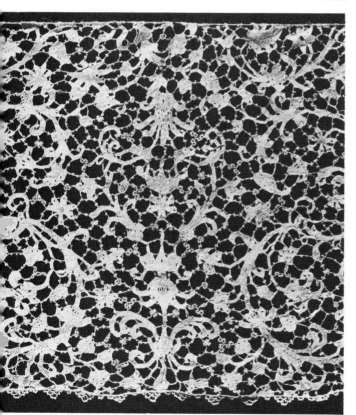

opinion with regard to the attribution and sequential history of certain laces. This disagreement is especially strong in the France-Venice-Flanders tangle. The late seventeenth and early eighteenth centuries seems to have been marked by a kind of rapid fire reciprocal imitativeness operating between them. Heavy laces were going out of fashion, fine were coming in; Baroque solidity was being replaced by Rococo frivolity; Venetian raised laces were excluded from France and rapidly becoming demodée; Flemish bobbin laces with their elfin rotundities of dream-like flowers were obsessing the market. France stole from Venice, and monopolized the French market with point de France; Venice tried to retaliate by copying France, squeezing her native voluptuousness into symmetrically constricted moulds, as in point de neige and point plat; France herself tried to shut out Flanders by imitating the light airiness of the popular bobbin laces with her reseau'd Alençon; Venice followed suit or, according to some authorities, provided the parental form, with reseau Venise. In short, designs, fillings and grounds became almost inextricably mixed, and the identification of reliably distinctive features has yet to be determined.

The interconnection of French and Venetian laces
1 It is known that the primary establishment of the points de France in 1665 was made possible by the settlement of a number of Venetian workers at various centres in northern France (see p. 185). That the lace

Fig. 195 *Symmetry:* **a** *point de France;* **b** *point de neige;* **c** *point plat, Venetian, part of an apron border.*

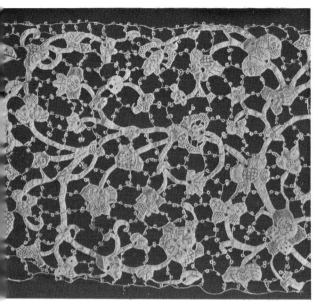

Fig. 196 **a** *A flounce of English needle lace with picoted bars.*
b *The garden of Eden. The legend reads 'As Adam's glory
and pore Eve's was done, Betwixt a rising and a setting sun'.*

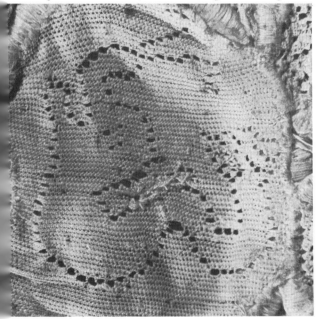

produced was initially strongly three-dimensional is
indicated by Palliser who describes the toilette made in
France for the marriage of the Prince de Conti and Mlle
de Blois, in 1688, as having raised work so high that the
stitches of the motifs could not be seen. There is an
obscurity here since the marriage in 1688 was between
François Louis de Bourbon (Le Grand Conti) and
Marie Thérèse. Mlle de Blois was not married until
1692, and then to M le Duc de Chartres.

Fig. 197 **a** *A dolphin, executed in a Venetian gros point lace
(reverse side). The motif is worked in close detached
buttonhole stitch with a straight return, not in 'hollie stitch'
(figs. 160b, 162),* ×4 **b** *Part of the legend of Judith and
Holofernes. The lettering, in antique Portuguese, may or may
not indicate place of origin.*

When a little later, the ex-patriate workers returned to Venice, point de France came under the influence of the great architectural designers Bérain, Le Brun and Bailly. Venice was now out in the cold, and her attempts to change with the times were scarcely successful. Her point de neige fripperies of snow crystals balanced one above the other in a kind of manic effulgence were impractical: they took far too long to make – an entire year might pass in the construction of one yard, and were impossibly expensive. The tortured complexities of the myriad excrescences could not compete with the plainer, coarser, yet more coherent and, in their way, grandiosely effective, point de France. As the seventeenth century ended, Venetian corallines attempted to follow the French trend towards flatness combined with a hexagonal meshwork of bars, but the design deteriorated rapidly into a haphazard contiguity of fragments giving a confused schizoid appearance to a lace which, judged by the minuteness of the work, should have been marvellously graceful (fig. 183b).

2 This disintegration of design might be regarded as reflecting the increasing disintegration of the Venetian Republic. The reseau'd form, or 'point de Venise à reseau' – in contrast to the bar'd form or 'point de Venise à brides' – demonstrates an unhappy mixture of old and new. It was perhaps an attempt to recapture the baroque stature and nobility of movement in a lightweight fabric, after the misguided venture into fragments and symmetry. But the juxtaposition of airiness and massivity simply appeared unbalanced and, in spite of the unparalleled workmanship, unattractive.

The lace called 'reseau Venise' is flat, with a ground of Alençon-type reseau ordinaire, the meshes pulled into square shapes, and running sometimes lengthwise, sometimes crosswise, of the lace (fig. 186a). The motifs are extremely densely worked with detached buttonhole stitch with a straight return, and there are many fillings, copiously varied. The extremely lightweight texture (see table on page 89), rivalled only by Flemish bobbin laces; the superb quality of the flax thread, probably from Flanders; and the incredible minuteness of the stitches (page 111) are other consistent features, as well as the motifs being separated from the ground by a line of holes which follow their shape (fig. 198). The latter feature persists even in forms which, because of the unusually thick structural outlining thread, appear raised; and any such raising itself can be seen on examination to be quite different from the separately added cordonnet of French needle laces. Apart from the anachronistic Baroque design, there are sometimes flower shapes which approximate to those of Alençon, sometimes to those of point de Sedan; sometimes the cones, tufted palms and peacock tails catch a spice of the

Fig. 198 *Reseau Venise, the twisted threads which form a line of small holes emphasizing the distinction between motif and ground, an important feature in a completely flat lace with an inconspicuous outlining thread.*

Orient, as in some of the densely patterned, near-groundless Brussels bobbin laces (fig. 199 & key photo 30.2 on page 154). This proves nothing more than what is already known, that imitation was rife, and that Venice in particular was desperately trying anything which might reverse the disastrous decline of her fortunes.

Reseau Venise was first attributed to Burano by the textile authority Dupont Auberville (author of *Ornamental Textile Fabrics*, 1877) who exhibited a number of examples at the Paris Exhibition of 1867. Burano's lace-making activities are to some extent a mystery. The tiny island is only five miles from Venice, yet so utterly divergent from that city in atmosphere, architecture and affluence that it tends to be thought of as another country. It tends to be judged too by its nineteenth-century productions which are coarse, with uneven thread, and somewhat lumpy inartistic designs. A writer in 1895 refers to it as an industry which has never been of much account. Yet according to Urbani, Burano in the sixteenth and seventeenth centuries was one of the principal seats of the 'celebrated lace manufacture of the Venetian provinces'; while Palliser quotes a seventeenth-century document as saying that 'punti in aria' were also called 'di Burano' and that they were noble, white, of excellent design, and of perfect workmanship. Carlier (1903) speaks of the 'finest needle lace in the world', a handkerchief then belonging to Queen Marguerite of Italy, who had revived the lace industry at Burano in 1874. Three lace makers, he says, had worked on it for nearly 20 years; it was so light that when closing the eyes one could not feel it touch the hand; and so fine that it could be shut into a golden casket no bigger than a nutshell.

It is small wonder that Belgian writers would prefer to believe that this lace was made in Flanders. Yet there is nothing in favour of that origin apart from the diaphanous texture, and the minuteness of working. The exquisite raised work of Venice established her as pre-eminent in the making of needle laces. Flanders, though not without needle skill, and famous for her cutworks ('ponti fiamenghi') in the sixteenth and seventeenth centuries, is incontrovertibly recorded c1700 only as a celebrated maker of bobbin laces. Such Brussels or Flemish needle laces as existed seem to have been neither plentiful, nor very highly regarded. Cole (1875) says of reseau Venise that 'It is now so rare that collectors tend to call it Old Brussels Point which it resembles. The Brussels needle lace however lacks the precision and extreme niceness of execution'. In the time of Louis XV, c1750, needle laces known as 'point gaze flamand' appeared, but they were grounded with bobbin stitches, and it seems likely that the needle part was made in France, and sent to Flanders for finishing, as was done occasionally for the fillings of Alençon's cheaper laces (*Dictionnaire du Citoyen*, 1761). Jourdain's opinion is that Brussels designs are distinctly floral, reseau Venise is not; Brussels fillings are less closely constructed and of less variety, their workmanship of a lower standard; and Brussels uses a slight cordonnet to cover the constructional outlining thread, so that it is not quite flat. The later editions of Palliser show a volte-face (fig. 200). But the above arguments in any case relate to mid-eighteenth century Flemish laces, and it is the early years with which, in reseau Venise, we are concerned.

Both Cole and Jourdain regard reseau Venise as beginning around 1700, and so antedating the French reseau'd laces. Paulis regards it as a Flemish lace, and as earlier still, on the basis of obscure quotations from the *Mercure Galant* of 1673 and 1678. The former refers to 'point de fil a reseau', the latter to a light clear 'point à la reine', newly popular with ladies as a head-dress. Although bobbin laces at this time had reseaux, there is no evidence that needle laces had progressed beyond bars. The similar word 'reseuil' was equated with filet in the sixteenth and seventeenth centuries; Palliser refers to point à la reine as a stitch; and the head-dress referred to could thus quite well have been of a fine silk gauze, or hand-made net, lightly embroidered.

These differences of opinion, and their supporting arguments, have been quoted in some detail to demonstrate how the criteria used in identification may need to be balanced against each other in trying to establish the geographical location, and date, of a lace. The various protagonists compare techniques such as

Fig. 199 *Reseau Venise with a Persian nuance.*

outlines, fillings and grounds; textures; designs; and documentary evidence. If in this case the result is not unanimity, the lack of agreement may be attributed at least in part to the paucity both of corroborative material and of examples for comparison.

When?
Quite a lot has been said about dating already because it was necessary to make sense of the geography, and also because the smaller range of techniques in needle laces throws a greater emphasis on the time sequence in distinguishing one lace from another.

Evidence for dating from technique
a Amount of ground. The same progression is discernable as in bobbin laces: no distinction between ground and motif (early punto in aria, fig. 180); the motifs touch so that there is no structural ground, and sometimes no space at all (fig. 181); a gradual spreading apart of the motifs as if pushed away by the ground, until by 1789 the Alençons were quite plain, with a little formal border and a scattering of tears (semé de larmes). In the nineteenth century, apart from the many imitations of the old, the design-ground ratio was readjusted at about 50–50..

Fig. 200 *A typical reseau Venise of Baroque design, from Palliser, 1910 edition called Brussels in her first edition, 1865.*

b Type of ground. Again the series – bars, reseaux, revival of bars – is as for bobbin laces. Needle lace reseaux appear to have developed later, not until the first years of the eighteenth century, and perhaps only when a reversal of fashion in favour of lighter forms made such a change desirable. The conversion may indeed have been influenced by the growing popularity of bobbin laces (figs. 182–189).

c Non-continuity is a universal condition in needle laces, except for the non-conforming hollie point. All the motifs were made as separate pieces, by a number of people, and then linked by a ground.

d Texture. As with bobbin laces, the finest threads belong to the second half of the seventeenth and early eighteenth centuries. Though the flax itself must have come from Flanders, the minuteness of the Venetian work excels anything found elsewhere, from 6000 stitches per square inch in gros point, to 10,000 in the amazing reseau Venise (see table on page 111 and pages 89 & 112).

Dating by design

a In the nineteenth century, copies of Venetian forms were made so prolifically in so many places that it is difficult to isolate distinguishing features. Sometimes the thread is inferior, thicker, or made of cotton. In many, however scrupulous the technique, the design is marred by an indescribable lifelessness (see chapter 8).

b It seems likely that early bobbin laces copied the designs of needle laces which, developing from embroidery, quite considerably antedated them. The two may thus at a quick glance be confused. Netherlands needle and bobbin laces are also similar (figs. 144a & 181b), and though to some extent after 1700 the major techniques went their separate ways, needle laces, like bobbin, conformed to the changing fashions of the passing years. The geometric mode appears in almost limitless diversity in the sixteenth- to early seventeenth-century punto in aria (fig. 201); the Baroque in Venetian and Spanish gros points in which the heavy design was intended to lie flat along the gowns it enriched (fig. 181a); and the architectural in point de France and some point de neige, in which the designs are vertically orientated, to hang perhaps gently gathered as deep flounces or the ends of cravats (fig. 195). Rococo, around 1700, was even more amenable to gathering, since the design was of discrete particles rather than an ordered whole (point de neige and coralline, fig. 202). Formal or stylized designs appeared in the flexible ribbon swathes of Alençon, and in the fine Argentan flounce worn by Queen Charlotte at her wedding in 1761 to George III of Great Britain; and these were mirrored by the eighteenth-century Mechlin bobbin laces (fig. 203). A thin Neo-Classical precision

marked the early years of the nineteenth century (fig. 204); to be followed later by the naturalistic designs of point de gaze and Youghal.

c Rarely, pieces of lace may incorporate direct clues as to their date of origin, and so throw light on other laces of that period (key photo 4 on page 139). Another example is the magnificent Austrian imperial bridal veil of Brussels point de gaze, made for the marriage of Rudolph, only son of the Emperor Francis Joseph I of Austria to Stephanie, daughter of the King of the Belgians, on 10 May 1881. Fig. 205, a detail of the veil, shows a lion rampant beneath the crown of Belgium, and the country's motto 'Unity is Strength'.

Dating from portraits and documents

a An early fresco in the Palazzo Pubblico, Siena, shows the figure of Peace resting against a cushion starred with geometric windows of reticella. The painting is by Ambrogio Lorenzetti (c1290–1348), and is thought to date from 1338–40.

b The carving on a tomb of 1426 in the Cathedral of Tarragon, north-east Spain, depicts kneeling mourners whose hooded vestments bear openwork braids or passements.

c A primitive form of punto in aria is said to be represented on the hem of a dress of one of the two courtesans in Carpaccio's painting of that name in the Museo Correr in Venice. Carpaccio died in 1525, and the work is thought to have been completed in 1515. All that is visible, however, is a design, and technically the decoration could have been achieved by a couched gold thread, a fringe caught together by knotting, or even a silk fabric interwoven at the border with precious metal in a type of geometric design later copied by both needle and bobbin laces of the sixteenth century.

d Punto in aria was mentioned in a sumptuary edict of the Venetian senate in 1476, much earlier than the lace is generally thought to have evolved. 'Punti in aere' is listed as a stitch in Tagliente's pattern book of 1527. But not until 1550 does it become unambiguously a lace in Pagano's *La Gloria e l'Honore di Ponti Tagliati e Ponti in Aere*, in which the title page actually illustrates the lace being made on a parchment, in traditional manner.

e The introduction of steel sewing needles, as opposed to ones made of drawn wire, in the mid-sixteenth century, undoubtedly influenced the development of openwork embroidery into an independent lace made without fabric foundation. In 1550 imported 'nidels the thousand' were taxed on a basis of 'xii d' (5p) in the Customs House book (Edwards and Nevinson).

f General George Washington, prior to his election in 1787 as the first president of the USA, ordered for his

Fig. 201 *Diversity in punto in aria.*

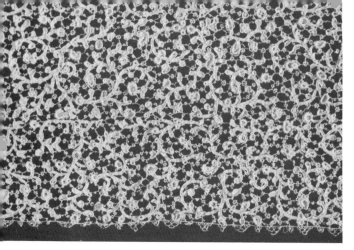

Fig. 202 *A flounce of point de neige, c1700. There is no sharp design to be obscured by gathering.*

Fig. 203 **a** *A flounce of Alençon made in the mid-nineteenth century, at the time of the Empress Eugénie. Though it shows naturalistic representations of flowers, it borrows the scrolled and garlanded formality of eighteenth-century forms.* **b** *Queen Charlotte's wedding flounce of Argentan, 1761, detail.*

Fig. 204 *The Neo-Classical forms of the First Empire:* **a** *Bed hangings (equipage du lit) of Napoleon 1, made for his second marriage, to the Archduchess Marie Louise of Austria, in 1810;* **b** *The coverlet. The ground swarms with bees, symbolic of Bonaparte, and it is bordered all around with the lilies of France. Alençon lace.*

Fig. 205 *Point de gaze, part of a veil made for a royal marriage in 1881. The provenance is unimpeachable, with 'Bruxelles 1880' worked in the lace on the right, and on the left 'Leon Sacré', the prominent lace dealer who organized its execution.*

204a

wife 'a cap, handkerchief, tucker and ruffles to match, of Brussels lace or point, proper to wear with a negligée of salmon-coloured watered silk with satin flowers'. This was in 1759, and though it is not clear whether the terms 'lace' and 'point' are being used as synonyms, or alternatives, it does help to reinforce the social acceptability of Flemish needle laces at that time. Washington himself wore Alençon lace for the painting of his portrait in 1797–9 (Morris and Hague).

g In the nineteenth and twentieth centuries records of revivals and of commercial vicissitudes are both clear and plentiful. They relate to the numbers of lace makers, the setting up of schools, production per annum, and exhibition pieces. Documents accompanied by actual laces survive from the Lefebure brothers of the 1870s, from Mrs Treadwin who died in 1892, and from the Imperial Lace School of Vienna whose needle laces were much praised at the 1900 Exhibition.

h Various modern books, such as by Risselin-Steenebrugen (1981), and by Abegg (1978), match up portraits with photographs of similar laces, and thus provide valuable help with dating.

205

EIGHT
Copying and Convergence

The copying of one lace by another over the centuries was motivated almost entirely by the prospect of commercial gain. Not until the second half of the nineteenth century did aesthetic, or research, copying begin. The former tried to recapture the beauties of the past, though on a gross scale; the latter to investigate their techniques.

Commercial copyings involved a pirating of designs, or textures. When one lace caught on in fashionable society, copyists did not hesitate to follow. The copyings were intended to produce an identical appearance, but were not necessarily by the same technique. In fact seven possible permutations can be distinguished:

1 *Same time – different area – different technique*
This covers all the nineteenth- and twentieth-century machine copies of contemporary bobbin and needle laces such as Bucks, Lille, Honiton, Mechlin, Valenciennes and Maltese copied in Nottingham or Calais on the Levers machines; bobbin Chantilly and needle Alençon copied at Lyon on the Pusher machines; torchon and Cluny on the Barmen; and Brussels Duchesse and Rosaline copied in Switzerland or Plauen on the Schiffli machines; also other copies made by knitting or crochet. There were in addition the convergent designs of Flemish bobbin and French needle laces around 1700 when deep flounces had become fashionable, notably a design which Marian Hague called the candelabra pattern. The meandering ribbon design was found in needle Alençon, and the bobbin laces Mechlin and point d'Angleterre (figs. 206–11). Earlier, the sixteenth-century punto in arias were copied by Genoese plaiting or braiding (fig. 123). There is some evidence that intagliatela may have been produced in Denmark (see 3 below).

2 *Same time – different area – same technique*
Extensive reference has been made to the interplay of French-Venetian influences at the end of the seventeenth century (see diagram on page 185). It is not always easy to distinguish between deliberate imitation and contemporary convergence inspired by the fashion trends of the period. Thus while we may say that the less successful Honiton copied the more successful Brussels in the 1880s, and that the ailing east Midlands laces seized on the flourishing laces of Malta to create

Beds Maltese, the relationship between Beds Maltese and Le Puy at much the same period was probably reciprocal. Abruzzi (central Italy) and Hainault (Belgium), on a more pedestrian level, share similar features in this century (fig. 212).

3 *Same time – same area – different technique*
The seventeenth century gros points of north-east Italy were copied by intagliatela, cloth shapes of flowers edged with buttonhole stitches and joined by bars; and the rose points by mixed laces (mezzo punto) in which gauchely folded bobbin tapes were infilled with buttonhole stitches. The aim of these was to save time (fig. 213). Late seventeenth-century Netherlands bobbin and needle laces converge in almost identical designs (key photos 5.1 & 22.4).

4 *Different time – same area – same technique*
In the nineteenth century, Bayeux in Normandy copied the eighteenth-century laces from nearby Alençon and Argentan, as well as a form of seventeenth-century point de France called in the 1870s 'point de Colbert'. In Italy, the sixteenth-century reticellas designed by the Bolognese Passarotti were copied in Bologna by the Aemilia Ars Society c1900 to 1929. The Scuola di Merletti at Burano copied seventeenth-century Venetian needle laces in the late nineteenth century (fig. 214).

5 *Different time – same area – different technique*
Seventeenth-century Venetian needle laces were copied in the nineteenth century by techniques which involved darning or cording (fig. 215, and see page 27).

6 *Different time – different area – same technique*
Raised Venetian laces of the seventeenth century were copied in the nineteenth century for commercial gain, or for exhibition purposes, at the Lefebure workshops in Bayeux, at convents in Ireland, at the Escuola de Puntaires in Barcelona, and at the Vienna Lace Centre. Flatter forms were copied in China and in Belgium as point de Venise (fig. 216). Seventeenth- and eighteenth-century Italian mezzo puntos, themselves a copy of Venetian needle laces, were copied by twentieth-century Belgium as point de Milan. Late nineteenth-century Burano made 'Burano Alençon', based on late eighteenth- or early nineteenth-century designs. Some of Mrs Treadwin's copies of antique

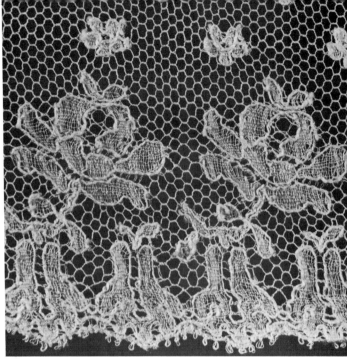

Fig. 206 **a** *Mechlin lace made by hand;* **b** *made on the Levers machine.* **c** *Honiton lace made by hand;* **d** *on the Levers machine – note that not only the shapes of the motifs but also the space-filling 'slugs and snails' and the braid at the neck edge, necessary in the slack bobbin lace to prevent it pulling out of shape but superfluous in the machine version, have been faithfully copied to provide the maximum verissimilitude. All mid-nineteenth century.*

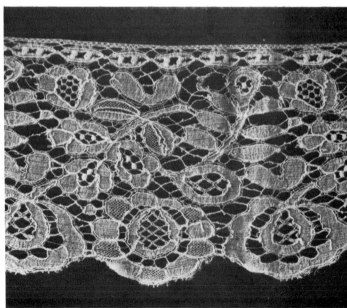

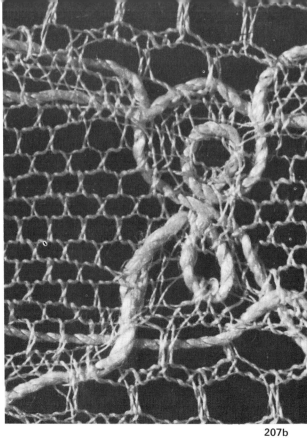

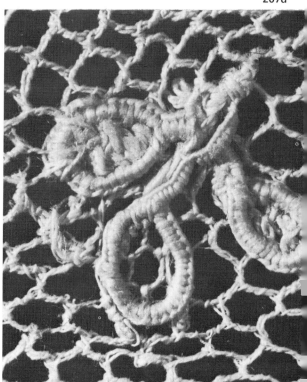

207b

Fig. 207 a *Alençon on the Pusher machine;* b *detail.* c *Alençon by hand;* d *and* e *details.* f *Chantilly lace made on the Pusher machine. All c1860.*

207d

207c

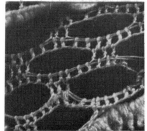

207e

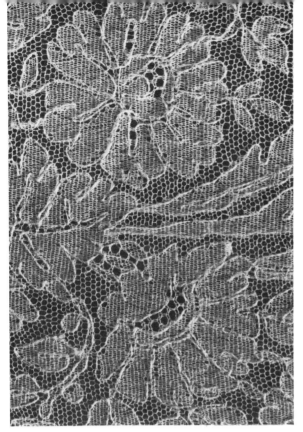

207f

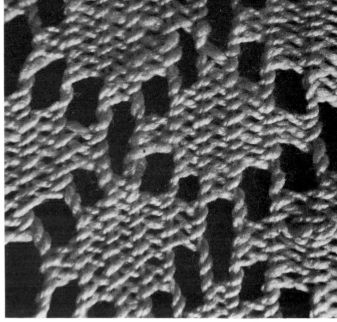

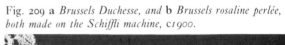

Fig. 208 *Torchon made on the Barmen machine,* c1920.

Fig. 209 **a** *Brussels Duchesse, and* **b** *Brussels rosaline perlée, both made on the Schiffli machine,* c1900.

209a

209b

Maltese Cross Antimacassar.

TERIALS—*Walter Evans & Co.'s Boars'-Head Crochet Cotton Nos. 12 or 14; Walker's Penelope Needle No. 3. Coarser size—Use Boar's-Head Cotton Nos. 6 or 8; Needle No. 2½.*
Doileys, Cushions, Toilets, &c., use Boar's-Head Cotton Nos. 14 or 20; Needle No. 4.
Church Lace, use Walter Evans & Co.'s Mecklenburgh Linen Thread.

THE SCROLL PATTERN.

Commence with 49 chain, turn, and missing the 2 last chain, work along the foundation chain,
reble in each stitch, 6 times); then 5 plain, 2 treble, 3 long, 2 treble, 10 plain, 2 treble, 1 long,

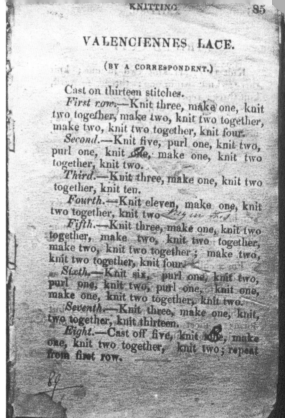

VALENCIENNES LACE.

(BY A CORRESPONDENT.)

Cast on thirteen stitches.

First row.—Knit three, make one, knit two together, make two, knit two together, make two, knit two together, knit four.

Second.—Knit five, purl one, knit two, purl one, knit one, make one, knit two together, knit two.

Third.—Knit three, make one, knit two together, knit ten.

Fourth.—Knit eleven, make one, knit two together, knit two.

Fifth.—Knit three, make one, knit two together, make two, knit two together, make two, knit two together; make two, knit two together, knit four.

Sixth.—Knit six, purl one, knit two, purl one, knit two, purl one, knit one, make one, knit two together, knit two.

Seventh.—Knit three, make one, knit two together, knit thirteen.

Eight.—Cast off five, knit one, make one, knit two together, knit two; repeat from first row.

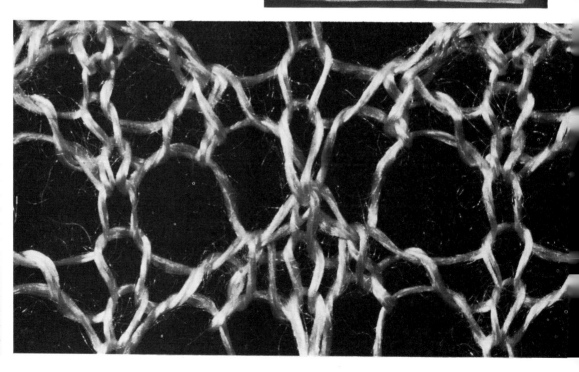

Fig. 210 a *Design and part instructions for making Maltese lace by crochet.* b *Valenciennes made by knitting.* c *A competent imitation of fond d'armure made in fine knitting with a silk thread;* d *detail. All 1860s.*

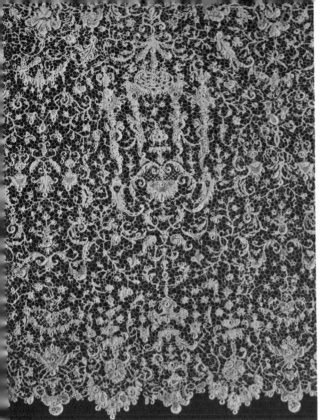

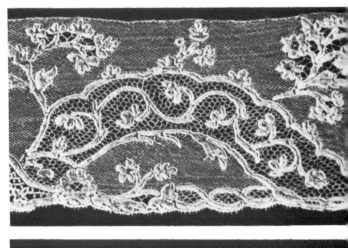

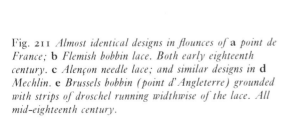

Fig. 211 *Almost identical designs in flounces of* **a** *point de France;* **b** *Flemish bobbin lace. Both early eighteenth century.* **c** *Alençon needle lace; and similar designs in* **d** *Mechlin.* **e** *Brussels bobbin (point d'Angleterre) grounded with strips of droschel running widthwise of the lace. All mid-eighteenth century.*

Fig. 212 a *Part of a Honiton lace collar giving an impression of the stylish proficiency of Brussels, but distinguishable by the rose shapes and the typical Devon fillings (see fig. 132e). b Hainault lace, second half twentieth century.*

Fig. 213 a *Intagliatela, the labour-saving cloth shapes incorporate buttonhole stitch petals to strengthen the deception. b Mezzo punto, bobbin tape joined and filled with buttonhole stitching; c detail. Late seventeenth/early eighteenth century.*

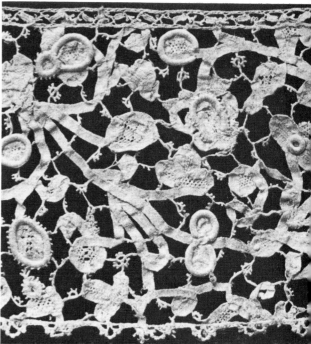

213b

213a

213c

214a

214b

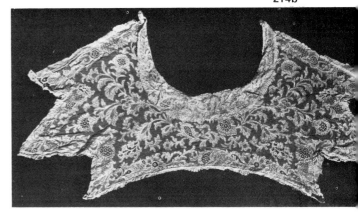

214c

Fig. 214 **a** *Aemilia Ars. The reticella form shows a mermaid, and two-headed eagles, the arms of Margarita Gonzaga da Este, Duchess of Ferrara. First quarter twentieth century.* **b** *A collar in the manner of reseau Venise, Burano, nineteenth century;* **c** *detail showing the chevron, reseau rosacé, and other typical filling stitches (compare fig. 193b).*

215c

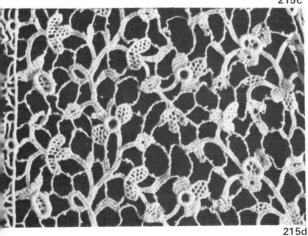

215a

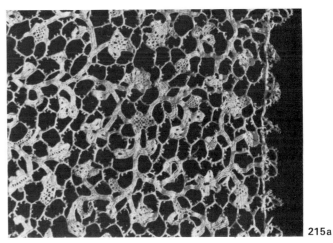

Fig. 215 *Venetian coralline* **a** *made by buttonhole stitching, c1700;* **b** *detail;* **c** *made by cording, c1880;* **d** *detail.*

215d

215b

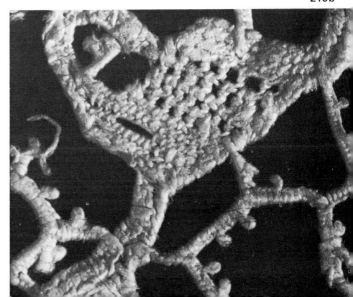

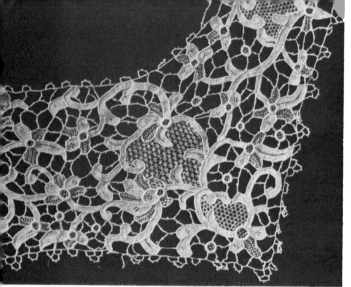

Fig. 216 Belgian point de Venise, early twentieth century.

Fig. 217 Gros point imitations: **a** on the Schiffli machine; **b** by Irish crochet; **c** detail of crochet chain stitch to compare with **d** needle lace buttonhole stitch; **e** sixteenth-century reticella copied by a knotting technique (puncetto), twentieth century; **f** Milanese bobbin lace with deer, hare and hounds, eighteenth century; **g** a remarkable similarity to **f** achieved with a woven braid and a needle lace 'Roman ground'; **h** detail of **g**, late nineteenth century.

217a

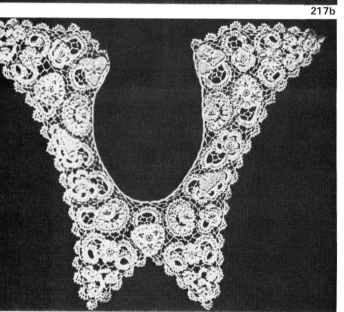

217b

217d

217c

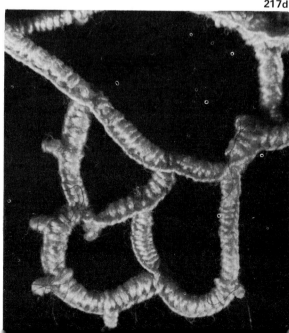

217e

217f   217g

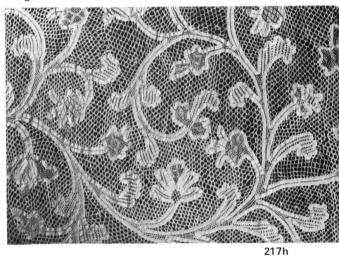

217h

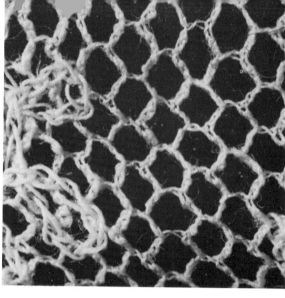

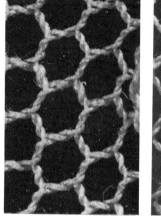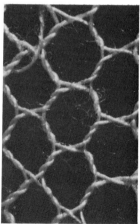

Fig. 218 **a** *A rare dress of warp frame cotton net made for a wedding in 1819;* **b** *detail.* **c** *Two-twist bobbinet.* **d** *Bucks point ground.*

Fig. 219 *So-called Greek lace, made by a mixture of buttonhole stitching, cording and needle weaving.*

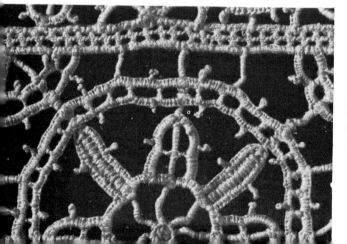

laces were bought by the lace dealer Samuel Chick and may, later, have passed as originals. The copies of sixteenth-century bobbin laces by Mme Paulis (1922) were for research purposes to resolve their techniques (fig. 146).

7 *Different time – different area – different technique*

The designs of late sixteenth-century Italian reticellas were copied in the 1880s by the Schiffli machine, and in this century by needle-knotting (puncetto) in north-west Italy. Seventeenth-century Venetian corallines were copied in mid-nineteenth century Ireland by crochet work; designs of eighteenth-century Milanese bobbin laces by the braid, or point, laces of the 1860s (fig. 217).

Apart from these, which relate to entire designs, the grounds alone might be copied by machine. Both two-twist bobbinet and the warp frame net give convincing illusions of Bucks point ground when seen from a short distance (fig. 218). The illusion was fostered at times

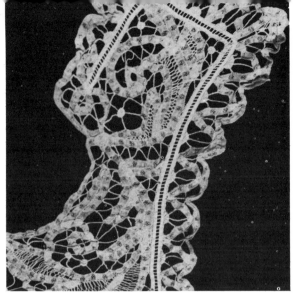
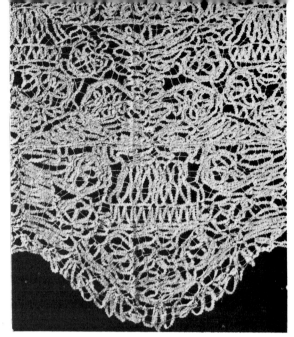

Fig. 220 *Braid laces:* **a** *Battenburg;* **b** *a copy of early eighteenth century Abruzzi bobbin lace made in wavy-edged tapes with minimal linkage;* **c** *page from a notebook thought to have belonged to Mrs Palliser and recording needle lace stitches for use in Branscombe (Devon) braid or Renaissance lace.*

Brussels Edging

1 ....
is common button hole stitch
worked from left to right.

2   Venetian Edging
is one button hole stitch and
then 4 tight stitches worked -
in the loop -
(enlarged to show manner of working)

2B Little Venetian Edging.
in the button hole loop
one light stitch is worked -

3   Sorrento Edging.
This consists of stitches worked
like little venetian edging at
alternate distances of the 8th and 16th
of an inch.

3 ✱ Sorrento lace repeated lines
of Sorrento edging, worked always

from left to right, with the two
close stitches always coming in
the long loop

4. Brussels Lace, is lines of the
Brussels edging worked from
left to right, and from right to left
the last row must be attached to the
braid by passing the needle through
at every stitch.

5 Venetian lace - lines of Venetian
edging, always worked from left
to right

5 ✱ a variety of this is worked
by working back from right
to left in Brussels edge so

6 English Lace   fasten
each little with a tight button hole
stitch then cross them over and under
generally 4 times round is enough for

by the net being so closely grafted on to hand-made Bucks or Lille edgings that the join was invisible.

The distinguishing features of machine laces have been discussed in chapter 2.

Names were copied, in addition to laces, and this adds profoundly to the confusion. Examples are the Belgian 'point de Venise', 'point de Milan', and 'point de Paris'; the abbreviation of 'Beds Maltese' to 'Maltese'; the name 'point d'Angleterre' used for a Brussels lace; 'point d'Espagne' for a lace from central France; and the mystifying use of 'Greek lace' which may never have been connected with Greece at all. Cole (1874) comments, 'At the present time the "Greek" lace which ladies delight in producing and using to decorate their five-o'clock tea-tables, very closely resembles the reticella lace' (fig. 219). The Spanish 'rosalina perlada' refers to point de neige with its mass of picots (pearls), while Brussels 'rosaline perlée' refers to a bobbin lace (key photo 30.3 on page 154). In late nineteenth-century Burano, point d'Alençon, Argentan, rose point de Venise, punto in aria, point de Bruxelles and point d'Angleterre were all made (Urbani).

There is a fairly small group of laces in which both bobbin and needle techniques appear together. These are called mixed laces. They are especially connected with:

a Brussels. Bobbin laces (point d'Angleterre) after 1750 frequently incorporated a few needle-made motifs, or fillings.

Duchesse, a coarser nineteenth-century lace, was similar.

Needle-made motifs were sometimes grounded with bobbin droschel in the second half of the eighteenth century.

Bobbin motifs grounded in needle-made 'gaze' ground produced nineteenth-century point d'Angleterre (key photo 2.3 on page 136).

Honiton, rarely, had a needle ground, made by twisting the thread once or twice around the needle to form the bar of each loop, and working LR, RL.

b The braid laces – also called 'point', 'renaissance', or 'tape' laces – were made mostly by amateurs, from the 1860s on. They used straight machine-produced, or rarely, bobbin-made tapes which, when coiled into interesting shapes, were filled and surrounded with buttonhole stitches of varying competence and complexity. Mrs Fanny Palliser (1805–78), daughter of Joseph Marryat, MP for Wimbledon, and of a Bostonian mother, made a collection of some of these stitches, taught the local Sidmouth women, and inspired Marianne, Viscountess Alford, to take such a strong interest that she prevailed on Queen Victoria to found the Royal School of Needlework, in 1874 (Morison) (fig. 220).

Index card

An index card can now be set out for needle laces (see pages 66 & 91):

Needle

14 Motifs made of: open detached buttonhole stitch – close detached buttonhole stitch – knotted buttonhole stitch

---

15 Ground: the design not the ground is made by holes.
No bars – the motifs touch across the open spaces
Bars – plain – picoted – forming a large mesh, hexagonal, sides curved – forming a small mesh the sides covered with buttonhole stitches (brides bouclées)
Reseau technique – LR, RL (point de gaze) – simple whip, square mesh – hexagonal mesh (Greek stitch) – the sides of the mesh twisted around with thread (brides tortillées)
Reseau direction – meshes made across width – meshes made along length

---

16 Decorative fillings – number – name(s) or photos

---

17 Outline – flat – padded and ornamented
– less padded but extended into numerous decorations – a hard rim with or without picots and completely covered with buttonhole stitches – untwisted strands held by spaced buttonhole stitches – a gimp couched along the border of each motif

---

18 Picots – forming raised spikes on the motifs – projecting from the cordonnet – attached to bars – none

---

19 Are there mixed techniques? – bobbin and needle – woven braid and needle – machine net and hand work

---

The sequence of numbering has been preserved for ease of reference, but obviously numbers 2–10 and 14–18 are alternatives, and no lace would need them all. Numbers 11–13 would be relevant to both bobbin and needle laces; and number 19 should be added to both sets of cards.

NINE

A Key to the Identification of Bobbin and Needle Laces

By the time that the index card questionnaires have been filled in, there should be a great deal of information available which can be applied to identification.

Using technical criteria to identify a lace is, as you will have gathered, quite straightforward. The allocation of a place name and a date on the other hand requires a good deal of memory work and mental matching up of not easily defined clues. In this robotic age one might well speculate whether a computer would help. If it were to be primed with every available piece of information on laces already known, then programmed to spot every relevant connection, it should be able to spew out names and dates at the touch of a keyboard.

But this Elysian time is not yet. There are too many unresolved problems of historical fact; too many lacunae in the data on structure; and too many disagreements on terminology, nomenclature and attribution for any computer to do other than respond endlessly, 'Ambiguity due to lack of adequate information'.

What is attempted in this chapter is something far more modest: a key to the identification of laces after the manner of a key for the identification of flowers in a flora. It does not pretend to be the last word, nor even the penultimate. It *does* attempt to emphasize the proper procedure for identification, which requires the same discipline and self-control needed to follow through step by step the investigations of a whodunnit instead of turning impatiently to the end, or in this instance to the illustrations, to find the – unsubstantiated and unexplained – answer.

Note: The numbers of the photographs in the key relate to the key sections. Figure references relate to the earlier chapters of the book.

Machine and embroidered laces must first be excluded, on the basis of chapter 2.

		Type of lace
1	The lace is constructed of buttonhole stitches.	4
	It has a predominantly woven, or plaited, look.	21
	It consists of a mixture of woven and buttonhole stitch techniques, or of either combined with a machine net.	2

2 There is a foundation of mainly smallish ($\frac{1}{4}$–$\frac{1}{2}$ in.) squares, formed either by the removal of threads from a woven cloth, or by the laying down of 4- to 6-strand plaited braids to make the outline; or by straight strands of threads buttonhole-stitched over. The cavities of the squares are partially filled with buttonhole stitch shapes (fig. 157).	16th to 17th century Reticella
The work as above, and at times no coarser, but the design stilted and, however closely it copies the original, unnatural (fig. 214a).	20th century Aemilia Ars
The woven-look part is a loom-woven lawn, the buttonhole stitches form decorative fillings inside white flowers of surface embroidery.	Ayrshire work 19th century
The woven-look part consists of bobbin-made motifs and bars, with scattered needle lace medallions.	Brussels Duchesse 19th century
The woven part consists of bobbin-made motifs, the ground is a fine regular 'gaze'.	Point d'Angleterre
The bobbin motifs are linked by an irregular needle-made net ground (rare).	Honiton
Buttonhole stitches form the motifs, the ground is a bobbin droschel joined stitch by stitch to the borders of the motifs.	18th century Needle Lace grounded in Flanders

2.1 *Ayrshire work, c1840: part of a fichu bearing the monogram of Queen Victoria.*

Brussels Hand-Made Lace.

DUCHESSE.

DUCHESSE Lace is a bobbin lace of fine quality, the sprigs resemble those of Honiton Lace and are united by brides. It is a very popular lace at the present age, and the effect of this lace is greatly beautified when Point de Gaze Motifs are inserted. It is made in Belgium and is now mostly in the hands of religious communities.

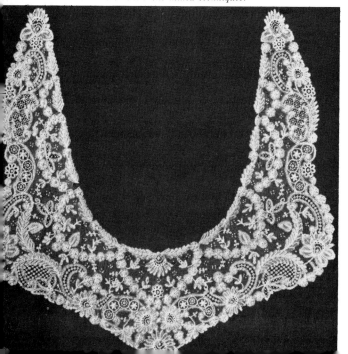

2.2 *Brussels Duchesse, early twentieth century:* **a** *a fan leaf, and* **b** *a page from a 1912 catalogue.*

2.3 *Point d'Angleterre, nineteenth century:* **a** *a collar, and* **b** *detail* × 10 *to show the mixed techniques.*

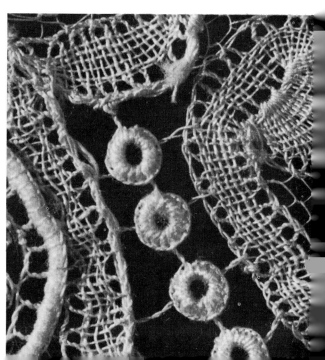

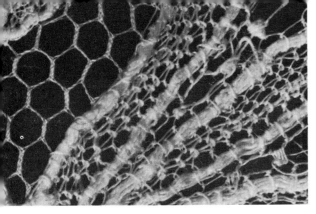

2.4 *Needle lace grounded in Flemish droschel, eighteenth century.*

2.5 a *Brussels bobbin and needle appliqué on net, nineteenth century; and* b *detail—note stitches used for attachment of motifs.*

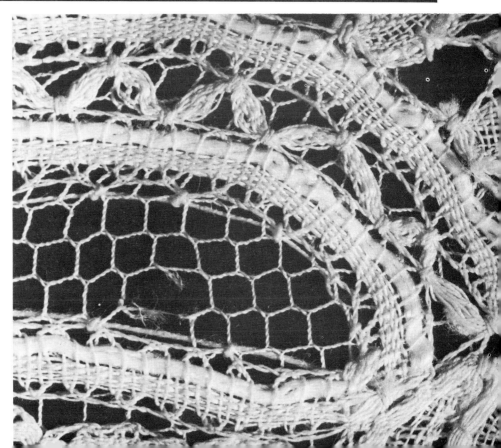

Needle or bobbin motifs are stitched to a droschel ground; the droschel passes across the back of the motifs, or has been neatly snipped away (fig. 119). | Late 18th century N. or B. appliqué on droschel

Needle or bobbin motifs are stitched to a droschel ground; the droschel passes across the back of the motifs, or has been neatly snipped away (fig. 119).	Late 18th century N. or B. appliqué on droschel
The bobbin- or needle-made motifs are stitched to a background of machine net.	19th century N. or B. appliqué on net
The woven part is a tape or braid manipulated throughout the lace to form a pattern; the buttonhole stitches form the fillings and ground.	3
3 The tape is hand-made, awkwardly folded, the pattern small, the bars elaborately picoted, the design flowing.	17th century Mezzo Punto
The tape is usually machine-made, rarely by hand, it may be straight or indented, softer, more neatly folded, or gathered, the bars usually plain, the design gross.	19th century Braid (renaissance, point) Lace
4 The lace is solid, the design formed by tiny holes, with no open ground.	Late 17th century to early 19th century Hollie Point
The solid part of the design is formed by buttonhole stitches and there are open parts but not crossed by a structural ground.	5
Design (solid) and ground (open) are quite distinct structures.	7
5 The open part is almost non-existent, the lace heavy, and either flat or with a slightly raised gimp, the design extremely compact.	17th century Netherlands
The design is slender, skeletal, like a geometric sketch, the lace often sharply dentate, fairly open but with no distinction into ground and motif.	16th or early 17th century Punto in Aria
There are clear solid motifs, and open spaces, but the motifs stretch outwards to touch each other so that no structured ground is needed to join them.	6
6 The lace is flat, of thickish thread closely worked, the designs barely representational, the border mostly straight.	Early 17th century Punto in Aria
The design, of stylized blossoms, is richly displayed, their rims heavily padded like great crescent moons, the thread fine and lustrous, the work minute with 6000 or more buttonhole stitches per sq. in. (fig. 181).	2nd quarter 17th century Venetian Gros Point
The work is stiffer, with seldom more than 4000 buttonhole stitches per sq. in., the motifs angular rather than rounded (fig. 193c).	*c.*1900 Viennese imitation of 17th century Gros Point
7 The ground is of bars.	8
The ground is a reseau.	(17) + 18
8 The bars are plain, or with a very few simple picots.	9
The bars from the motifs meet in the open spaces to form a complex pattern of loops and picots.	10
The bars meet to form large, more or less regular meshes, each side purled with tiny picots.	16
The bars are reduced to a small hexagonal mesh, each side covered with buttonhole stitches.	17
9 The design motifs are old.	17th or 18th century lace regrounded
The design is stiff, angular and frequently crude, the thread fairly thick.	19th or 20th century Belgian/Chinese Point de Venise
10 The outlines of the motifs are conspicuously raised.	11
The lace is quite flat, or with isolated slightly raised decoration.	14

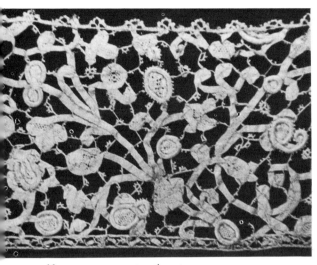

3.1 *Mezzo punto, seventeenth century.*

3.2 *Braid lace collar, nineteenth century.*

4 *Hollie point, 1739.*

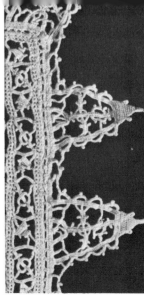

5.1 *Netherlands needle lace, seventeenth century.*

5.2 *Punto in aria, sixteenth century.*

6 *Punto in aria, seventeenth century.*

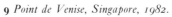

9 *Point de Venise, Singapore, 1982.*

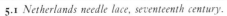

11   The thread is very fine, the stitches almost microscopic.

The thread is coarser, sometimes brownish, the designs similar to 12 but stilted.

The motif size is fairly small, stiff and symmetrical, forming a pattern like curving acanthus, or astragals moulded in plaster, the texture less supple than 12, the thread less fine.

12   19th century Burano
imitations of 17th century

19th century Point de
Colbert

---

12   The motifs are large, 2 in. or more across, the padded outlines further decorated with fancy embellishments.

The motifs are smaller, about 1 in. across, the padding less extreme, but the smaller decorations more varied and fanciful, the design like burgeoning rambler roses.

The motifs are tiny, about $\frac{1}{2}$ in. across, tiered upwards like fretted paper doileys, the design often symmetrical and static, though bewilderingly intricate.

13

2nd half of 17th century
Venetian Rose Point

17th century Venetian
Point de Neige

---

13   The design is bold, floral and stylized, sometimes incorporating pictorial insets of mythological scenes.

The motifs are slightly smaller, but with exaggerated intermittent raising like curved fungoid excrescences split into spore-like pustules, large S-shaped caterpillars encircled with hairy rings, and sometimes long wormy picots like loose trails of vermicilli.

2nd half of 17th century
Venetian Gros Point

2nd half 17th century
'Spanish'

---

14   The thread is fine, nearly 5000 stitches per sq. in.

The thread is thicker, with 2000 or fewer stitches per sq. in., the colour off-white, the design usually coarse, angular and naive, though with some variations of fillings, and figures may be represented.

15

17th century English
needle lace

---

15   The motifs are a little less than 1 in. across, tenuously star-like on smoothly flowing stems (see fig. 195c).

The motifs are minute, barely $\frac{1}{4}$ in. across, like narrow random pathways, the design obscured and scarcely discernible in the picoted ground (fig. 215).

17th century Venetian
Point Plat
Late 17th century
Coralline (Venetian)

---

16   The lace is flat, the meshes of bars curved like the scales of a fish, the motifs floral and naturalistic, the petals shaded by close and open textures, the fillings copied from various sources, the thread thickish.

The lace is mainly flat but with some, usually slight, raising; the motifs small and symmetrical, at times representing tiny people, animals, or musical instruments (figs. 183a, 195a and 211a).

The motifs have a slightly raised outline oversewn with buttonhole stitches, the design is tumultuous with crowded shapes of bursting fruits packed with a multitude of fillings, the texture fine.

The design is flat and fragmented as in Coralline 15, but with more fragments and fewer stalks, the thread sometimes coarser, the ground simpler.

The stalks are oversewn with spaced buttonhole stitches which connect with the ground, the work is comparatively slack.

19th century Youghal

17th century Point de France

17th century Point de Sedan

Early 18th century Coralline
18th century Flemish
Coralline

---

17   The hexagonal meshes have each a central inclusion (reseau rosacé), the thread is fine, the design of well-conceived but slightly angular flowers, their edges hardened by a tightly twisted gimp thread with close buttonhole stitching.

18th century Argentella

11 *Burano imitation of earlier lace, nineteenth century.*

12.2 *Venetian point de neige, seventeenth century.*

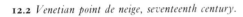

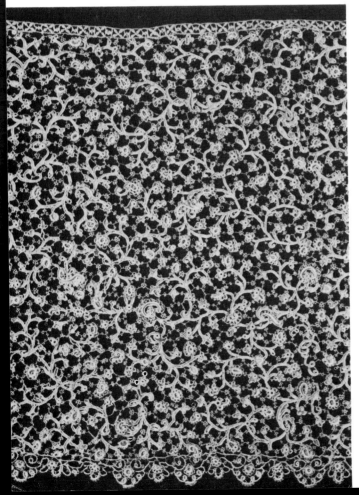

12.1 *Venetian rose point, second half seventeenth century.*

13.1 *Venetian gros point with picoted bars, second half seventeenth century.*

13.2 *Spanish gros point, second half seventeenth century.*

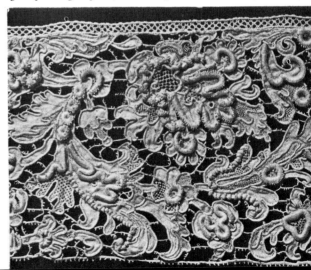

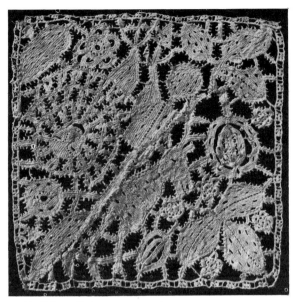

14 *English needle lace, seventeenth century.*

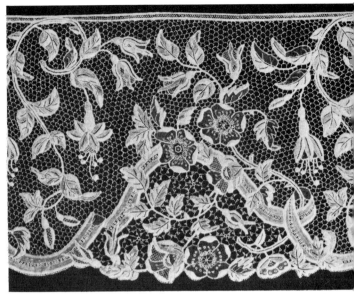

16.1 *Youghal, nineteenth century.*

16.2 *Point de Sedan, late seventeenth century.*

16.3 *Flemish coralline, early eighteenth century.*

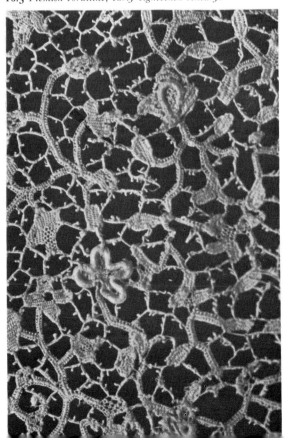

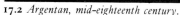
17.2 *Argentan, mid-eighteenth century.*

17.1 *Argentella, early eighteenth century.*

17 (cont.) The meshes are smaller, with no central inclusions, but with every side closely covered with buttonhole stitches (brides bouclées), the rest as above.

As above, but the thread heavier, the design florid, sometimes bombastic or sentimental.

The mesh is sufficiently fine and regular to be called a reseau; every side is twisted around with thread, imitating the Argentan texture (brides tortillées, fig. 185c and d).

18th century Argentan
19th or 20th century Argentan

Some 19th century Alençon

18 The stitches are worked from left to right, and from right to left, the bars of the loops being twisted twice in one row, and once in alternate rows. The design is floral and naturalistic, often with separately made rose petals attached in a layered manner; the range of fillings is proportional to the quality of the lace; the whole fairly loosely textured, the gimp threads held by spaced buttonhole stitching.

The reseau stitches are worked in one direction only, the sides of each loop being twisted twice. The return thread whips over the lower part of each loop, and is sometimes left slack to give a hexagonal mesh, sometimes pulled tight to form a square one (reseau ordinaire).

The thread is exceedingly fine.

19th or 20th century Brussels
Point de Gaze

19
20

19 The thread is fine, but not exceptionally so. The small motifs are close and neat, outlined with a firm cordonnet made hard and spiky with picots. The design is like a simplified Argentan or Argentella, the mesh may be square or hexagonal.

The thread is coarser, sometimes fluffy and uneven, the design of lumpy sprigs grouped around bullock's hearts, or representing touristic scenes of the Doge's Palace, or gondolas. The mesh is very square and worked along the short axis of the lace.

As above, but the design is more traditionally French.

The general appearance is of a magnified reseau Venise, with the mesh worked lengthwise, no additional cordonnet, and typical filling stitches, though the design has a nuance of Belgian influence in a few floral enclosures with picoted bars (fig. 214b and c).

18th and some mid-19th
century Alençon

19th or 20th century Burano
19th or 20th century Burano
Alençon

19th century Burano

18 *Brussels point de gaze, nineteenth century: the technique and fillings are characteristic but it imitates some features of Alençon design.*

19.1 *Alençon, eighteenth to nineteenth century.*

19.2 *Burano, a tourist piece worked with the Doge's Palace, 1930s.*

19.3 *Burano Alençon, late nineteenth century.*

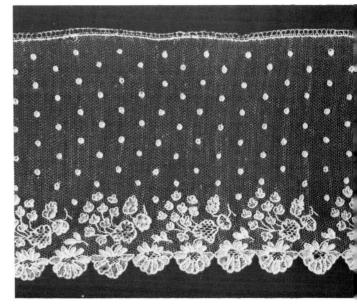

20 An entire lappet of this lace would weigh only a fraction of an ounce (see table on page 89). The lace is completely flat, with a graceful full-blown design of conventional fruits and flowers, and a multitude of fillings; there may be 10,000 buttonhole stitches per sq. in.	**Early 18th century Reseau Venise**

21 There are threads forming a design, and spaces forming a background, but there is no structural distinction into motif and ground.	22
The lace has solid motifs, the open grounds are structured.	23

22 The design incorporates thin braided strands articulated together in a geometric manner, and the heading is sometimes sharply dentate.	**16th century Genoa**
The design is like serrated teeth, the interior partly braided and partly woven (figs. 146 and 147).	**16th century Venice**
The heading is of rounded scallops of compact wholestitch with some internal braiding and sometimes heavy oval point d'esprit.	**Early 17th century Genoa**
The heading is of rounded or gently pointed scallops, closely designed as in the portraits by Van Dyck.	**1st half 17th century Flemish collar lace (some may be English)**
The heading is almost straight, the lace very dense, intricate with almost no open spaces and of a massive solidity; the parts are joined by brief close sewings, or by knots (fig. 145a).	**17th century Netherlands**
The substantial clothwork forms the background in which the geometric design appears as holes (as in cutwork and hollie point) (fig. 126b).	**18th century or earlier Scandinavian**

23 The ground is made by bars.	24
The ground is a reseau. (Note: the reseau names used are inclusive of variations.)	31

24 The bars are made in continuity with the motifs.	25
The threads which join the motifs are not the same as those which make them (i.e. the lace is non-continuous).	26

25 The threads are of corn-coloured or black silk, the linking bars short, either braided or twisted, the design geometric in the manner of ornamental tiles, and incorporating the Maltese cross.	**19th or 20th century Maltese**
Black silk, white flax, or gold thread are used; the ground is of ornamental bars arranged to form large decorative meshes; the design may have big oval point d'esprit strung out in rows or applied flat to the surfaces of flowers; it may have reseau'd medallions inset like cameos, or be markedly Art Nouveau.	**19th or 20th century Le Puy**
The threads are usually of linen, sometimes silk or cotton, the designs influenced by other centres such as Bruges, Honiton, Le Puy and Cluny, but basically simple, sometimes with lobed floral representations. There may or may not be a gimp. Both larger oval and smaller square point d'esprit may occur, sometimes embossed on the surface in a three-dimensional manner. Traditionally there is a nine-pin border.	**19th or 20th century Beds Maltese**
The threads are fairly coarse; the design includes divided trails and/or rosettes of oval point d'esprit, a simple braided heading, and short braided bars. It may be black or white (figs. 131d and 132c).	**19th or 20th century Cluny**
There are applied surface oval point d'esprit on half-stitch ovals, the bars sometimes regularly enough arranged to be thought a reseau, though a very large one (fig. 212b).	**20th century Hainault**
The bars form a plaited ground of tallies (point d'esprit), regular enough for a reseau.	**19th century Plaited Beds**

20 *Reseau Venise, early eighteenth century.*

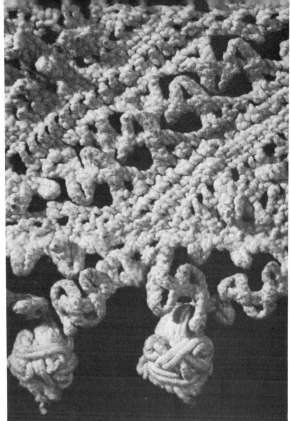

22.1 *Genoese bobbin lace, sixteenth century.*

22.2 *Genoese bobbin lace, early seventeenth century.*

22.3 *Flemish collar lace, early seventeenth century.*

22.4 *Netherlands bobbin lace, seventeenth century.*

25.1 *Maltese, nineteenth century.*

25.2 *Le Puy, second half nineteenth century.*

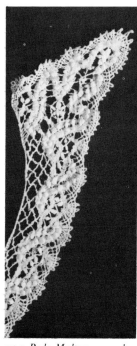

25.3 *Beds Maltese, second half nineteenth century.*

25.4 *Beds with a plaited ground (or tallies), mid-nineteenth century.*

26 The pattern takes the form of a sinuous maze or U-bend trail; there may be a central gimp or a central strand of colour. The bars are short, caught by sewings at one end, at the other continuous with the adjacent trail

There is no gimp, the lace is flat.

There is occasionally a gimp, in parts, but outlines of raised work are more characteristic.

	19th or 20th century Russian, Slavic, Katherine of Aragon
	27
	28

---

27 The lace is so heavily textured as to appear almost unperforated; the extremely short connections are scarcely distinguishable from the wholestitch designs (figs. 145a, section 22 above).

The design is of massive curves representing lily petals, made mainly of wholestitch, linked by a very few short bars

The design is more obviously floral, the bars a little longer, often double, braided and with a few picots; the texture very closely worked wholestitch.

The design is fragmented, only occasionally representative of reclining Oriental figures slippered and turbanned, of pavilions, camels and black-amoors, all on a minute scale; the more elaborate pieces strikingly similar to the candelabra designs of point de France (fig. 211a and b); the bars single, and picoted along one side only.

The design is of strong sweeping lines of wholestitch forming stems which sprout at intervals into trilobed halfstitch buds. Often named after the lace-making centre near Milan where the Scuola d'Art Mobile e del Merletto is situated, but claimed also by Belgium, and so described by Steinmann of London, as 'Bruges'.

The sinuous lines curve back on themselves, they are broad and lack buds.

	17th century Netherlands
	17th century Milanese
	Early 18th century Milanese
	Late 17th to early 18th century Flemish with Brides Picotées
	20th century Cantu
	20th century Bruges Russian

---

28 There may be either raised work or a fairly inconspicuous gimp, or both.

There is raised work only.

	29
	30

---

29 Traditionally the motifs are of roses, thistles and shamrocks, sometimes of lilies of the valley, ferns, birds and butterflies; the bars may be braided and picoted, or twisted, or a snatchpin thread may move in a zigzag manner from one motif to the next, linking them together. In the best, the raised and rolled work emphasizes the veins of leaves and the separation of flower petals; but the motifs may be ill-matched, badly assembled, of different proportions, tension and even colour of the thread – the lace then has no raised work but instead a thin shiny gimp.

There is a ground of leadworks which might be regarded as bars or reseau (rare).

The texture is of closely worked wholestitch in good but slightly thick thread, the large flat flowers are outlined with a neat gimp, the leaves elongated trefoils, the whole well assembled but very plain, the bars snatchpin.

Leaves and petals are emphasized with raised work, there may be additional lightly attached decorations. The texture is heavy compared with **30** Brussels bobbin; the designs may be delicate and naturalistic, but in comparison with the cottage charm of Honiton they are ornate and polished (see also **2**).

	19th or 20th century Honiton
	Honiton
	19th or 20th century Bruges Flower Lace
	19th or 20th century Brussels Duchesse

20 *Russian lace, part of a black silk stole bought in Archangel, 1899.*

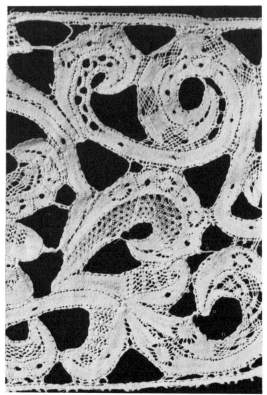

27.1 *Milanese, seventeenth century.*

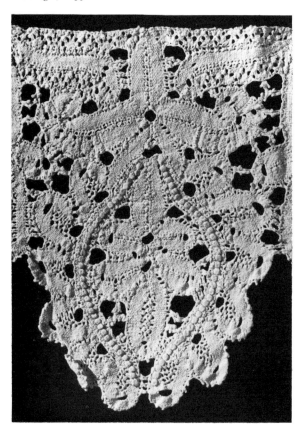

27.2 *Milanese with double bars, early eighteenth century.*

27.3 *Flemish, or Milanese, with brides picotées, eighteenth century.*

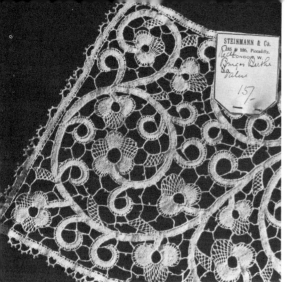

29.1 *Honiton with picoted bars, nineteenth century.*

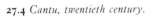

27.4 *Cantu, twentieth century.*

27.5 *Bruges Russian, twentieth century.*

29.2 *Honiton with a ground of lead-works.*

29.3 *Bruges flower lace, a choker collar designed to fit the shape, c1900.*

29.4 *Brussels Duchesse,* **a** *part of a fall cap, and* **b** *an advertisement.*

30   The thread is extremely fine, the design delicately floral, strengthened with raised work, the open spaces narrow as cracks and crossed by the shortest of bars.

Called Point d'Angleterre – 17th century 'Opaque' Brussels bobbin

    The design is similar to the above but on a much larger scale, the texture loose and lightweight. Used mainly for flounces and cravat ends (see also **58**).

18th century Brabant

    The raised work takes the form of small circular buttons centering the flowers. The bars may be thin and sparse, or thick, made of wholestitch and crinkly edged.

*c*1900 Brussels Rosaline

31 The threads of design and ground are continuous.	32
The threads of design and ground are non-continuous.	52

32 The motifs are outlined with a gimp thread.	33
The motifs have no outlining thread.	46

33 The ground is a fond simple.	34
Other grounds.	37

34 The threads are silk.	35
The threads are linen or cotton.	36

35   The thread is matt, the colour mostly black (rarely white), the motifs of halfstitch, the gimp of several untwisted strands, the design of naturalistic garden flowers beautifully rendered, sometimes crossed with parallel curved lines like railway tracks and said to have been inspired by that innovation. The units of a large construction are made in odd shapes to fit together inconspicuously around the main portions of the design.

19th century Chantilly

The thread is lustrous, often of two thicknesses, cobwebby in the fragile ground and heavier to emphasize the design of simple flower heads which repeat at short intervals. For large pieces, straight strips about 4 in. wide are joined together. Black or silvery white.

19th century 'Spanish' Blonde

The texture and thread are similar to the above, but the design is lighter and less repetitive, with alternations of wholestitch and halfstitch giving a shadowed effect.

19th century Blonde de Caen

36 The ground is mostly plain. The design clings to the heading and is sometimes 4 in. or more deep. The attractive rounded shapes are like an eclectic code representing beehives, wedding bells, and lords and ladies. Traditional fillings are mayflower and honeycomb (fig. 81). There may be square point d'esprit (tallies) as fillings, or in the ground. There is a typical footing.

19th or 20th century Bucks, Northampton, Downton

There is little plain ground; the designs are as pretty and as obscurely representational as in Bucks, but often extending across the width of the lace from footing to heading, and with more abandon; the flowers haloed with point d'esprit.

18th century Lille, 19th century Tonder

The design is much reduced, often formed only by gently manipulated gimps caught between the reseau threads, the ground frequently diapered with point d'esprit.

*c*1800 Lille

37 The ground is one of the variations of five-hole. 38
Other grounds. 39

38 The texture is for the most part heavy, the design a simple triptych sometimes representing a pot of flowers flanked by birds. A gimp is not always present (see **49**).

18th century Antwerp (Anvers)/Flanders

The texture is extremely light and supple, the floral design plump and rounded, with enclosures of lobed quatrefoils.

*c*1700 Mechlin

39 Torchon ground. 40
Other grounds. 41

40 The design is geometric with fans, spiders and halfstitch lozenges, the angle 45°. A gimp is not always present.

Some 20th century Torchon e.g. Swedish

The design is lumpily floral, the angle 40° (rare) (fig. 102).

Late 18th century Mechlin

41 Point de Paris ground. 42
Other grounds. 43

42 The lace is of black silk with delicate floral designs, the ground known as 'fond chant' (fig. 116).

18th century Chantilly

The description, apart from the ground, is as 37.

18th century Antwerp (Anvers)

The texture is lighter than above, the design freer and less formal, usually of very simply represented flowers.

19th century Point de Paris (Normandy)

The general texture is light, the wholestitch slightly loose, the motifs representational, or commemorative, of beasts, coats of arms, dates and flags of the Allies.

19th or 20th century Point de Paris (Belgium)

Rarely, this ground is found in Bucks (Kat stitch or wire ground) especially in the rather coarse black laces.

19th century South Bucks

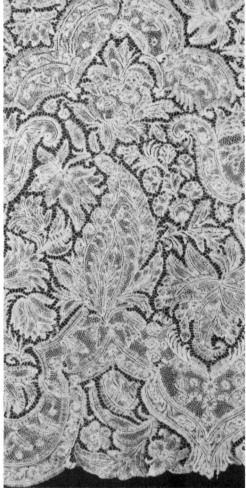

30.1 *Brussels bobbin (point d'Angleterre), late seventeenth century.*

30.2 *Brabant, a flounce 0.57 m deep, first half eighteenth century.*

30.3 *Brussels rosaline, c1900.*

35.1 *A fan leaf of Chantilly, reputed to have belonged to Julia, wife of the 7th Viscount Powerscont (1864–1931).*

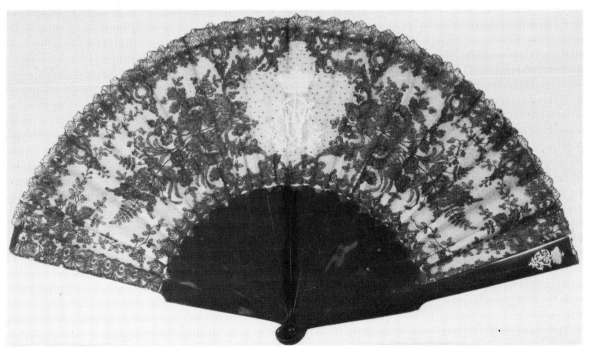

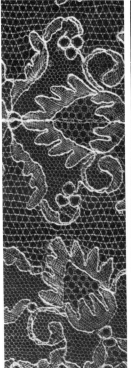

36.1 *Bucks point, the 'Wreath', a South Northants design worked as a handkerchief edging by Winifred Millar* MBE, *c1960.*

35.2 *Spanish blonde, nineteenth century.*

35.3 *Blonde de Caen, nineteenth century.*

36.2 *Lille, eighteenth century.*

36.3 *Tonder, nineteenth century.*

36.4 *Lille, early nineteenth century.*

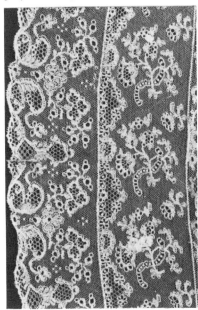

36.2

36.3

36.4

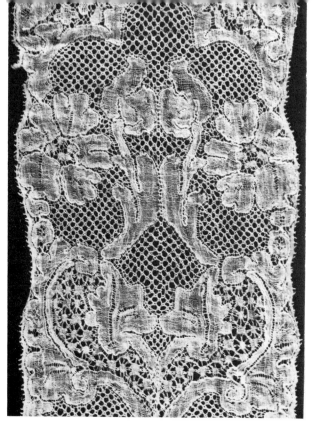

38.1 *Mechlin, c1700.*

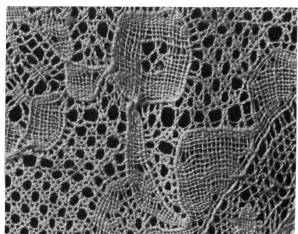

38.2 a *Antwerp with a gimp; and* b *detail.*

40 *Torchon with a gimp, twentieth century.*

42.1 *Antwerp, eighteenth century.*

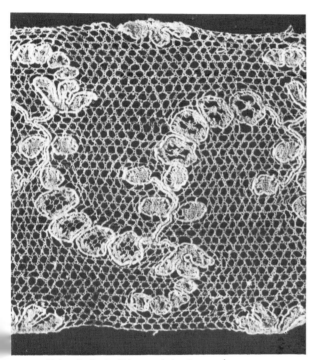

42.2 *Point de Paris (Normandy), nineteenth century.*

42.3 *Point de Paris (Belgian), twentieth century.*

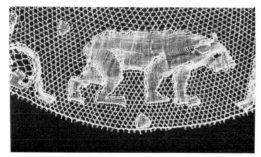

42.4 *Bucks with kat stitch ground, nineteenth century.*

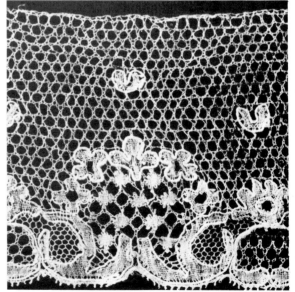

43 'Spanish' ground, as group I (iii) (see page 52).

44

Oeil de perdrix, and Mechlin ground

45

44 Coloured silks and gold thread are often used; the design may include two-headed eagles, or be otherwise pictorial.

Rare examples in black and white thread, either with the patterns formed mainly by gimps or with halfstitch motifs, are known from (fig. 148).

17th to 19th century Spanish
19th century Bucks,
Erzegebirge and Ipswich
(Mass.)

45 Oeil de perdrix (snowball) ground: a rare ground the design is similar to 38.1, and almost weightless.

Mechlin ground: the design chubbily floral or softly angular with little ground; exceptionally light.

The ground occupies up to 50 per cent of the lace; there is a design of arc-like ribbons in the manner of French Alençons.

The Mechlin ground is very extensive, with regularly arranged sprigs; the design is Neo-Classical, or a line of rose heads (fig. 206a).

Late 17th century Mechlin

Early 18th century Mechlin

Mid-18th century Mechlin

*c***1900 Mechlin**

46 The thread is silk; the black form frequently has no gimp (compare 35).

The thread is linen, the lace diaphanously light, with a minute line of pinholes entirely surrounding each part of the design.

The thread is linen, sometimes cotton, the lace heavier.

19th century 'Spanish' Blonde

47
48

47 The ground is five-hole, the designs flowing, well balanced, and of great delicacy, sometimes with snowball fillings.

Rarely, the ground is round Valenciennes.

The ground is oeil de perdrix, which appears to melt into the insubstantial design, blurring its form (fig. 68).

*c***1700 Valenciennes**
Early 18th century
Valenciennes

*c***1700 Binche**

48 Round Valenciennes ground, rarely found in continuous laces, but occasionally in heavy forms.

The lace is heavy, filled with a tripartite design of closely bunched flowers flanked by mirror images, the ground round Valenciennes.

There is an uninteresting design repeat in a round Valenciennes ground.

Five-hole ground.
Square Valenciennes ground.
Torchon ground.

17th to mid-18th century
Flemish Peasant

Mid-17th century 'Dutch'
19th century False
Valenciennes

49
50
51

49 A gimp is occasionally present (see 38).

Wool thread is used, sometimes coloured; the design is geometric with bars or triangles set at a 45° angle, sometimes with a cartwheel of oval point d'esprit.

18th or 19th century Antwerp
(Anvers)

19th century Yak

50 The thread is white, the wholestitch like closely woven linen, the design precise and well regulated in the French manner.

The design is neat, close and well executed but repeating at frequent intervals.

18th century Valenciennes
Mid-19th century
Valenciennes

51 As 48 Dutch but with a torchon ground.

The lace is geometric, at a 45° angle.

A variation of this ground is sometimes made plain, either at a 45° or a 90° angle, then decorated by darning. The locality is uncertain, probably

Mid-17th century Dutch
19th or 20th century Torchon

20th century Brazil

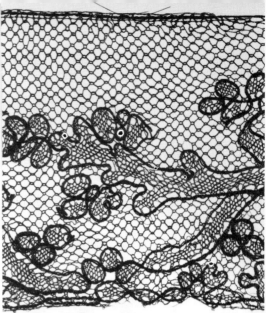

44.1 *Spanish bobbin lace, using gold thread, eighteenth century.*

44.2 *German lace with Spanish ground, late eighteenth century.*

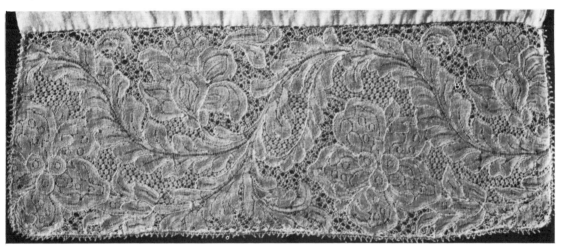

45.1 *Mechlin with oeil de perdrix ground, late seventeenth century.*

45.2 *Mechlin, early eighteenth century.*

45.3

45.4

47.1

46

45.3 *Mechlin, mid-eighteenth century.*

45.4 *Mechlin c1800.*

46 *Black Spanish blonde with no gimp, nineteenth century.*

47.1 *Valenciennes with five hole ground, reputed to have been a gift from Queen Anne (1702–14) to the Foliott family.*

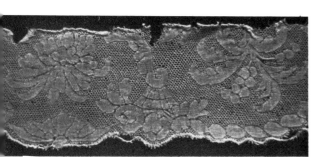

47.2 *Valenciennes with round Valenciennes ground, early eighteenth century.*

47.3 *Binche, c1700.*

48.1 *Flemish peasant lace, early eighteenth century.*

48.2 *Dutch lace, mid-seventeenth century.*

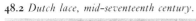

48.3 a *False Valenciennes, with* **b** *detail of ground, nineteenth century.*

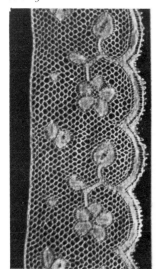

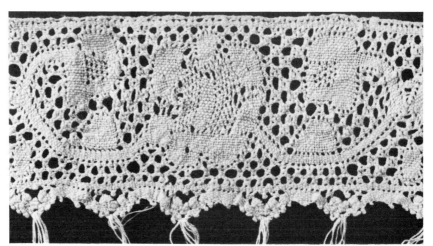

49.1 *Antwerp, eighteenth century.*

49.2 *Yak, in white wool, with a blue rosette of 'leaves',* c*1870*.

50.1 *Valenciennes, late eighteenth century.*

50.2 a *Valenciennes, mid-nineteenth century, and* **b** *detail of ground.*

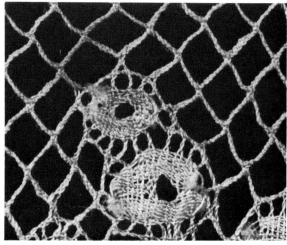

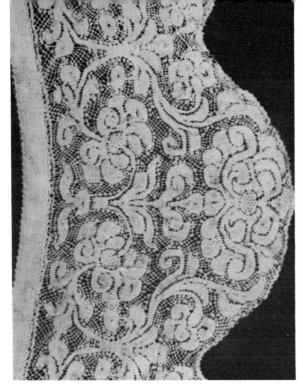

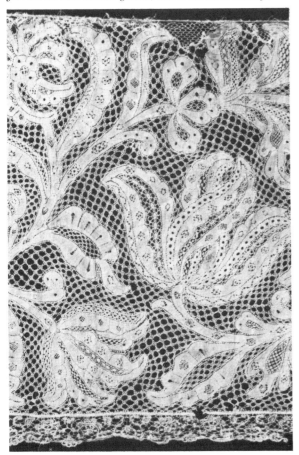

51.1 *Dutch with torchon ground, mid-seventeenth century.*

51.2 *Torchon, twentieth century.*

51.3 *90° torchon ground, made plain and then darned, Brazil, twentieth century.*

54.1 *Milanese, first half eighteenth century.*

54.2 *Milanese/Flemish, mid-eighteenth century.*

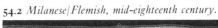

54.3 *Valenciennes, non-continuous, late nineteenth century, a flounce 300 cm deep.*

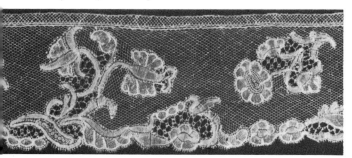

58.1 *Brussels bobbin (point d'Angleterre), eighteenth century.*

55 *Ghent, a kind of non-continuous Valenciennes, nineteenth century.*

57 *Honiton with reseau, first half nineteenth century.*

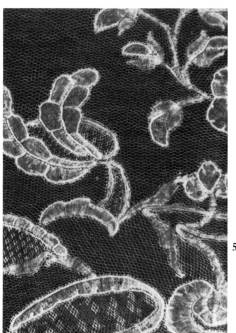

58.2 *Devon, c1770.*

58.3 *Brabant, eighteenth century.* 59 *Brabant 'Valenciennes'.*

| 52 | The lace is flat. | 53 |
| | The lace has raised work. | 56 |

| 53 | Round Valenciennes ground. | 54 |
| | Square Valenciennes ground. | 55 |

| 54 | The design is bold, flowing and with many varied stitches. | **First half 18th century Milanese** |

The design is a bit skimped, lanky and gauche, perhaps amateur and ecclesiastical, but sometimes approximating to the candelabra form of point de France flounces (see **27** Flemish); occasionally there are raised point d'esprit. **Mid-18th century Milanese or Flemish**

The texture is close, precise and very neat, with more enterprising designs aping those of 17th century Valenciennes on a much larger scale, fillings numerous and very well executed (at Ghent or Bayeux?). **Late 19th century 'Valenciennes'**

| 55 | The lace similar to a good quality 19th century continuous Valenciennes **50**, but the design more naturalistic and floral, often though not always enriched with numerous fillings. | **2nd half 19th century Ghent** |

56	Needle or bobbin made net ground.	57
	Droschel ground.	58
	Square Valenciennes ground.	59

57 The bobbin reseau imitates a fond simple but is less regular. The needle ground is worked LR, RL, but is a bit haphazard (see 2). The bobbin motifs have a needle made 'gaze' ground 2.	**1st half 19th century Honiton** **Rare 19th century Honiton** **Late 19th century Brussels** **Point d'Angleterre**
58 The ground is attached to the motifs by sewings, and worked in regular narrow ($\frac{1}{4}$ in.) strips, joined by point de raccroc, and arranged lengthwise or widthwise of the lace; the texture is exceedingly fine.	**18th century Brussels Point** **d'Angleterre**
The ground is of fine thread but worked at odd angles; the design may strongly resemble 18th century Brussels point d'Angleterre, or it may be completely disjointed.	**18th to early 19th century** **Devon**
Found in large (24 in. deep) flounces, loosely textured and lightweight. The design from a distance is stable and impressive, mainly of bouquets of idealised flowers 30.	**18th century Brabant**
The droschel continues across the back of the motifs or, if not entirely, it shows signs of having been cut away beneath them rather than of having been joined by sewings. Bobbin or needle motifs are fixed to the ground 2.	**Early 19th century Brussels** **or Honiton appliqué**
59 Non-continuous 'Valenciennes', with raised work using ten-stick, and other techniques, rare (see page 64).	**19th century Brabant** **'Valenciennes'**

PART 2 CARE

TEN
The Problems of Conservation

Most of the antique laces which survive today date from the sixteenth, seventeenth and eighteenth centuries. One might well think that if they have already lasted for two, three or four hundred years without any particular problem, what is the current conservation brouhaha all about?

For one thing, the greater part of those laces have *not* survived. Leaving aside the vast quantities burned by the Customs men, buried with the dead, or lost in battle, some may well have been killed as it were by kindness, by the very efforts intended to keep them fresh and vital. Of the endless shiploads of lace produced during those fecund years there are relatively few pieces remaining. However, existence is a process of ageing. The degrading cannot be stopped, only speeded up or slowed down, at best put into near-suspension.

In essence, lace care, or conservation, is concerned with finding out:

a What factors accelerate the wearing-out process;
b How to minimize the effect of those factors.

It might be salutary to look first at some of the cleaning methods of the past. The credo, 'Cleanliness is next to godliness', goes far back. There are numerous entries in Queen Elizabeth I's wardrobe accounts of the washing and getting up of ruffs. The Flemish starcher who settled in London in 1570 charged £5 to teach young ladies the art of stiffening fine lawn and lace. Henri III, the dissolute younger son of Henri II of France, each day with his own hands heated the poking stick to set the flutes of his ruffs because he did not trust his servants to do it perfectly. In the *Ladies Pocket Book* for 1762 there are directions for getting mildew out of linen, sandwiched between a paragraph on 'To make currant shrub' and 'To keep green peas all the year'. In the early nineteenth century the treatment of lace was, if not callous, at least robust. *Cranford* relates how in the 1820s a piece of lace was swallowed by a cat, boiled, spread on a lavender bush, and left in the sun to dry: four traumatic experiences from which we can today recoil only in horror. But sun and boiling water were common practice in the nineteenth century. Mrs Treadwin, whose establishment at 5 Cathedral Yard, Exeter, specialized not only in making lace for special commission, including some for Queen Victoria, but also in cleaning and refurbishing old and recent laces, has the following advice (slightly abridged):

Procure in the first place a plain white earthenware slab of 8 or 10-in. square, through which small holes have been pierced about an inch apart; then take a piece of book muslin or, what is preferable, a piece of common bobbin-net cut about 4 in. larger than the slab, with a double hem run with tape. Smooth out carefully the piece of lace . . . and cut its exact shape and size in paper . . . fold the lace, lay it on the slab, and cover it with the piece of net or muslin tying it tightly over the lace with strings at the back of the slab, very tightly to keep the lace smooth. Next get ready an Earthenware Foot Tub or large vessel, but on no account is it to be made of tin, zinc or any other metal. Into this pour about a gallon of cold water and add to it 3 ounces of soap, which should be well dissolved . . . . Gard's Sapoline is the best soap for the purpose – then put the slab into the water and leave 12 hours. Before taking the lace out wash it over with the palm of the hand for at least 5 minutes . . . place in another tub with perfectly clean water and wash with the hand in the same way for two minutes . . . then put the lace into a copper (not iron) boiler with a gallon of water with 4 ounces of soap dissolved in it. Set the boiler on the fire, being sure that the side of the slab having the lace on it is uppermost, in other words nearest the cover. Let it remain on the fire to boil for at least 2 hours. Now take out the slab and the lace and place them again in the tub, into which should be poured a gallon of hot, but not boiling, water; dissolve in this water 2 ounces of soap, wash the lace with the palm of the hand again. . . . Untie the strings . . . turn the lace upside down without unfolding it, replace the net/muslin cover as before, wash for 5 minutes with the palm of the hand . . . replace in a tub of clean cold water . . . wash until quite free from soap.

Her additional notes for cleaning may be summarized: If it is very dirty, change the water several times, adding fresh soap each time, and boil at least 12 hours, *or* leave the slab with the lace exposed to the sun. As it dries, throw clean soapy water over it to keep it damp. Repeat for one or two days.

For 'finishing', Mrs Treadwin recommends spreading the lace face down on a check cloth (so that it can be correctly aligned) on a flat 2×4 foot board, then smoothing it over the cut-out paper until it occupies the original shape, then ironing just the edges to prevent the pin holes showing. For raising the relief work she

Aficot, the narrow end of which is used for raising the picots or applied petals in three-dimensional laces. The broad end is sometimes used to give an artificial gloss or polish, especially to needle laces.

suggests using a small curved bone or ivory instrument (see diagram). With this the fringes or loops of the lace can be raised up, and held with pins. She adds, 'I do not recommend the raiser being used for the purpose of glossing the lace. This is frequently done, but is a pernicious practice' – but one which, pernicious or otherwise, is perpetuated by the lace makers of Alençon today.

Sun treatment is recommended also by Thomas Wright (1919), after the lace has been stitched around a bottle covered in flannel, placed in soapy water and smoothed with the hand. The bottle with the lace is then stuck on the end of a stick in the garden and left to bleach and hazel (i.e. to dry and sweeten).

Advice in fact was almost as varied and prolific as the types of lace themselves. It was all a serious business: for lace to appear dirty was undoubtedly in 'poor taste', indeed socially a disaster. The popular Weldon's magazines were loaded with directions, such as the following:

'When laces that have been laid away for some time show signs of mildew, the best restorative to use is a solution of spirits of ammonia and water, which rub on gently but thoroughly with the aid of a soft toothbrush.'

'To whiten lace that has become discoloured sew it in a clean linen bag and lay in pure olive oil for 24 hours. It must then be boiled in soapy water for about 20 minutes, and afterwards rinsed in lukewarm water. . . .'

'Stains can be removed from lace by moistening the spots with oxalic acid and placing the lace on a hot iron covered with three or four folds of linen, then steep the lace in lukewarm water in which it must be rinsed several times, after which press out the moisture between folds of linen or a towel and pin on a board to dry.'

'To freshen black lace wash in stale beer or coffee and rinse in cold water. If any stiffening is required, a little loaf sugar dissolved in cold water will make a better stiffener than starch. Potato water is very good for stiffening large pieces of lace, such as that used for skirts etc., and is made by grating a raw potato in cold water.'

'Never touch lace with an iron, but pull out each point carefully with the thumb and forefinger and, if possible, pin out flat on a board to dry.'

If some of these procedures now seem to us destructive, it must be remembered that the perpetrators had but one object in mind, fashionability, which included a perfect cleanliness. Conservation, or preservation, was not at all their concern: they were advising on lace to be worn. There was no reason for them to be concerned with future generations, whom no doubt they could not even have imagined as being unable to obtain lace. Dicey as the livelihood of lace makers had been throughout the nineteenth century, society ladies must have found it inconceivable that lace should ever be out of fashion. If they looked ahead, it would be as far as the next season's rapidly changing fashions, which fostered the urge to get as much wear as possible from each piece of lace before it became outmoded.

Today, the attitude to lace is quite different, and becoming more so. Until lace interest was revived in the 1960s, it had scarcely been made commercially, by hand, for 30 years. At the same time, intensive researches of the late nineteenth and twentieth centuries had shown convincingly that antique laces were irreplaceable. It was realized that the fine flax thread could no longer be retted, or spun, or perhaps even grown; that the hours of work necessary were quite incompatible with modern ideas of industry; that the rate of pay was ludicrously low. No one any longer had the single-mindedness, or social vulnerability, to spend a lifetime of ceaseless work in uncomfortable conditions for minimal reward only in order that others might strut in social splendour sporting the fruits of their labours.

The attitude to lace, now, can fairly be expressed as: 'What can't be replaced must be encased', which is fine as long as it doesn't develop into 'What is conserved can't be observed', and there is just a slight danger of this happening.

The admirable attitude of condemning anything which might contribute in any way to the harming of lace has led to the compilation of a blacklist of potentially destructive forces which has grown to impressive proportions: dust, gaseous impurities, light, dryness, wetness, heat, cold, insects, mildew, and above all people. The mini-atmosphere of the human persona can inflict many wounds, by oil and acid from hands, moisture and fungal spores from the breath, dust and solid particles from hair and clothes. Moreover the human eye needs light to study the lace.

As if this were not enough, the experiences of preservation from the distant past, as well as the detailed results of modern researches, have shown that the ideal conditions for lace storage would be to wrap it as neatly, securely, darkly and inaccessibly as a mummy in its sarcophagus within an Egyptian tomb. The tendency to cosset lace, resulting from all this, is proving to be a strong inhibiting influence, and is discouraging the effort of 'unearthing' the lace either for individual study or for public exhibition.

We should perhaps at this point reconsider the question of the purpose of conservation. To say that we conserve lace in order to preserve it is to say no more than that we breathe in order to remain alive. We need to ask ourselves:

1 For whom is it being conserved? For what far distant time, or for what hermetically sealed creature from outer space whose emanations cannot harm the fabric, are we saving it?

2 Is the future more important than the present?

3 Is private research more important than public enjoyment?

4 Whatever method is chosen for cleaning, storage or display, can we be certain there will be no unforseen side effects?

It may sound extreme, even obsessional, to say that lace must never be washed unless it is so filthy that the dirt in it might rot it; that it must never be lifted except by a supporting sheet beneath it; that all contact and friction for example by brushing against it must be avoided; that it must be minimally folded; that if rolled this must be done gently between sheets of acid-free tissue; that if exposed to light this must be as dim as possible and free of ultra-violet rays. Between this and the spirited Treadwin attitude is a whole world of disagreement. The following chapters aim to set out the sources of this change of view and then, in the light of that information, to try to decide what action or non-action should be taken in relation to any particular piece of lace.

ELEVEN
Cleaning

What most people want to know about the care of old lace sounds quite modest, namely, 'Should I wash it, and if so how?' Simple as it may sound, such a question cannot be answered in isolation. It necessitates in fact quite complex considerations.

Cleaning an old lace is likely to change it, probably in an irreversible way, and although if the lace is stained, mildewed, odoriferous or badly crumpled the change may be for the better, any unnoticed fragility or fibre weakness such as consumption by moth or carpet beetle could cause it to rupture and fall apart, which would certainly be for the worse.

Those extremely rare 'new', i.e. never used, laces of the past, keep with their structure a crispness of design and freshness of preparation which even a single cleaning will destroy for ever. The preserving of this pristine quality is, because of its scarcity, more valuable than absolute cleanliness.

Apart from this, the important question is, 'What end result are we aiming for?' If a piece of lace is justifiably to be regarded as consumable ephemera, a disposable commodity, then what is done to it must be left to the initiative of the owner who may wish to wear it, to dress a doll with it, or to make it into boudoir cushions. Such laces, and how to treat them, are considered in chapter 14, but not here, where the advice might be misunderstood, or misapplied to laces which more properly should have preservation orders slapped on to them.

Cleanliness alone is never an adequate excuse for exposure of the lace to potentially harmful water and cleansing agents, to the dangers of shrinkage, tearing, over-whitening, loss of lustre, residual particles, under- or over-drying, and thread stress. The earnest desire to avoid such deleterious effects may well take us a good deal nearer to godliness than the cleanliness itself. The aim of cleaning should be purely to put the lace into such a state that its chances of survival over many years are improved, not diminished. It is said that the proof of the pudding is in the eating, and so it may be assumed that the proof of the cleaning is in the resultant appearance. Antique lace boiled, for example, in Napisan loses its character, the ivory glow of its antique flax is replaced by a bluish-white glare foreign to its nature and destructive of its design. It will no longer be representative of its place of origin or of its time. Financially its value is halved, quartered, perhaps even decimated.

Even when the result looks alright one must bear in mind that damage resulting from wrong treatment may not be apparent for some time just as severe indigestion may follow only slowly the engorgement of the pudding. An obvious example is the long-term effect of inadequate rinsing so that chemicals are left in the fabric to continue indefinitely their action on the threads.

Suppose, then, it has been decided that a piece of lace must be cleaned. It may be either wet cleaned or dry cleaned and the following should be carefully noted.

Wet Cleaning (Washing)

Water

Research has shown that the ideal water is pure and non-ionic, in other words water which has been distilled away from all the salts (such as calcium or magnesium bicarbonate or sulphate) which harden it, from the iron impurities which may stain it, and from all the other impurities which in however mild a form may act as corrosives. In the past rain water was recommended, but though soft this may, in its passage through the atmosphere of an industrial area, have acquired a number of undesirable solutes.

The effect of water on lace varies according to the nature of its constituent fibres. Hand laces, up to the early nineteenth century, were made almost entirely of linen, occasionally of silk, wool or metal thread.

The structures which go to make up linen threads are the peripheral bast fibres which run the whole length of the stem and root of the flax plant, and provide it with flexible support. They are extracted by a rather smelly rotting process known as retting. Under the microscope the bast fibres can be seen to be made up of many narrow tapering cells slotted together into long strands. They have thin central cavities and thick walls constructed of cellulose strengthened with a little lignin or wood. The proportion of lignin present varies in different parts of the plant. It is never large – 3.8% in

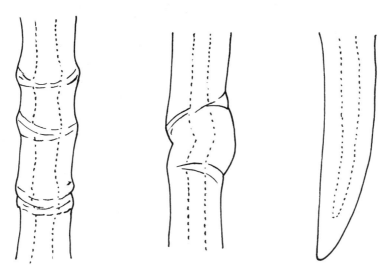

the root, 2.36% in the middle stem, and 1.64% in the stem tip (Hanausek) – but enough to contribute to the heavy cool suppleness which characterizes good linen as opposed to cotton thread. Carefully prepared fibres when first separated from the plant are quite smooth, but examination of the threads from almost any linen lace reveal nodular deformities rather like arthritic knuckles which constitute points of weakness or incipient dislocation (see diagram). The source of these distortions is uncertain, but harshness of treatment at some point must have been responsible. Linen threads may thus be subject to breaking, even fragmentation, during retting if this is hastened; during spinning if the air becomes too dry; during the making of the lace if too much strain is put upon it; and during storage over a long period in sub-ideal conditions.

When linen threads are immersed in water a certain amount of liquid is absorbed, causing swelling. If the fibres are already weak through age or maltreatment, the increased pressure is likely to result in rupture. The more closely worked the lace is, the greater will be the pressure of one strand against another, and therefore the greater care will be needed to avoid damage.

The effect of immersion in water on fibres is measured in terms of their breaking-strength i.e. the weight needed to be applied to them before they will snap. Reassuringly, in healthy fibres of linen, the wet fibre may be 10 to 30% stronger than the dry so that the water itself will not harm them. Degraded (weakened) fibres on the other hand may be only half as strong when wet, so that if they are to be washed at all it must be with consideration (see 'Handling'). The absorption of water by the threads increases with temperature, and the use of cold water is therefore often recommended. If warm is used, the maximum temperature should be between 21 and 27°C (70 and 80°F).

In the case of cotton each fibre from the seed boll is between 12 and 64 mm long, depending on type. The walls of the fibres are thin, the large central cavities

a and b The node-like protruberances on flax fibres form areas of incipient weakness. c The tapering end of a fibre. Width of fibre 30μm (3/1000 mm).

filled with air, making the thread warmer and lighter in weight than linen. Here there is no danger of fragmentation, though the finished product fluffs more easily by the springing out of the tiny fibres from the spun thread. Also, cotton was not used for bobbin or needle laces before the nineteenth century, and so its properties are not relevant to really antique laces. The fibres of cotton, like those of healthy linen, are stronger when wet.

Wool fibres are weaker when wet, and also tend to shrink and harden in response to high temperatures, or even changes of temperature in water. However, woollen laces significantly older than a hundred years are scarcely likely to be found.

Silk, like wool, is chemically a protein, and so quite distinct from the plant cellulose fibres cotton and linen. When wetted it may swell to nearly one-fifth of its former size. It stretches, and at the same time becomes weaker. As with wool, little silk lace earlier than the nineteenth century survives.

The dirt (or soil) remover
Simple soaking in water will often cause the release of tiny insoluble particles caught in the lace fibres, and also allow the extraction of soluble dirts. More stubborn dirts, however, may require some added lever to prise them free. Such a lever may be provided by a soap or detergent.

As a general rule all the plant and animal fibres used for lace react favourably in mildly alkaline conditions measured at an H^+ concentration of 10^{-10} (usually written pH10, which stands for *potenz Hydrogen*, or strength of hydrogen-ion concentration. See page 177). More strongly alkaline, or more acid, conditions are likely to have a destructive effect.

Soaps, which are compounds of fatty acids and metal hydroxides (e.g. olive oil or oleic acid plus caustic soda or sodium hydroxide), are fairly strongly alkaline, and this may cause wool laces to shrink or felt. To counteract this, Caulfield (1887) suggested using for wool, in addition to $\frac{1}{4}$ lb of soft soap, 1 tablespoon of ox gall, and $\frac{1}{2}$ pint of Gin. Some soaps may dissolve satisfactorily only at fairly high temperatures, such as 70°C, which for antique laces is too high for safety. Also, with hard water, soaps form an insoluble scum which is difficult to remove from the lace. If soft or distilled water is used this problem does not arise.

The so-called detergents do not have these disadvantages. 'Detergent' in the seventeenth century meant simply a 'cleansing agent', and thus included soap. Today the contradistinction between soap and detergent is a commercial one. The distinction in fact is between the soap based on naturally occurring oils (olive oil, palm oil, coconut oil) and the synthetic detergents derived from petroleum oil. The synthetic detergents most commonly used for washing clothes are described as anionic, meaning that they work on the surface of the fabric by means of a negative ionic electrical charge, as indeed does soap itself. Both are therefore known as 'surfactants', an abbreviation for 'cleaning by surface activity'. Both act by their attraction to the surface of the lace being strong enough to displace the dirt particles so that these break free as a fine suspension and are rinsed out leaving the lace clean.

Synthetic detergents have an advantage over soap in being more stable, and more effective cleaners. Their disadvantage is that the lather they produce is difficult to disperse, and some may remain in the lace.

Both soaps and detergents frequently need agitation of the water and the lace in order fully to remove the dislodged dirt. The preferred surfactant therefore is saponin, a naturally occurring glucoside obtained from the plant *Saponaria* (Soapwort), or from the bark of the South American tree *Quillaja saponaria*, and others. It forms only a slight lather; cleans well without agitation – an extremely important property when dealing with fragile textiles; and has no adverse reaction with hard water. It is described as a non-ionic detergent since it does not dissolve to form ions. American conservationists recommend this, or other non-ionic detergents such as Orvus WA paste in a 1% solution, DW 300, Igepal CA Extra, or Ivory Liquid. In Britain the non-ionic Lissapol N, or Vulpex, are most commonly used. Only very low concentrations are needed, such as 0.5%, or 1 fluid ounce per 10 pints of water. They must be well mixed to form a homogeneous solution, before the lace is added. As many as three changes of the washing water are used, but with the minimum of disturbance to the textile itself.

Digestive enzymes are sometimes used to remove stains caused by organic substances such as egg or blood. 'Parazyme' is a mixture of enzymes which break down both starch and proteins into soluble products which can then be flushed away with warm water. Such reagents should be used with caution on silk or wool fibres which are, like the stains themselves, a form of protein.

Whitening: a question of colour

It is recommended that the compounds mentioned above, obtainable from specialist suppliers, should be used to wash lace. Supermarket detergents have all kinds of additives to enforce a stark cleanliness upon family clothes, bed- and table-linen. These additives often take the form of fluorescents which are simply whiteness-adders rather than dirt-subtractors. Such 'optical whiteners' obtain their effect by reflecting invisible ultra-violet beams, giving a perceptible blue-white tinge. They are a modern development and have no place with antique laces. Ordinary commercial detergents therefore should not be used.

The original degree of whiteness of sixteenth-, seventeenth- and eighteenth-century laces is very hard to establish, and so to reconstruct. Some eighteenth-century records refer to 'nuances' of white, and to a scale of prices according to the one desired. The general opinion is that a slight greyness or yellowness remaining after a wash, though perhaps less historically accurate than a shade nearer to snow-white, is preferable to subjecting the lace to chemical whiteners which may make it look brash and, in addition, may harm the fibres.

Experiments have shown that ordinary commercial bleaches, such as sodium hypochlorite, may severely damage plant fibres (flax and cotton) by reducing the degree of polymerization (or DP). What this means is that the enormously large molecules of cellulose which compose the fibres are broken into shorter lengths, thus they hold together less well and are weakened. This reduction in their power of holding together is sometimes described as 'loss of viscosity'. Chlorine bleaches have an even more disastrous effect on the animal protein fibres wool and silk, causing at the best a yellowing rather than a whitening effect, and at the worst their complete chemical disctruction. Such bleaching also removes the lignin from flax, leaving only cellulose, and so destroys much of the characteristic properties of old linen.

Hydrogen peroxide on the other hand produces almost no degradation of the fibres; its whiteness does not become dingy with time; and because it acts fairly slowly the degree of whiteness can be controlled by stopping the process at any point. For bleaching by immersion, a 0.5% solution is commonly used; for application to isolated spots, a 1% solution. Hydrogen peroxide acts by releasing oxygen, and can be used to remove stains such as blood. Sodium perborate, marketed in the United States as Snowy Bleach, releases hydrogen peroxide when dissolved in water, and has the advantage of being easier to package, and more stable, than the liquid form. Treatment of lace with hydrogen peroxide should never be carried out in sunlight (see page 180).

Isolated stains may be removed by water-soluble reagents, or by non-water-soluble ones. These latter are usually known as dry cleaners. However since, dry or not, they occur as fluids, both types will be mentioned briefly here:

Stains of iron rust may be removed by 1% oxalic acid, followed if necessary by 0.5% acetic acid, sponged off with hot softened water. For cotton, linen and wool, but not silk, 1 volume of hydrofluoric acid diluted with 3 volumes of water may be used, sponged off again with hot water. The iron mould or foxing caused by fungal growths can be treated with a mild bleach solution such as Chloramine T, left for one to two hours, then completely removed with distilled water.

For mud stains, hydrogen peroxide made alkaline with ammonia, followed if necessary by 0.1% ammonia, followed again if necessary by 2% hydrochloric acid (for wool only) can be tried, then sponged off with warm water.

Water-soluble acid stains such as tea, coffee, beetroot and fruit juices can be removed with 5% borax.

For grease, either trichlorethylene or white spirit (non-water-soluble); for candle wax, placing the lace between sheets of brown paper and pressing lightly with a warm iron melts the wax which is then drawn by capillarity into the compressed fibres of the paper.

For red ink on any fibre except silk use methylated spirits or, for cotton and linen only, Chloramine T. For grass stains, an ethereal oil such as eucalyptus can be used, and this is also effective, with patience, on thick oils from machinery or creosote.

To prevent the reagent spreading beyond the required area it can be stiffened with a paste of carboxy-methyl-cellulose. This is called spot-bleaching. The lace must be closely watched for an hour or two if necessary, and then the whole piece thoroughly rinsed, a process which will need great care if the lace contains any coloured threads.

Three other aspects of the colour of lace should be mentioned:

a Ecru. In the early, and again in the late, nineteenth century it was the practice to tint lace to achieve a pale brown effect, which was known as ecru (literally, unbleached). The following directions 'to colour lace . . . which of late has become much the fashion' are by Mrs Treadwin. The lace should first be cleaned, 'then take $\frac{1}{4}$ lb of the very best coffee – inferior coffee will not produce the same shade – infuse it by throwing 6 pints of quite boiling water on it, let it remain for about $\frac{1}{2}$ hr, strain it through a piece of thick muslin, then throw the coffee over the lace until it is thoroughly saturated – in fact there is no objection to put the slab [see page 167] entirely in the coffee for a few minutes, and this should be done immediately after the starching or stiffening, but the quality of the colour to which lace should be brought imitates that of pure unbleached linen thread'.

Unfortunately this ideal was not always achieved: much ecru lace is quite hideously dark, and sometimes patchy. The artificial colour is difficult to remove, and though the temptation to be heavy-handed in lightening it may be strong, advice should be sought before irremediable harm is done.

b Black. The dye used to achieve a black effect is acid. It can be accepted directly by the protein fibres silk and wool, but not by the cellulose flax or cotton which are, as it were, allergic to acids (see page 88). These latter fabrics require a mordant, i.e. a gluing agent which by one means or another sticks the dye onto the fibres. One of the commonest mordants is an iron salt which when boiled with the thread forms a sticky trivalent iron hydroxide. When the acid dye, such as haematein from the Logwood tree (*Haematoxylon campechianum*), is added, it forms an insoluble mass which coats the fibres. The dye is not fully permanent: the iron hydroxide slowly converts to ferric oxide, giving the lace a rusty appearance, while the acid of the dye insidiously penetrates the fibres, and rots them, as well as sometimes exuding a sharp unpleasant odour. Good quality black silk may be almost completely water fast, for example Maltese stoles and Spanish Bobbin mantillas may retain their intense ebony sheen with remarkable tenacity. Black machine laces, however, through incompetent dyeing, or poor quality cotton fibres, tend to produce massive 'bleeding' whenever the lace comes in contact with water. Mrs Treadwin's recipe for washing black lace was to soak it in diluted eau de Cologne, and then briefly in beer. If the black lace is ironed 'do so over paper, otherwise if the iron touches the lace it will gloss it, which is very objectionable'.

c Other colours. Colour is not commonly found in antique laces, except perhaps in those of East Europe, Scandinavia, or the Mediterranean shores, where red and azure, green, brown, saffron and pink may at times be found. Before any wet cleaning is attempted each colour should be carefully tested for water-fastness. This is done by gently rubbing a small area with a piece of white cloth, or cotton wool, dampened with water, followed by a similar treatment with the chosen dirt-remover, for example a non-ionic detergent. If the cloth remains clean for each colour, washing is possible; if it stains, dry-cleaning, or even no cleaning, is advisable.

Handling

During the cleaning process, the lace should be handled as little as possible. Picking up a piece of lace imposes a strain on the fibres that are taken hold of. They are dragged down unevenly by the dangling weight of the unsupported part. When wet, fibres absorb water, so that their weight is heavier, and the strain greater, and frail pieces of old lace may break apart.

It is advisable therefore before immersing lace in water to support it for example between two fairly rigid pieces of nylon gauze, placed above and below it and tacked around, so that the whole sandwich is firm enough to be lifted without distortion. This has at the same time the advantage of allowing free access of both water and cleaning substance.

Some movement of the water or of the lace is obviously necessary in order to wash away the dislodged or dissolved dirt and to bring fresh detergent in contact with the surface. Since the lace itself is immobilized, gentle stirring of the water will circulate, without harming it. Vertical movement of the lace in the water by bobbing it gently up and down with pressure from, for example a sponge has the same effect, though perhaps with more risk of drag and pull on the fibres as they are forced with or against gravity.

When the lace is removed from the water after the final rinse, it can be released from its sandwich. It should not be wrung or squeezed, which would strain it unevenly, but should be laid flat on a surface. Small or very fine pieces can be 'floated' out, and gently straightened while supported in a pool of water. Large or thicker pieces can be softly blotted with cotton cloths or special paper towels.

Lace which is thought too fragile to be put right into water can sometimes be rested on a flat surface and dabbed with a weak saponin solution, then with clear water. If even this is considered too vigorous, and yet the lace is badly crumpled, a repeated gentle spraying with an atomizer which produces just a fine mist of water will gradually soften the fibres without the added weight which would strain them. Over a period, perhaps of several days, the creases are gradually smoothed away. A mild blasting with steam such as may be used for heavy fabrics is seldom necessary for lace. If it is used, it is important that the lace should be quite clean, or the damp heat will seal in any dirt.

Drying and smoothing

A formica surface can be used for the wet-stretching of lace. Treadwin's method of restoring it to its original shape with the guidance of a template (see page 167) is still sometimes used. Large pieces, especially those made at least partly of machine net are best stretched evenly on softboard covered with polythene sheeting (for waterproofness, and also because the board is acid) and pinned at equal intervals around the edge using brass pins. The use of even the best stainless steel pins is not recommended because of the harmful effect of iron on natural fibres (see page 177). The pins, needless to say, go only through the spaces of the lace, not through its fabric. Even pinning is not universally approved of: slight shrinkage as the lace dries causes a pull on the pin-fixed parts, drawing the edges into undulating points. Where the lace is three-dimensional, gentle lifting by some implement such as Treadwin described on page 168 is necessary throughout the drying process, even though this may take several hours. Only in this way can the tiny crowns and spikes of picots, in Venetian laces for example, be set in their little starry whorls well above the general lace surface. In more recent forms such as point de gaze with its separate rose petals, or the Hainault laces with their adhering wheatears, constant attention is also needed to avoid a dog-eared, lop-sided look. Finger-drying is sometimes the best treatment, the warmth of the fingers pressing and smoothing the lace like the softest of irons. The hands must be washed every 10 minutes to avoid contamination by oil or sweat. To ease the tedium of this long process a hair dryer can be used, not too fiercely, so that its warmth will speed evaporation and its breeze blow away the saturated air. Care should of course be taken that the lace is not hardened by over-drying, and so made brittle.

The voices which through the years have recommended ironing, albeit over a padded board, and under thicknesses of cloth, are being gradually stilled.

Dry Cleaning

Solvents

White spirit, turpentine, benzene and trichlorethylene are especially useful where water is not effective, for example in the removal of grease stains, for coloured laces where the dyes run in water, and perhaps for fragile fibres since they are absorbed to a lesser extent than water and therefore cause less swelling and less strain on the gross, and molecular, fibre structure. This last is controversial: though no specific and detailed results are available, it is at least possible that the chemical nature of some of the fluids may harm the fibres.

These solvents can be used as spot-cleaners by dabbing the stain with a piece of cotton wool. However, there is a possibility that, the stain once dissolved, the dirty liquid instead of passing back into the cotton wool will be sucked by capillary action through·the microscopic tubes of the lace fibres, and so spread the discolouration. Cleaning the lace over blotting paper – itself a compacted mass of tiny capillary tubes – may correct this tendency.

In some cases the entire lace may be immersed in the solvent, and then spread as described on page 174. See also page 173.

Vacuuming

A low suction cleaner may be useful in removing minute solid particles of dust which could in time abrade the fibres. The lace is never vacuumed directly, but only through a thin firm gauze known as monofilament screening. This screening frays easily, and the edges must either be bound, or sealed with a hot wire which melts and glues the marginal threads.

The use of French chalk, fuller's earth, baking powder, potato flour and other granules, to which particles of dirt may adhere and then be removed, are not recommended, as their own removal from the lace is seldom easy, and the shattering effect of shaking or brushing can be more harmful than the dirt itself.

As you will have gathered from chapter 10, a number of the older books on lace, some of which have now been reprinted, contain sections on cleaning. All of these are best ignored. The conscientious research into every aspect of lace conservation has mostly taken place within the last 30 years. It has shown convincingly that the procedures recommended in good faith by the authors of the past are for the most part deleterious in the long term.

TWELVE
Storage

It may be hoped that the two preceding chapters will have demonstrated that the care of lace is no esoteric mystique emanating from the faery nature of the lace itself. The rules and recommendations, which may at times seem to take the form of negative commands, have developed out of carefully controlled scientific experiments, pioneered in Washington DC, New York, Holland and England. They all really boil down to the nature of the fibres of cellulose and protein which make up the lace, and to the various factors which may reduce their strength. When the fibres are harmed, the lace fabric itself inevitably will be weakened, tenderized or degraded. A knowledge of these harmful factors and the effects which they produce is therefore of the greatest importance. Many, such as light, humidity, temperature fluctuation, air impurities, saprophytic fungi, and the degree of acidity of the immediate environment, are chemically damaging; others, such as voracious insect or rodent pests, gritty particles, and uneven strain have instead a physically adverse effect.

The general action of all the chemically deteriorating agents for cellulose fibres (flax and cotton) is to reduce their degree of polymerization. Healthy cellulose is built up of huge molecules (polymers) which hold well together. They are said thus to have a good degree of viscosity. The immediate effect of harmful factors is to split these large molecules into smaller ones (= reduction of their degree of polymerization). This in turn reduces the degree of viscosity, or holding together power, and so inevitably results in weakness. The chemical distruction of protein (silk and wool) fibres is sometimes of quite a different kind, but no less devastating. It is called denaturing, and is quite literally a change of nature which robs the protein of its normal state and function. The molecular structure is not so much diminished as irreversibly disorganized. One everyday example is the transformation of the protein egg-white from a translucent liquid to an opaque solid by the application of heat.

The degree of polymerization of the fibres can be measured directly before and after treatment only if the change is fairly large. Other criteria of fibre weakening can also be used such as the tearing or breaking strength (the weight in grams needed to rip the fibres apart); or folds to rupture (how many times a fabric can be folded and unfolded before it splits).

The results of all the experiments put together lead to conclusions of immense significance. By considering the factors proved to be harmful to lace, and then negating them, the ideal conditions for lace storage can be determined, and there is at least then a chance of establishing them, at any rate to the nearest approximation.

Factors Harmful to Lace
Gritty particles
These if left in the lace during storage may cut into the fibres by persistent pressure, or by any movements however slight. They are best removed by vacuuming through a gauzy screen (see page 175), and then making sure, by storage in dust-free and dust-proof containers that the problem does not recur. If the lace is exposed to the air for any length of time, as during an exhibition, or a prolonged study session, it should be vacuumed again before being returned to storage. This cleaning is really a pre-storage, or inter-storage, problem. So is the removal of dissolved dirts perhaps discolouring the lace. The choice between cleaning and not-cleaning is simply a question of whether it is more harmful to remove the dirt or to leave it in; which procedure in fact will most prolong the life of the lace.

Gaseous impurities
If filtration of the air entering the storage and study rooms is possible, up to 95% of the suspended dirts can be removed. The removal of gaseous impurities, however, may be extremely expensive, involving the passage of air through activated carbon filters, or water sprays.

One of the main pollutants is sulphur dioxide, a by-product of the burning of coal, coke or oil for either domestic or industrial purposes. It was estimated that for the year 1953 the total of sulphur compounds poured out into the British atmosphere was equivalent to 9 million tons of sulphuric acid. On the European continent, the problem is even more acute since drifting air currents may carry the gas in massive quantities from one country to another.

Acid-alkali gradient.

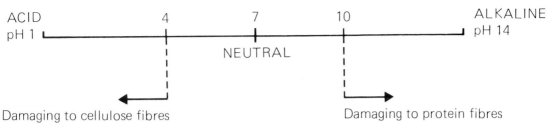

ACID
pH 1

4   7   10

NEUTRAL

ALKALINE
pH 14

Damaging to cellulose fibres

Damaging to protein fibres

It is the acid which sulphur dioxide so readily forms in the presence of even the smallest quantity of water that is the real menace to textiles. The acid has a digesting effect on cellulose, converting it little by little to glucose which will dissolve in any moisture present so that slowly but surely the whole structure is eroded away. Isolating the lace in air-tight cases, though not ideal, is a relatively inexpensive way around the problem. Better still, if the case is filled with an inert gas such as nitrogen which would be incapable of producing any action on the fibres, harmful or otherwise.

Iron is known to catalyze, or speed up, the conversion of sulphur dioxide to sulphuric acid. It is therefore essential that iron nails, tacks, pins or clips should not come into contact with stored textiles, or extensive rotting may take place around them. This property of iron is yet another contributing factor to the frequent disintegration of black cotton or linen laces in storage, since the iron of the mordant encourages attack by any sulphur dioxide in the air.

Another pollutant, of more significance in the United States than in Europe, is ozone. In Los Angeles for example the peculiar atmospheric conditions allow the sun to act on the blanket of exhaust fumes pumped out by the myriad cars to form a kind of oxygen known as ozone. Ironically, some of the filters designed to remove air impurities themselves generate ozone through friction with metal and plastic, which favours the release of positively charged particles. The gas acts by weakening the molecular structure of the cellulose (see pages 172 and 176).

Acids and alkalis
Of these two, the greater danger is from acidity. Urban air is almost invariably acid. Paper, cardboard and softboard, which may be used for wrapping or mounting, are acid. Therefore cardboard tubes should be covered with acid-free tissue, and the lace sandwiched with it, then encased in acid-free glassine, tied with acid-free tape, and stored in acid-free drawers or boxes.

Acids and alkalis are merely the opposing ends of a gradation of hydrogen ion concentrations in aqueous solution. The more hydrogen ions there are, the more acid will be the solution; the fewer hydrogen ions, the

more alkaline. Somewhere between the two is an area which is neither acidic nor alkaline and which is described as neutral. The concentrations of hydrogen ions are measured in terms of molecules per litre. The actual amounts are necessarily very small, such as .0000000001, or 10^{-10}. This is more usually represented as pH10 which means quite simply *potenz* (power, strength) of hydrogen, but is a convenient shorthand. pH3 (or 10^{-3}) would mean .001 hydrogen molecules per litre, a large amount, and therefore acid (see diagram).

One of the objects of washing lace prior to storage is to render it neutral, i.e. pH7, which is the safest condition for it to be in. Test papers are available for measuring pH. They are simply placed against the wetted lace and the resultant colour matched against a chart.

Cellulose is more susceptible to acid than proteins are, and is likely to be damaged by anything stronger than pH4, the acidity resulting from sulphur dioxide pollution. Silk exposed to light tends to deteriorate more rapidly if the acidity is greater than pH3.5, while wool may only be seriously damaged if the acidity exceeds pH1.2. It seems likely, however, that damage by a strong acid over a short period might be equated with damage by a weaker acid over a longer period.

The risks at the other end of the scale are far less great: alkalis do not normally appear in the atmosphere, and are only likely to infiltrate the textile during some perhaps misguided washing process, and to be extensively harmful only if inadequately rinsed out.

Humidity and temperature
These two factors are considered together since the amount of water vapour which the air can hold is directly proportional to the temperature: the higher the temperature the more can be held, and vice versa. If the air at any temperature is holding as much water vapour as it possibly can, it is said to be saturated. If it becomes as it were over-filled, it will overflow as droplets of condensation. If on the other hand it is not quite full of gaseous water, then a measure is needed as to how much is there. An actual measurement in terms of cubic centimetres, or whatever, would not be particularly helpful, since what one needs to know is how relatively

dry or wet the air is, i.e. how near to, or how far from, saturation and condensation. This figure, which is the percentage of vapour actually present in the air relative to the total amount which could be present at that temperature, is called the relative humidity (RH):

$$\frac{\text{Amount of water vapour actually present}}{\text{Amount of water vapour that could be held}} \times 100 = \%\text{RH}$$

A low percentage, such as 5% RH indicates dry air, a high percentage such as 90% RH wet air. The water vapour actually present is measured directly by a simple hygrometer. The amount that could be held at a particular temperature is read off from hygrometric tables. The temperature of course is measured by a thermometer, either in °C (centigrade or Celsius) or °F (Fahrenheit). 0°C = 32°F. 100°C = 212°F. To convert one into the other:

$$°C \rightarrow °F$$

$$°C \times \frac{9}{5} + 32$$

$$\text{e.g. } 10°C \times \frac{9}{5} = 18 + 32 = 50°F.$$

$$°F \rightarrow °C$$

$$°F - 32 \times \frac{5}{9}$$

$$\text{e.g. } 50°F - 32 = 18 \times \frac{5}{9} = 10°C.$$

The generally recommended RH for storage is 55% at a temperature of 20°C (68°F). Under these conditions growth of moulds, mildews and bacteria is retarded or even prevented, though resting spores may 'hibernate' awaiting a return to favourable conditions. If the RH increases, the spores may burst out of their long sleep and browse avidly through the textile structure. If the RH decreases the fibres may become desiccated, and brittle.

It is important that the temperature should be kept as constant as possible. A sharp fall in temperature would raise the RH until it approached and perhaps even passed the saturation point. The modest 55% humidity at 20°C for example would make the air 75% saturated if the temperature fell to 16°C, and over 100% at 8°C, i.e. there would be condensation. The actual amount of water vapour has not changed, the cooler air is simply not able to hold so much.

Quite apart from the revitalizing effect which this increased humidity might have on saprophytic growths, the variations cause the fibres to writhe microscopically, swelling and shrinking as they absorb water from the air and lose it again. Granules of silica gel near, though not in contact with, the stored textiles, absorb moisture from the air and so to some extent guard against sudden changes of RH. The crystals need to be dried out as they become wet.

Living pests

a If sufficient moisture is present, fungi and bacteria tend to treat lace as bed and board. They feed by external digestion, that is by the conversion of the nourishing carbohydrate or protein of the fibres into calories and growth units by means of which they can extend themselves in all directions. The digestion of the textile causes a weakness, or rotting. The accompanying chemical changes may also result in localized staining, and the running of colour, though this latter is irrelevant to most laces.

Fungicides can be used to kill off the invaders. But some have undesirable side effects, from the hardening of protein fibres (wool and silk) by formaldehyde, to the degeneration of man's liver by prolonged exposure to high concentrations of paradichlorbenzene. Penta-dichlorophenol produces a weak acid and may therefore damage cellulose, and the same is true of other fungicides which contain chlorine. Naphthaline on the other hand is slightly alkaline, and so may damage protein.

Because of the miniscule nature of the tiny resting spores, the fungicide vapours may not reach them unless they are actually impregnated into the fabric. Salicylanilide, related to aspirin, is sometimes used; and experiments on bombarding the growths with ultra-sonic waves have been attempted, but since any vibration may have a shattering effect on the cellulose molecules themselves the lace may suffer more by this impact than may the moulds, or indeed than it would from the mould's depradations.

A chilling temperature of 5–10°C, with a 55% RH, discourages fungi, but is also adverse to human comfort, and though it might be preserved in purely storage areas, any study under warmer conditions must constitute a hazard.

Fumigation by thymol prior to storage involves prolonged exposure to warm thymol vapour in a special fume cupboard. For private use, small containers of thymol crystals left open wherever lace is stored are better than nothing.

b A high moisture content also provides an incentive for invasion by various insects such as clothes moths, carpet beetles, silver fish and termites. These breathe by minute air tubes which are sufficiently delicate to be harmed by excessive dryness. Either the adults, or larvae, have strong jaws and a rapacious appetite. Their onslaught can cause an immense amount of damage in a relatively short space of time, while their small size enables them to creep in through almost invisible crevices. The problem of excluding them from storage areas is that quite a number of methods known to be lethal to the insects are also harmful to the textile itself so that to use them would simply be substituting one type of damage for another.

Chemical insecticides come in a wide range. Some are specific to one insect e.g. clothes moth, others kill insects indiscriminately; some are effective for only a few weeks then must be renewed, others are said to last for 20 years; some may be used in contact with the lace, others must be kept separate; some are regarded as harmless to people, others are known from experiments with rats to have a high toxicity. The comparative toxicity of the compounds is expressed as LD_{50} (Lethal Dose 50%). This is the weight of the insecticide per kilogram of body weight which kills 50% of the experimental animals when administered orally. Thus an LD_{50} of 100 (DDT) means that 100 milligrams will dispatch half the animals (often rats); an LD_{50} of 2950 (paradichlorbenzene) means that 2,950 mg will be needed to produce the same result; and an LD_{50} of 56 (DDVP, dichlorvus) that only 56 mg would be needed (Leene). Obviously the lower the figure, the less of the compound is needed, and therefore the more toxic it may be assumed to be.

These insecticides may be sprayed over floors, walls and ceilings, but commercial aerosols contain too little of the active ingredient to be effective on a large scale. Fumigation of new acquisitions which may be contaminated with resting stages of the pests would need to be carried out in special chambers using for example ethylene oxide ($LD_{50} = 330$).

There are strong arguments for avoiding the use of insecticides, and concentrating on exclusion rather than extermination.

Light

The cleansing effect of light was, as you will have gathered, well known to the ancients. It whitened the lace, and its powerful ultra-violet radiations with sufficiently long exposure killed off the moulds and mildews and the glued-on moth eggs nestling invisibly among the threads.

What people of that time did not know, and what only relatively recent study has revealed, was the devastating effect of those same beneficent rays on the very fibres of the lace itself. Light, as a result, has now been relegated to the rank of a prime destroyer of textiles.

Both ends of the spectrum are harmful. The blue end, and the ultra-violet beyond, provide the light energy for the chemical degradation of cellulose and protein, while the infra-red waves provide a destructive heat energy. The relevant experiments have involved the measurement of the tearing strength (see page 176) of plant and animal fibres before and after exposure to sunlight. For the tearing strength to be diminished by half requires only 200 hours exposure in the case of silk, 940 for cotton, 990 for flax, and 1200 for wool. The general conclusion is that all light, any light, is harmful to textiles.

However, conservators cannot work in the dark, neither can lace be studied without being visible, and so some compromise has to be achieved. An obvious step is to exclude the most harmful rays, the ultra-violet (often abbreviated to UV), and this can be done by screening windows against daylight, and the use of UV filters (such as UF-3 Plexiglas, or Perspex VE) over artificial light sources. Fluorescent lighting is less heat-productive than tungsten and so is preferable. The total exclusion of UV will mean that plants drop dead since they lack the potential for photosynthesis, and the incarcerated workers may suffer a Vitamin D deficiency, but neither problem is insoluble.

To calculate the degrading effect of any particular lighting (referred to as photodegradation) requires a fairly simple arithmetic. The illumination of a surface is defined in terms of the quantity of visible light falling per second on a unit area. If that unit area is 1 sq.m., then the measurement is in lux (or metre-candles), i.e.:

1 lux = 1 unit of illumination (or lumen) per sq.m.
Similarly, 1 foot-candle = 1 lumen per square foot.
The relation between these two measurements is approximately 1 foot-candle = 10 lux.

The illumination of a surface is measured with a photometer, using a photo-electric cell. Most conveniently, the photometer can be graduated to give direct readings either in lux, or in foot-candles.

Brilliant sunlight has an illumination value of 100,000 lux. Around 200–500 lux may be necessary for close study, 30–90 lux for comfortable reading, 10 is sufficient to prevent bumping into objects, while strong moonlight may be as low as 0.1 lux (Daith).

All these illuminations, however weak, are harmful. Fortunately, however, there appears to be a direct relationship between the strength of the light and the time of exposure to it. Thus, if 200 hours exposure at 100,000 lux weakens silk by 50% it should be possible to calculate by inverse ratio how many hours exposure at 500 lux would be needed to produce the same effect: the answer would be 40,000 hours.

The recommended level of illumination for museums, however, is only 50 lux, which would give a life expectancy (or a 50% reduction of it) of 400,000 hours. At say 8 hours a day 5 days a week, this is equivalent to 10,000 weeks of exposure to light. So, if the lace were actually displayed in an exhibition all through the year it might be expected that its strength would be halved in a little less than 200 years. But a three-month exhibition period for any particular piece would be more likely, extending its life expectancy to some 770 years. And this of course is not its full expectancy.

A similar calculation for the natural fibre most resistant to light, i.e. wool, predicts that an exposure of 40 hours a week, 3 months of the year, at 50 lux, would require 4615 years for its tearing strength to be reduced by half. This remarkable figure is still an understatement. The photometer measures only visible light, and so cannot take into account the fiercely destructive UV effect, or the strong heat of unscreened sunlight. In the cool UV-free museum atmosphere, what enormous correcting factor would be necessary to arrive at the true potential endurance of lace thus cosseted? It must extend onwards almost into infinity, and make the lace seem near eternal.

This is no reason for throwing caution to the winds. Some antique laces may already have used up a large part of their strength through a combination of all the possible deleterious effects over the centuries. They may not indeed have many years to go. But to estimate exactly how long requires an experiment to calculate their current degree of polymerization by molecular weight assessment (see page 176) and this would use up several inches, or grams, of the fabric, which is likely to be more than should be sacrificed. It is thus simpler to treat all old laces as equally perishable.

The actual effect of light on the fibres is mainly a reduction of the degree of polymerization, and accompanying loss of viscosity, of the molecular structure. The process has been found to be accelerated by the presence of oxygen (hence the harmful effects of ozone, or of hydrogen peroxide in sunlight); and of moisture (hence an additional reason for controlling RH); by certain metals; and by a rise in temperature.

THIRTEEN

Stacking and Display

The question which must now be considered is how to combine the maximum preservation of the lace both with the maximum accessibility for students, and the maximum enjoyment for the public at large. We should never lose sight of the fact that lace is being preserved for people.

The two topics of how to pack the lace away out of sight, and how to spread it out on view, are being considered together since they are really two aspects of the same thing. In both cases the exclusion of the potentially harmful factors considered in the last chapter has to be taken into account; in stacking to be as nearly as possible eliminated, in display to be reduced to a minimum.

The principle of stacking is to alleviate fibre stress so that there is no drag, or pressure, on the lace at any point.

Flat storage
Small flat pieces of lace are best spread in shallow drawers between layers of acid-free tissue. A coating of polyurethane varnish will seal in any possible exudations from the wood. The shallowness of the storage space will prevent too many pieces being stacked one on top of the other with consequent crushing of those at the bottom of the pile. The drawer should not be filled so full that squashing is needed to close it. The opaque, or translucent, issue will make the laces difficult to see, but a clear label can be attached to each piece of paper, and a list in order of position placed inside the drawer. Although many people do not approve of labelling the lace itself by any means whatsoever, it is nevertheless very helpful when assorted pieces have been removed from their resting places, and then returned again. Stick-on labels are certainly undesirable, but small tags

A small tag attached through a space in the lace by a soft embroidery thread. The tag need bear no more than a reference number.

carefully tied through some hole near the end of a piece of lace are no hazard unless very carelessly handled (see diagram). The use of polythene bags for storage is also controversial. The great advantage is that the lace can be seen through them, which makes selection of a particular design, technique, or stitch a great deal easier. But if the lace is at all damp the restricted air circulation may encourage mildews; the plastic has a static attraction for dust; and the long-term effect of the loss of plasticizer which causes gradual deterioration of the bag itself has not been sufficiently investigated to know whether it may cause harm to the lace. If such bags are used it is preferable to leave the ends open – but then there is another school of thought which holds that containers should always be airtight.

Raised pieces of lace can be stored in a similar manner provided either they are on a shallow surface on their own or, if there is a shortage of space, resting on the top of one or more layers of flat laces so that any crushing effect on them is eliminated.

Rolled storage
For longer pieces of lace too large to fit straight and flat into the storage box or drawer, rolling is on the whole preferable to folding which, even when the fold is internally padded, and a sharp crease avoided, still produces an uneven stress in the folded areas. For rolling, a cardboard or plastic tube is used, well covered with acid-free tissue, since cardboard itself is acid. The lace, spread rather like a Swiss roll with acid-free tissues is wrapped gently around, right side outwards. The whole is then enclosed in a glassine shell, labelled, tied, and rested in drawers or boxes, or on slatted shelves which can slide in and out for ease of reaching. This last is possible because of the firm carapace of the outer glassine, and the tape which gives ease of picking up the specimen. The advantage of this method is that the shelves can be adjusted so that the minimum of space is wasted, and because the laces are arranged in a single layer there is no pressure of one upon another. The disadvantage is that to get out one piece of lace the door of the storage cabinet must be opened, and all the contents exposed, however briefly, to light and the storage room atmosphere. One would need to be

slightly paranoid to worry greatly about such exposures. The dangers, however, should always be borne in mind.

Shaped pieces
Big shawls, veils and mantillas can only be stored flat if large areas are available. For shapes other than square or rectangular, rolling may be tricky and patience-straining, but it is not impossible. Long rolls can be supported safely on vertical racks. Folding is to be avoided if possible, but if there is really no alternative then padding at every crease with tissue is essential.

With costume pieces such as collars, baby caps or provincial bonnets, more space is needed. Elaborately shaped collars cannot be rolled. They can be arranged as they would be in wear, and placed on a flat surface, with tissue to bolster the bends. Alternatively they can be mounted around plexiglas shoulders, or on plexiglas heads moulded to the appropriate size and shape. The obvious disadvantage here is cost, and space-consumption. The advantage is that the lace is immediately available for study or display. Such modelled laces can be stored in units larger than, but otherwise similar to, the dust-fungus-insect-damp-light- and acid-free containers described for flat laces above, though of narrow depth, and with widely spaced shelving.

Display
During temporary or permanent exhibitions glass-fronted cases in which the lace is exposed on a coloured ground of acid-free tissue can simulate safe storage conditions fairly closely. The main hazard then is light, without which the lace is invisible. While an overall impression of the design of the lace can probably be gained by a low illumination, an appreciation and magnification of the minute thread techniques must need a considerably higher intensity. However, as explained in chapter 12, illumination × duration is the operative factor, and a brief exposure to strong illumination can be equated in harmfulness with long exposure to weak illumination. For example television, or photography, of the lace using spotlights may require an illumination of 4000 lux. This, in half an hour, would have the same destructive effect as 40 hours at 50 lux. Spotlights, in addition, generate heat, which is bad. In this connection it may be mentioned that the photo-copying of pieces of lace, sometimes done for exhibition hand-outs, inflicts both intense light and heat, and so for rare pieces of lace cannot at all be recommended.

The display cases should ensure as far as possible static conditions of temperature, relative humidity, stillness of air, and so forth. Push-button lights may be arranged for individual cases, or small black-out curtains which can be pulled back as required. Flat glass-topped cases can be covered with roll-back material. The advantage of these precautions is that because of the protection of individual pieces the general level of illumination can be raised making the exhibition area a bit less like a gloomy and somewhat depressing cave strewn with eerie obstacles and reflected gleams slipping like will-o'-the-wisps over surfaces of perspex or glass. A black background to lace shows it up well, and has the advantage also of minimizing the reflected light.

Framing lace
If space is no object, or at least not a serious restriction, the framing of pieces of lace may provide a convenient method of storage as well as of display. Inevitably there is some difference of opinion as to the best technique. One quick and easy method is as follows:
A backing layer of plexiglas (perspex) perforated with holes for air circulation is lined with a slightly smaller piece of coarsish muslin, then with a smooth colourfast fabric such as polyester cotton. This coloured fabric should be large enough to fold about $1\frac{1}{2}$ inches over the back all the way around, so that it can be glued firmly to the perspex. The lace is centred on this fabric, then covered with a second sheet of perspex the same size as the first, and the whole clipped together. The contact of the lace with the covering perspex produces gentle and even pressure combined with ease and safety of handling, and ease of removal. For raised laces the same method can be used but with the insertion of a mount equal in depth to the elevation of the lace so that the top of the lace just touches the covering perspex (see diagram).

Darkish background colours are recommended for antique laces, such as black, midnight blue, earth brown or maroon. Light colours would show up any spots or discolouration, and exaggerate the off-whiteness of the old fibres, making them look dingy. Linen can be used as a backing instead of polyester-cotton, but it has the disadvantage that it absorbs moisture rather readily from the air, and as a result it 'moves', dragging the lace either with it or against it. The risk of damage is probably minimal since antique laces themselves are of linen thread and so may be assumed to absorb and release water to more or less the same extent, and to be little disturbed by the movement behind them. Even so, the different construction of the two fabrics, single element for lace and double for woven linen (see chapter 1), can distort the pull and lead to stress.

If the frame is to be hung, rivets and hooks can be attached to the backing perspex. Alternatively a shaped strip of wood or perspex can be joined to the top at the back, to slot over a wall fitting. If instead of clips a wooden frame is put around the perspex, it can be

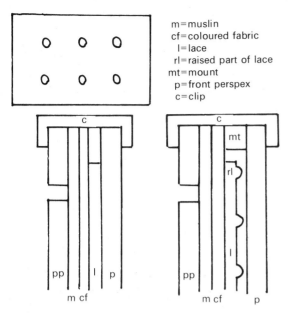

m = muslin
cf = coloured fabric
l = lace
rl = raised part of lace
mt = mount
p = front perspex
c = clip

a *The perforated backing perspex, of whatever size is needed.*
b *and* **c** *Sketches to show the layers involved in framing lace, side section:* **b** *flat lace,* **c** *raised lace.*

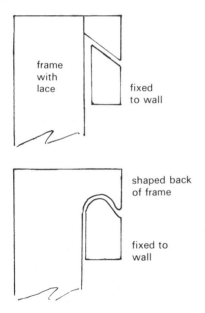

frame with lace

fixed to wall

shaped back of frame

fixed to wall

Sketches to show two ways of hanging framed lace. In **a** *a bevelled strip is glued to the back of the frame. In* **b** *the wooden frame is gouged out and the hollow groove fits over a correspondingly shaped baton fixed to the wall.*

grooved out at the back to be slipped over a wall fitting in a similar manner (see diagram).

If, for whatever reason, it is thought advisable to stitch the lace to the backing fabric, great care must be taken that the fixing of spaced points on the lace by the stitches does not cause a differential pull. The use of a surgical needle to attach the lace is unnecessary, even undesirable, since its shape makes it difficult to locate the entry and emergence of the needle sufficiently accurately that it never touches the threads but passes only through the meshes or other spaces of the lace. It is thus likely that the delicate fibres will be pulled or torn by misplacement. A safer and easier method is to stretch the washed and dried coloured backing fabric over a frame, making sure that warp and weft threads are aligned parallel to the edges. Only a moderate tension in the material should be aimed at, and the sewing needle should be passed straight through, at right angles to the cloth and lace, so that each stitch is two separate movements, through and back. A little slack should be left in the thread at each stitch. When the attachment of the lace is complete, remove the cloth from the supporting frame, tack it to the coarsish muslin (page 182), then glue to the perspex as described above, making sure once again that the warp and weft lines are strictly parallel to the perspex sides. The controversy over how airtight the framing should be will not be entered into here. The advantage of a minute gap between lace and covering perspex is that it avoids undue pressure; the disadvantage is that some static effect may be generated causing unstitched parts of the lace to rise towards the perspex, dragging at the parts which are fixed. Anti-static polishes can be used, and the danger is probably very small, except perhaps for silk laces.

Hanging lace
Exposure of lace to the atmosphere, even the carefully regulated atmosphere of a museum, should be avoided as far as possible. However, it may occasionally happen that lace requires to be hung, for example to spread out a very large piece so that the full impact of its design can be appreciated. One method of supporting the lace in this event is to line it with some pre-shrunk material turned over at the top to form a sleeve through which a rod can be passed and used to hang it. Instead of making a sleeve, the fluffy half of a velcro strip can be stitched to the top of the lining, while the hooked half is stapled to a baton on the wall. The two parts can then be easily pressed together, and so support up to 7 lb weight per inch. Detachment is also easy, since only the lining material is pulled, not the lace.

Yet another possibility is to attach a broad band of webbing to the upper border of the lace, using a zigzag backstitch which will exert the minimum pull. But this method is not really desirable, even using a weak sewing thread which will give way under strain before the lace itself does: the insidious drag as the lace hangs must eventually cause damage.

FOURTEEN
Last Words of Advice

As a supplement to the foregoing chapters on care, just a little will be added about what might be called non-preservation-worthy laces. The rigorous recommendations for cleaning, storing, stacking and display should not rule out all possibility of the lace being enjoyed by wearing, any more than it should rule out enjoyment by viewing.

What is vitally important is that only certain laces should be worn, i.e. those in great supply, of no outstanding artistic merit, or rarity, or research value. The constant aim should be to preserve everything which can never be replaced, so that it can survive for study and appreciation by succeeding generations. Plenty of lace will be left which is delightful to wear, and yet expendable.

Lace then must first be identified (see part I). Very probably you will be able to do this yourself by perusing the text and illustrations of this book, or *The Identification of Lace*, or *A Dictionary of Lace*. Should conviction as to its identity still elude you, it would be best to take the lace to a museum which has a lace specialist. There, its nature could be explained, and probably also some information concerning its commonness or otherwise could be acquired.

Until the identity of the lace is known, no action should be taken to wash, iron, dry clean or otherwise interfere with it. If, ultimately, your decision is that it will be no great loss to the world, that is the time to consider its preparation for wear, or other consumption.

If be washed it must, then a very gentle method is to support the lace on a sheet of polythene, and soak it in two or three changes of cold water until there is no longer any discolouration. Lift it by the polythene into a container with a very weak solution of Stergene in barely lukewarm water, and circulate it gently. Rinse several times with distilled water – this can be poured through it until no lather remains. Spread the supporting polythene on soft board, ease the lace into its proper shape over the surface, and pin with brass pins, or Newey's stainless steel bridal pins, until it is dry.

If this treatment does not make the lace clean or crisp enough for your requirements, the decision to be more violent is yours. If you wish to boil, bleach, use commercial detergents, dye or iron it, on your head be it. Plenty of nineteenth- and early twentieth-century laces have been treated in this way, and have survived.

The only question is, for how long? There is no doubt at all that violence will shorten a lace's life, but in its function as a fashion accessory such a consideration is not particularly relevant. The main recommendation is simply to be aware of what you are doing and of why you are doing it, to act in short with knowledge, and not in ignorance.

1 Silk laces need special care since they are hypersensitive to heat, bleach and strong soaps.

2 If ironing is done it should be from the wrong side (this better shows up the design of the lace) and over a cloth (which will prevent too hard a pressure, and the risk of ripping). Even when ironing is thought to be essential, care should be taken that the lace is not completely crushed. Lace, however smoothly made, is in low-relief, and to squash it utterly flat destroys its character.

3 Diamond-shaped nets (the machine three- or four-twist bobbinets) should not be ironed, only pinned, since they pull out of shape very easily, and the billowing bulges which result are extremely difficult to get rid of.

4 Carrickmacross lace, whether a decorated net or a guipure (fig. 26), is merely a muslin or lawn fabric cut into shapes around a bounding cord. The muslin roughly handled will fray; when washed it may shrink and pull away from the cord. Catching the point of the iron against the thread in attempting to get out the creases will have the same effect. It is a pretty lace, but very impractical, and so even if regarded as ephemeral it should be treated with care.

Appendix

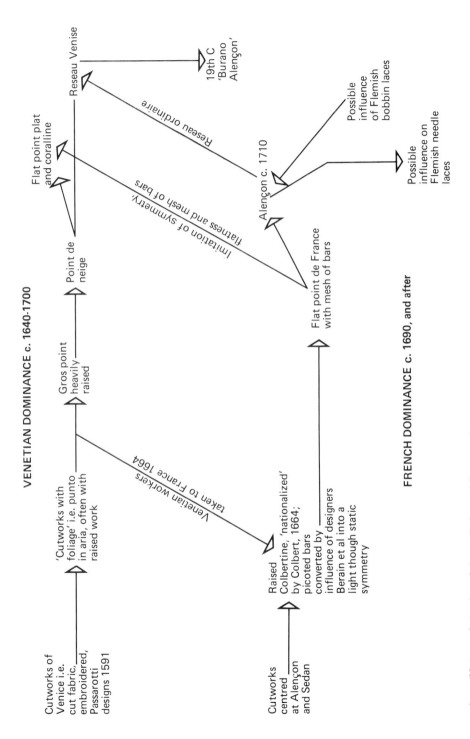

VENETIAN DOMINANCE c. 1640-1700

Cutworks of Venice i.e. cut fabric, embroidered, Passarotti designs 1591

'Cutworks with foliage' i.e. punto in aria, often with raised work

Gros point heavily raised

Point de neige

Flat point plat and coralline

Reseau Venise

19th C 'Burano Alençon'

Réseau ordinaire

Imitation of symmetry, flatness and mesh of bars

Venetian workers taken to France 1664

Cutworks centred at Alençon and Sedan

Raised Colbertine, 'nationalized' by Colbert, 1664; picoted bars converted by influence of designers Berain et al into a light though static symmetry

Flat point de France with mesh of bars

Alençon c. 1710

Possible influence of Flemish bobbin laces

Possible influence on Flemish needle laces

FRENCH DOMINANCE c. 1690, and after

A possible interrelationship of the needle laces of France and Venice, partly based on Cole (1875) and von Henneburg (1930).

CONSERVATIONISTS

United Kingdom

Textile Conservation Centre Ltd, Apt. 22, Hampton
Court Palace, East Molesey, Surrey KT8 9AV
Royal School of Needlework, 25 Princes Gate, London
SW7 1QE
North-west Museum and Art Gallery Service, Griffin
Lodge, Griffin Park, Blackburn BB2 2PN
Judith Doré, Castle Lodge, 271 Sandown Road, Deal,
Kent
The Textile Restoration Studio (Jacqueline Pickford), 5
Oxford Road, Altrincham, Cheshire WA14 2DY
Kysnia Marko, Textile Conservation Studio, Metropolitan
College of Craftsmen, Enfield Road, London N1

United States of America

Mary Ballard, Detroit Institute of Arts, 5200 Woodward
Avenue, Detroit, Michigan 48202
Pat Collins, Textile Conservation Centre Inc., Houston,
Texas

Betty LaCasse, 37 Prescott Avenue, White Plains, N.Y.
10605
Marguerite Morgan, Studio I, 6 Highland Cross, New
Jersey 07070
Helen von Rosensteil, Restorations, 382 Eleventh Street,
Brooklyn, New York 11215
Therese Schoenholzer, 501 West 43rd Street, New York,
N.Y. 10036

Conservation Suppliers:

Frank W. Joel Ltd, Oldmedow Road, Hardwick Industrial
Estate, Kings Lynn, Norfolk PE30 4HH, Great Britain

MUSEUMS WITH LACE

The following list is arranged alphabetically first in order of
countries and then of cities or towns within those countries.
No attempt has been made to indicate the size of the
collection, nor whether it is the museum's practice to keep
some lace always on display. Intending visitors should
therefore first consult the curator to check what, and how
much, they might be able to see.

Austria
Vienna. Österreichisches Museum für angewandte Kunste.
Australia
Adelaide, South Australia. Art Gallery of South Australia.
Melbourne, Victoria. National Gallery of Victoria.
Sydney, New South Wales. Museum of Applied Arts and
Sciences (The Power House).
Belgium
Antwerp. Provinciaal Textielmuseum, Vrieselhof, Oelegem.
Bruges. Kantcentrum. Gruuthuse Museum.
Brussels. Musées Royaux d'Art et d'Histoire. Musée de
Costume et Dentelles.
Canada
Saint John. The New Brunswick Museum.
Toronto. The Royal Ontario Museum.
Denmark
Copenhagen. Drager Museum. Museum of Decorative
Arts. Samling på Rosenborg.

France
Alençon. Musée de la Maison d'Ozé. Musée de la
Peinture.
Argentan. Abbeye Notre-Dame.
Bayeux. Musée Baron Gérard.
Calais. Musée de la Dentelle.
Le Puy. Centre d'Initiation à la Dentelle du Puy. Musée
Crozatier.
Lyon. Musée Historique des Tissus.
Paris. Musée des Arts Decoratifs. Musée de Cluny. Musée
Nationale des Arts et Traditions Populaires.
Germany
West Berlin. Kunstgewerbemuseum.
Holland
Amsterdam. Rijksmuseum.
Rotterdam. Museum Boymans-Van Beuningen.
Hungary
Budapest. Iparmuveszeti Museum.
Ireland
Dublin. Museum of Ireland.
Italy
Florence. Palazzo Davanzati.
Milan. Poldi Pezzoli.
Venice. Museo Correr. Scuola di Merletti, Burano.
Portugal
Lisbon. Gulbenkian Museum. Museu Nacional de Arte
Antiga.

Spain
Barcelona. Museo de Puntas y Encajes.
Sweden
Lund. Kulturhistoriske Museum.
Stockholm. Livrustkammaren.
Switzerland
Appenzel. Town Museum.
Berne. Abegg-Stiftung.
St. Gallen. Textilmuseum.
United Kingdom
Aylesbury, Bucks. Buckinghamshire County Museum.
Bath. Museum of Costume.
Bedford. Cecil Higgins Art Gallery.
Broadclyst, Devon. Killerton House.
Budleigh Salterton, Devon. Fairlynch.
Cambridge, Fitzwilliam Museum.
East Molesey, Surrey. Embroiderers' Guild, Apt. 41a, Hampton Court Palace.
Edinburgh. Royal Scottish Museum.
Exeter. Royal Albert Memorial Museum.
Glasgow. Camphill Museum (Burrell Collection).
Guildford, Surrey. Guildford Museum.
Honiton, Devon. Honiton and Allhallows Museum.
Liverpool. Merseyside County Museum.
London. London Museum. Royal School of Needlework. Victoria and Albert Museum.
Luton. Museum and Art Gallery.
Manchester. Platt Hall. Whitworth Art Gallery.
Nottingham. Industrial Museum, Wollaton Park. Museum of Costume and Textiles.

Olney, Bucks. Cowper and Newton Museum.
Padiham, Lancs. Gawthorpe Hall (Rachel Kay-Shuttleworth Collection).
Salisbury, Wilts. Salisbury and South Wiltshire Museum.
Tiverton, Devon. Tiverton Museum.
Waddesdon, Bucks. Waddesdon Manor.
Yelverton, Devon. Buckland Abbey.
York. Castle Howard.
United States of America
Boston, Mass. American Institute of Textile Arts. Isabella Stewart Gardner Museum. Museum of Fine Arts.
Chicago, Ill. Art Institute.
Cleveland, Ohio. Museum of Art.
Detroit, Mi. Detroit Institute of Arts.
Greenfield Village, Mi. Henry Ford Museum.
Hartford, Conn. Wadsworth Atheneum.
Houston, Texas. Museum of Fine Arts.
Indianapolis, Ind. Museum of Art.
Ipswich, Mass. John Wipple House.
Lubbock, Texas. Texas Tech University Museum.
Minneapolis, Minnesota. Institute of Art.
New York. Brooklyn Museum. Cooper-Hewitt. Metropolitan Museum of Art.
Philadelphia, Pa. Museum of Art.
Rhode Island. School of Design.
Richmond, Va. Valentine Museum.
Washington DC. Daughters of the American Revolution Museum. Smithsonian Institution.
USSR
Leningrad. Hermitage.

Bibliography

Abegg, Margaret. *Apropos Patterns for Embroidery, Lace and Woven Textiles*. Berne, 1978.

Ballard, Mary. 'The Care of Textiles'. *Art and Antiques*, 1982.

Boulard, Felix. *The Needlepoint and Lace of Alençon*. Alençon, n.d.

Broeckhove, M. *De Gentse Kant*. Gent, 1973.

Buck, Ann. *Thomas Lester, his Lace and the East Midlands Industry, 1820–1905*. Ruth Bean, 1981.

Calavas, A. (ed.). *Dessins de Broderies*. Paris, n.d. but *c*1910.

Carlier, Antoine. *Les Valenciennes*. Bruxelles, 1902.
 – 'Les Dentelles á l'Aiguille', *Bulletin des Metiers d'Art*. III. 1903–4.
 – *Les Duchesses*. Bruxelles, 1910.

Caulfield, S.F.A. and Saward, B.C. *Encyclopaedia of Victorian Needlework*. Dover Publications, 1972 reprint.

Chaleyé, J. *Methode d'Enseignement de la Dentelle aux Fuseaux*. Le Puy, 1946.

Channer, C.C. *Lace Making in the Midlands*. 1900.

Cole, A.S. *Ancient Needlepoint and Pillow Lace*. London, 1875.

Daith, C.B. *Light*. English University Press, 1974.

'Devonia'. *Honiton Lace*. Robin and Russ reprint, 1977.

Dillmont, Thérèse de. *Encyclopaedia of Needlework*. Birmingham, n.d.

Duncan, Kate C. 'American Indian Lace Making', *American Indian Art Magazine*, vol. 5, no. 3, 1980.

Earnshaw, Pat. *The Identification of Lace*. Shire, 1980.
 – *A Dictionary of Lace*. Shire, 1982.

Edwards, Joan and Nevinson, J.L. 'The Rates of the London Customs House in 1550', *Costume*, 4, 1970.

Emery, Irene. *The Primary Structure of Fabrics*. Textile Museum, Washington DC, 1966.

Eve, G.W. *Decorative Heraldry*. Bell, 1908.

Finch, Karen and Putnam, Greta. *Caring for Textiles*. Barrie & Jenkins, 1977.

Fraser, Antonia. *King Charles II*. Weidenfeld and Nicolson, 1979.

Glover, Jean. *Textiles: their care and protection in Museums*. Mus. Ass. Sheet, no. 18, 1973.

Godet, Alfred. *Quelques dates concernant la dentelle aux fuseaux Neuchâteloise*, 1982.

Hanausek. *Microscopy of Technical Products*. Chapman and Hall, 1907.

Hannover, Emil. *Tønderske Kniplinger*. Host and Sones Forlag, 1974.

Henneberg, Baron Alfred von. *The Art and Craft of Old Lace*. Batsford, 1931.

Johnstone, Margaret Taylor. 'Ragusa'. *Needle and Bobbin Club Bulletin*, vol. 10, no. 1, 1926.

Jourde, Michel. 'Perfectionnement à la Mise en Carte: IV. Quelques Fonds', *La Dentelle*, no. 9, March 1982.

Leene, J.E. (ed.). *Textile Conservation*. Butterworth, 1972.

Lefebure, Auguste (ed.). *La Collection de Dentelles au Musée des Tissus de Lyon*. 1909.

Lefebure, Ernest. *Les Points de France*. New York, 1912.

Lewis, Fulvia. *Lace*. Remos Sandron. Firenze, 1981.

Mailand, Harold F. *Considerations for the Care of Textiles and Costumes*. Indianapolis Museum of Art, 1980.

Morison, Stanley. *Splendour of Ornament*. Lion and Unicorn Press, 1968.

Morris, F. and Hague, M. *Antique Laces of the American Collectors*. New York, 1926.

Murphy, William S. *The Textile Industries*. Gresham, 1910.

Nordfors, Jill. *Needle Lace and Needle-Weaving*. Van Nostrand Reinhold, 1974.

Nunn, Robin and West, Alan. *The Making of String and String Bags after the Manner of the Aborigines of West Cape York Peninsula*. Victoria, Australia, 1979.

Paulis, L. *La Dentelle aux Fuseaux*. Lamertin, 1921.
 – 'Le Drochel', *Needle and Bobbin Club Bulletin*, vol. 7, no. 2, 1923.
 – 'Le Pompe', *Needle and Bobbin Club Bulletin*, vol. 6, no. 1, 1922.
 – *Les Points à l'Aiguille Belges*. Bruxelles, 1947.

Petersen, Gunvor and Dich, Minna. *Amagersyninger*. Drager Museum, n.d., but *c*1980.

Plenderleith, H.J. *The Conservation of Antiquities and Works of Art*. OUP, 1956.

Powys, Marian, *Lace and Lace Making*. Gale, Detroit, reprint, 1982.

Raventos Ventura, Antonia and Monserrat. *Puntas*. Barcelona, 1967.

Ricci, Elisa. *Old Italian Lace*. Heinemann, 1913.

Risselin-Steenebrugen, M. *Trois Siècles de Dentelles*. Brussels, 1981.

Simeon, Margaret. *A History of Lace*. Stainer and Bell, 1979.

Stringer, June. 'Some Distinctive Styles of Needle Lace', *The Lace Maker*, Australian Lace Guild, vol. 2, no. 2; vol. 2, no. 3; vol. 3, no. 2, 1980–82.

Treadwin, C. *Antique Point and Honiton Lace*. Ward, Lock and Tyler, *c*1874.

Urbani, C.M. *A Technical History of the Manufacture of Venetian Laces*. Venice, 1882.

Verhaegen, Pierre. *La Restauration de la Dentelle à Venise et l'Ecole de Burano*. Bruxelles, 1908.

Wardle, Patricia. 'A Lace Society and a Lace School', *Lace*, no. 5, Jan. 1977.
 – *Victorian Lace*. Ruth Bean reprint, 1982.

Weldon's Practical Torchon Lace. no. 124, vol. 11, n.d.

Whiting, Gertrude. *A Lace Guide for Makers and Collectors*. Dutton, 1920.

Index